Regulation and Compliance

Past Examination
Questions and Answers

Winter 2008

LEARNING MEDIA

BPP House
Aldine Place
London W12 8AA

Tel: 0845 0751 100

E-mail: learningmedia@bpp.com
Website: www.bpp.com/learningmedia

Published September 2008

ISBN 9780 7517 5431 5

British Library Cataloguing-in-Publication Data
A catalogue record for this book
is available from the British Library

Published by

BPP Learning Media Ltd
Aldine House, Aldine Place
London W12 8AW

www.bpp.com/learningmedia

Printed in Great Britain by
WM Print
42-47 Frederick Street
Walsall
W Midlands, WS2 9NE

Your learning materials, published by BPP Learning Media are
printed on paper sourced from sustainable, managed forests.

£125.00

Contents

Winter 2007

Section A

1. Summarise what is meant by the term 'insider' in the Criminal Justice Act 1993. **(3 marks)**

2. How would an authorised firm be classified? List two circumstances under which they may be treated differently. **(3 marks)**

3. Describe S19 of FSMA. **(2 marks)**

4. Explain the scope of the FSA's market abuse regime. **(3 marks)**

5. Briefly describe churning. What type of customers does the rule cover? **(2 marks)**

6. What are the key money laundering offences and their relevant penalties? **(5 marks)**

7. Describe the rules requiring firms to send out confirmation notes and periodic statements. **(4 marks)**

8. Outline the split of responsibilities between home and host regulators under the MiFID regime. **(4 marks)**

9. Describe the role of a DPB. **(2 marks)**

10. Describe the MiFID CASS rule relating to the reconciliation of client money. **(2 marks)**

(Total 30 marks)

Section B

Answer Question 11 and any ONE of the other three questions

11. (a) Tim and Bob are fund managers at Banks plc. They have been close friends for many years. Tim is highly regarded in his field and has been appointed as a non-executive director of several financial institutions, including Banks-r-us.

At a recent board meeting of Banks-r-us Tim discovers that Banks-r-us have suffered serious financial losses as a result of recent failed investments in Eastern Europe. This is likely to have a significant impact on the capital adequacy of Banks-r-us. Tim is personally of the view, although this was not discussed at the meeting, that the regulators are likely to step in and close down Banks-r-us.

Tim tells Bob of his concerns for the future of Banks-r-us in strictest confidence. Tim is aware that the fund that Bob manages has a significant holding in Banks-r-us, but is unaware that Bob holds a significant number of shares in Banks-r-us in his personal share portfolio.

Bob keeps all his personal shareholdings secret from everyone. The following day Bob sells small blocks of shares in Banks-r-us, firstly from his personal portfolio and, subsequently, from the fund that he manages. Bob is hoping that the share price in Banks-r-us will not move. Shortly after Bob had sold all the shares the Stock Exchange halted all trading in the shares of Banks-r-us because of the high volume of trading in Banks-r-us shares and the fall in the value of the shares. The Stock Exchange has commenced an investigation into all-share trading in Banks-r-us. The regulator has also announced that the financial probity of Banks-r-us is under investigation.

   (i) Identify any criminal and other legal consequences for Tim and Bob **(6 marks)**

   (ii) Advise Tim and Bob on the likely consequences of their actions in terms of their regulatory status and any ethical considerations **(4 marks)**

(b) Ginger works as a clerk in the Private Client department at Banks plc. Fred wants to open a new account at Banks plc and offers Ginger the use of his villa in the Cayman Islands if she will open the account quickly without completing the usual formalities. Fred says that he wants to buy a new boat. To obtain a 25% discount on the purchase price of £1 million he has to transfer the monies from the new account at Banks plc to a Swiss bank account within 48 hours.

Ginger was very concerned about this transaction and sought advice from Irving, the senior clerk. Irving has been working very hard on another project and has not attended any of the compulsory training courses held at Banks plc for the last three years. Senior officials have turned a blind eye to this because Irving is a long-standing employee. Irving thought that it was better to let the transaction go ahead but decided to notify the compliance officer of this unusual transaction. The account was opened and the funds were duly transferred. The compliance officer was away at a training course and was not aware of the transaction authorised by Irving until his return. Fred has disappeared and it has not been possible to contact him. The compliance officer is very concerned about this transaction and now seeks your advice on the matter.

   (i) Advise the compliance officer on the potential liability for Ginger, Irving and the firm.
   (7 marks)

   (ii) Identify the management controls that you would recommend are improved.
   (3 marks)

   (Total 20 marks)

12. Agatha Carpentras, a retail client, telephoned Brown Jones, a firm of brokers. She asked the firm to sell shares on her behalf. Brown Jones effected the deal by buying some of the shares as principal and selling the remainder in the market as agent. The total due to Agatha amounted to £28,000. Four days after effecting these transactions, Brown Jones sent Agatha a letter and contract confirming the deal, together with the transfer documents. The latter were completed and returned promptly by her with the relevant share certificates.

Two weeks elapsed during which time Agatha heard nothing from Brown Jones. She then telephoned the firm and was told that her funds were available. She was asked whether she would prefer to reinvest the money in a combination of gilts and options or, alternatively, whether she would prefer the cash. The firm's employee with whom she spoke emphasised several times that, as a widow, she should have her money working for her on the market. Agatha requested Brown Jones to pay a quarter of the sum into her bank account and to retain three quarters to invest on her behalf. The firm sent Agatha a cheque for £7,000 drawn on its current account and placed £21,000 into a client bank account (designated as such).

Brown Jones subsequently purchased from that account options and gilts and when it received the gilt certificates, the firm (which was temporarily financially embarrassed) used them as collateral for its bank overdraft. Brown Jones has since been declared insolvent.

(a) Identify the rule breaches that have occurred **(16 marks)**

(b) Advise Agatha on the procedures for and prospects of her retrieving her money. **(4 marks)**
(Total 20 marks)

13. Target plc is a medium-sized UK public company with a single class of shares listed by the UKLA and admitted to trading on the LSE. It operates in the computer and microelectronics area and is engaged in a substantial research programme. The research programme has been expensive and resulted in low profits and a depressed share price, even though there are indications that some of the research has been fruitful and should lead to innovative new products within two or three years. Companies operating in the same field include Swift Move plc (a listed company), Chancer Limited and Opportunist Limited. Opportunist, which has two subsidiaries, Quickbuck Limited and Speedy Limited, is controlled by the Pampas twins, David and Alex, who are chairman and managing director, respectively. The following events occur.

(a) On Monday, 4 June, Swift Move acquires privately a 9.5% holding in Target at a price of 150p per share, its holding duly being notified to Target on the evening of Thursday, 7 June, although this only becomes known in the market the following Monday.

(b) On Tuesday, 5 June, Chancer and Opportunist, together with the Pampas twins and Sir Charles Tiger, reach an understanding with Swift Move that, if through share purchases, or otherwise, they assist Swift Move to obtain control of Target, Chancer and Opportunist will get free use of the fruits of Target's research. Market purchases of Target shares are effected as follows.

6 June – Chancer buys 2% of Target. Quickbuck buys 2.3% of Target.
7 June – Sir Charles Tiger buys 2.5% of Target. Speedy buys 0.6% of Target. One of the Pampas twins buys 2% of Target.

(c) On Monday, 11 June, and on the following morning, James Megapocket, chairman and chief executive of Swift Move, buys shares of Swift Move.

(d) At noon on Tuesday, 12 June, Swift Move publicly announces its intention to make an offer for the whole of the issued share capital of Target, other than 19% already owned, on the basis of two Swift Move shares for every three Target shares. James Megapocket privately instructs his brokers, within a specified limit, to buy Swift Move shares whenever necessary to keep the market price of Swift Move shares sufficiently high. Analyse and comment on the regulatory issues arising and specify any breaches that you consider have occurred for each day's transactions. **(20 marks)**

14. A wealthy Greek shipowner, Mr Stavros Popocros, is a customer of the Shipping Department of the authorised firm you work for. Mr Popocros' ships' main cargo is sugar. Mr Popocros speaks some English, but this is not normally a problem since his relationship manager in the Shipping Department, Christos Wotolos, is also Greek.

Mr Popocros is considering buying sugar futures, on a regular basis, on NYSE.Euronext (formerly Euronext.liffe) in order to hedge against any loss of business to a rival firm in transporting sugar, and asks Mr Wotolos to help him execute the deals.

As an aside, Mr Popocros has used a rival firm to execute Eurobond orders for him in the past, but has heard that your firm's Treasury Department is highly rated and is considering using them for his future Treasury and capital market needs.

Your firm is a member of NYSE.Euronext. Mr Wotolos is not approved by the FSA. Treasury is a separate legal entity from the Shipping Department.

No one in Treasury speaks Greek. Mr Wotolos is concerned about disclosing too much information about his customer directly to the futures desk, since he fears that Treasury may deal directly with Mr Popocros in future, bypassing Mr Wotolos, with the result that the latter will lose his percentage of commissions charged by Treasury.

Mr Wotolos now calls you (the compliance officer) to explain that he will be passing Mr Popocros' orders to Treasury for execution only. Furthermore, Mr Popocros is loath to sign any documentation, unless it is in Greek. Mr Wotolos asks you to assure him that there are no compliance issues with this course of action.

(a) What alarm bells are ringing, and what compliance issues need to be considered?

(14 marks)

(b) Having identified the issues, what are your possible courses of action? Of these, choose your best course, and justify your reasons. **(6 marks)**

(Total 20 marks)

Section C (Answer ANY TWO of the four questions)

15. What challenges are posed by the increased use of the internet for selling financial services products? **(15 marks)**

16. Regulators are increasingly focusing on the responsibilities of the management of investment businesses. Why has the regulator taken such an approach, what are these responsibilities, and are the regulators correct to impose such responsibilities? **(15 marks)**

17. 'The function of financial markets is to enable investment to be directed, in appropriate amounts, to the different destinations where it can be effectively employed. In order for this to occur, the markets must operate and be seen to operate, in an open, transparent and fair manner. The (Financial Services and Markets) Act includes important measures for the FSA to deal with market abuse.'

    Discuss. **(15 marks)**

18. To what extent have the UK 'gold plated' MiFID requirements and will the harmonisation arising from MiFID be worthwhile? **(15 marks)**

Summer 2007

Section A

1. Summarise what is meant by the term 'insider' in the Criminal Justice Act 1993.   **(3 marks)**

2. How would an authorised firm be classified? List two circumstances under which they may be treated differently.   **(3 marks)**

3. Describe S19 of FSMA.   **(2 marks)**

4. Explain the scope of the FSA's market abuse regime.   **(3 marks)**

5. Briefly describe churning. What type of customers does the rule cover?   **(2 marks)**

6. What are the key money laundering offences and their relevant penalties?   **(5 marks)**

7. Describe the rules requiring firms to send out confirmation notes and periodic statements.   **(4 marks)**

8. Outline the split of responsibilities between home and host regulators under the ISD regime. Briefly state how this will change under MiFID.   **(4 marks)**

9. Describe the role of a DPB.   **(2 marks)**

10. List the types of client bank account that a firm may open.   **(2 marks)**

Section B

Answer Question 11 and any ONE of the other three questions

11. (a) Tim and Bob are fund managers at Banks plc. They have been close friends for many years. Tim is highly regarded in his field and has been appointed as a non-executive director of several financial institutions, including Banks-r-us.

At a recent board meeting of Banks-r-us Tim discovers that Banks-r-us have suffered serious financial losses as a result of recent failed investments in Eastern Europe. This is likely to have a significant impact on the capital adequacy of Banks-r-us. Tim is personally of the view, although this was not discussed at the meeting, that the regulators are likely to step in and close down Banks-r-us.

Tim tells Bob of his concerns for the future of Banks-r-us in strictest confidence. Tim is aware that the fund that Bob manages has a significant holding in Banks-r-us, but is unaware that Bob holds a significant number of shares in Banks-r-us in his personal share portfolio.

Bob keeps all his personal shareholdings secret from everyone. The following day Bob sells small blocks of shares in Banks-r-us, firstly from his personal portfolio and, subsequently, from the fund that he manages. Bob is hoping that the share price in Banks-r-us will not move. Shortly after Bob had sold all the shares the Stock Exchange halted all trading in the shares of Banks-r-us because of the high volume of trading in Banks-r-us shares and the fall in the value of the shares. The Stock Exchange has commenced an investigation into all-share trading in Banks-r-us. The regulator has also announced that the financial probity of Banks-r-us is under investigation.

  (i) Identify any criminal and other legal consequences for Tim and Bob **(6 marks)**

  (ii) Advise Tim and Bob on the likely consequences of their actions in terms of their regulatory status and any ethical considerations **(4 marks)**

(b) Ginger works as a clerk in the Private Client department at Banks plc. Fred wants to open a new account at Banks plc and offers Ginger the use of his villa in the Cayman Islands if she will open the account quickly without completing the usual formalities. Fred says that he wants to buy a new boat. To obtain a 25% discount on the purchase price of £1 million he has to transfer the monies from the new account at Banks plc to a Swiss bank account within 48 hours.

Ginger was very concerned about this transaction and sought advice from Irving, the senior clerk. Irving has been working very hard on another project and has not attended any of the compulsory training courses held at Banks plc for the last three years. Senior officials have turned a blind eye to this because Irving is a long-standing employee. Irving thought that it was better to let the transaction go ahead but decided to notify the compliance officer of this unusual transaction. The account was opened and the funds were duly transferred. The compliance officer was away at a training course and was not aware of the transaction authorised by Irving until his return. Fred has disappeared and it has not been possible to contact him. The compliance officer is very concerned about this transaction and now seeks your advice on the matter.

  (i) Advise the compliance officer on the potential liability for Ginger, Irving and the firm.
  (7 marks)

  (ii) Identify the management controls that you would recommend are improved.
  (3 marks)

12. Agatha Carpentras, a private customer, telephoned Brown Jones, a firm of brokers. She asked the firm to sell shares on her behalf. Brown Jones effected the deal by buying some of the shares as principal and selling the remainder in the market as agent. The total due to Agatha amounted to £28,000.

Four days after effecting these transactions, Brown Jones sent Agatha a letter and contract confirming the deal, together with the transfer documents. The latter were completed and returned promptly by her with the relevant share certificates.

Two weeks elapsed during which time Agatha heard nothing from Brown Jones. She then telephoned the firm and was told that her funds were available. She was asked whether she would prefer to reinvest the money in a combination of gilts and options or, alternatively, whether she would prefer the cash. The firm's employee with whom she spoke emphasised several times that, as a widow, she should have her money working for her on the market. Agatha requested Brown Jones to pay a quarter of the sum into her bank account and to retain three quarters to invest on her behalf. The firm sent Agatha a cheque for £7,000 drawn on its current account and placed £21,000 into a client bank account (designated as such).

Brown Jones subsequently purchased from that account options and gilts and when it received the gilt certificates, the firm (which was temporarily financially embarrassed) used them as collateral for its bank overdraft. Brown Jones has since been declared insolvent.

(i) Identify the rule breaches that have occurred. **(16 marks)**

(ii) Advise Agatha on the procedures for and prospects of her retrieving her money. **(4 marks)**

13. Target plc is a medium-sized UK public company with a single class of shares listed by the UKLA and admitted to trading on the LSE. It operates in the computer and microelectronics area and is engaged in a substantial research programme. The research programme has been expensive and resulted in low profits and a depressed share price, even though there are indications that some of the research has been fruitful and should lead to innovative new products within two or three years. Companies operating in the same field include Swift Move plc (a listed company), Chancer Limited and Opportunist Limited. Opportunist, which has two subsidiaries, Quickbuck Limited and Speedy Limited, is controlled by the Pampas twins, David and Alex, who are chairman and managing director, respectively. The following events occur.

(a) On Monday, 4 June, Swift Move acquires privately a 9.5% holding in Target at a price of 150p per share, its holding duly being notified to Target on the evening of Thursday, 7 June, although this only becomes known in the market the following Monday.

(b) On Tuesday, 5 June, Chancer and Opportunist, together with the Pampas twins and Sir Charles Tiger, reach an understanding with Swift Move that, if through share purchases, or otherwise, they assist Swift Move to obtain control of Target, Chancer and Opportunist will get free use of the fruits of Target's research.

Market purchases of Target shares are effected as follows.

■ 6 June – Chancer buys 2% of Target. Quickbuck buys 2.3% of Target.

■ 7 June – Sir Charles Tiger buys 2.5% of Target. Speedy buys 0.6% of Target. One of the Pampas twins buys 2% of Target.

(c) On Monday, 11 June, and on the following morning, James Megapocket, chairman and chief executive of Swift Move, buys shares of Swift Move.

(d) At noon on Tuesday, 12 June, Swift Move publicly announces its intention to make an offer for the whole of the issued share capital of Target, other than 19% already owned, on the basis of two Swift Move shares for every three Target shares. James Megapocket privately instructs his brokers, within a specified limit, to buy Swift Move shares whenever necessary to keep the market price of Swift Move shares sufficiently high.

Analyse and comment on the regulatory issues arising and specify any breaches that you consider have occurred for each day's transactions.

(20 marks)

14.   A wealthy Greek shipowner, Mr Stavros Popocros, is a customer of the Shipping Department of the authorised firm you work for. Mr Popocros' ships' main cargo is sugar. Mr Popocros speaks some English, but this is not normally a problem since his relationship manager in the Shipping Department, Christos Wotolos, is also Greek.

Mr Popocros is considering buying sugar futures, on a regular basis, on Euronext.liffe in order to hedge against any loss of business to a rival firm in transporting sugar, and asks Mr Wotolos to help him execute the deals.

As an aside, Mr Popocros has used a rival firm to execute Eurobond orders for him in the past, but has heard that your firm's Treasury Department is highly rated and is considering using them for his future Treasury and capital market needs.

Your firm is a member of Euronext.liffe. Mr Wotolos is not approved by the FSA. Treasury is a separate legal entity from the Shipping Department.

No one in Treasury speaks Greek. Mr Wotolos is concerned about disclosing too much information about his customer directly to the futures desk, since he fears that Treasury may deal directly with Mr Popocros in future, bypassing Mr Wotolos, with the result that the latter will lose his percentage of commissions charged by Treasury.

Mr Wotolos now calls you (the compliance officer) to explain that he will be passing Mr Popocros' orders to Treasury for execution only. Furthermore, Mr Popocros is loath to sign any documentation, unless it is in Greek. Mr Wotolos asks you to assure him that there are no compliance issues with this course of action.

(i)   What alarm bells are ringing, and what compliance issues need to be considered?

(14 marks)

(ii)   Having identified the issues, what are your possible courses of action? Of these, choose your best course, and justify your reasons. **(6 marks)**

Section C

(Answer ANY TWO of the four questions)

15.   What challenges are posed by the increased use of the internet for selling financial services products?   **(15 marks)**

16.   Regulators are increasingly focusing on the responsibilities of the management of investment businesses. Why has the regulator taken such an approach, what are these responsibilities, and are the regulators correct to impose such responsibilities?   **(15 marks)**

17.   'The function of financial markets is to enable investment to be directed, in appropriate amounts, to the different destinations where it can be effectively employed. In order for this to occur, the markets must operate and be seen to operate, in an open, transparent and fair manner. The (Financial Services and Markets) Act includes important measures for the FSA to deal with market abuse.'

Discuss.   **(15 marks)**

18.   To what extent have the UK decided to 'gold plate' the MiFID transposition and will the harmonisation arising from MiFID be worthwhile?   **(15 marks)**

Winter 2006

Section A (30 Marks)

Answer ALL questions in this section

NB: FSMA = Financial Services and Markets Act 2000
FSA = Financial Services Authority
FSA Handbook = FSA's Handbook of rules and guidance

1.   Specify the consequences of breach of the general prohibition imposed under s19 of the FSMA.
(3 marks)

2.   With what requirements must a firm comply in order to treat an individual as an intermediate customer.
(3 marks)

3.   List four categories of exempt person under the FSMA.
(2 marks)

4.   List four of the regulated activities and four of the specified investments covered by the FSMA.
(4 marks)

5.   Identify three principles contained in the FSA Handbook which apply to individuals carrying out significant influence functions.
(3 marks)

6.   Explain the purpose of the 'Know your customer' (KYC) requirement imposed under the 'Conduct of Business' COB sourcebook.
(3 marks)

7.   List three types of collective investment schemes covered by Part XVII of the FSMA.
(3 marks)

8.   Identify six disciplinary sanctions available to the FSA under FSMA.
(3 marks)

9.   What are the principal types of conduct that may constitute market abuse under the FSMA?
(3 marks)

10.   List six of the required pieces of information that must appear on a confirmation issued to a private customer under the FSA Handbook.
(3 marks)

Section B (40 Marks)

Answer question 11 and ONE other.

11.   Tony Adams is an analyst at Premier Investment Bank plc covering the pharmaceuticals sector. Tony is shortly to publish a single stock piece on Gooner Pharmaceuticals plc and has diligently carried out fundamental research into the company. However, unlike some of his peers, he has a negative view of the stock and is thinking of downgrading his recommendation, principally because he is not sure whether Gooner's new drug, Zapazit (a revolutionary treatment for acne) will receive FDA regulatory approval in the USA. His draft forecast figures are considerably below the market consensus and, following Premier's revised and more open approach to recommendations, he plans to downgrade from "hold" to "reduce".

Gooner Pharmaceuticals plc are shortly to enter their close season and Tony is keen to issue his report as soon as possible. He has arranged to meet with the Finance Director, Brian Bull, to discuss his draft.

When Tony arrives, he finds that Gooner's Head of R&D, Dennis Bergen, and an analyst (Will Jonson) from Hotspur Investment Bank will also be present at the meeting. Hotspur Investment Bank is broker to the company and their regular updating report is due to be published shortly after the meeting. Previous reports have been upbeat and Jonson expects to maintain this stance. Jonson asks how Zapazit was progressing with the FDA. Dennis looks uncomfortable but is immediately interrupted by Brian who says that that they are restricted in what they can say because of the UKLA Guidance on the dissemination of price sensitive information. The rest of the meeting is fairly bland and nothing is said which changes Tony's negative stance on the stock.

After the meeting, Brian escorts Tony to his car and, whilst shaking his hand, says, "I think I know what you're thinking and you may well be right."

(a)   How should Tony act to preserve his own reputation for integrity?   **(3 marks)**

(b)   Following the meeting, what considerations should Jonson give before issuing his report?
                                                                                (5 marks)

(c)   How should Premier's Compliance Department respond to Tony's request for guidance if he reports his visit and what aspects might they consider ?   **(5 marks)**

       Following the meeting, Jonson is uncomfortable with his position and delays publication of his report. He is then pressured by senior management of Hotspur to proceed and is advised that Gooner is unhappy that he has not issued his normal positive report.

(d)   What are the relevant issues to consider?   **(7 marks)**

12.   You are the compliance officer of a newly established hedge fund manager in the West End of London. You are asked to advise on each of the following:

(a)   The sales force would like to start calling potential new clients and advertising their new fund range immediately.   **(5 marks)**

(b)   How should the firm classify its investment clients under the FSA rules?   **(5 marks)**

(c)   Explain the documentation that has to be entered into before the firm can conduct any regulated activities on behalf of any of its clients.   **(5 marks)**

(d)   If the client wishes to invest in high risk products on a discretionary basis, what further action is required?   **(5 marks)**

13. You are a compliance officer in a firm of hedge fund managers and become aware that one of your firm's most senior traders (Rapier) has been approached by a salesman from an investment bank, who is seeking market feedback on a forthcoming issue of US$ securities issued by a Brazilian Bank in New York.

Although you have not been approached for advice as to the impact that these discussions could have on Rapier's trading activities, which generate a significant portion of the firm's income, a number of concerns spring to mind.

(a) What might these concerns be and why? **(5 marks)**

You discuss these concerns with your boss who says that he will have a word with Rapier. As a result of this, you are approached by Rapier, who tells you that he has been an active borrower and short seller of stock in the Brazilian bank for some time and suggests that there is no reason why he should not continue to trade in this manner.

(b) What advice would you give and why? **(5 marks)**

Rapier also suggests to you that he believes that his trading activities are permitted as he is not trading in the UK.

(c) How would you respond and why? **(5 marks)**

Shortly after your conversation with Rapier, the Brazilian securities are issued and as a result of his short position, Rapier has booked the firm a substantial profit.

Nevertheless, you remain concerned at the position in which Rapier may have placed both himself and the firm.

(d) Explain what further issues may arise and their possible regulatory consequences.
(5 marks)

14. The Frankfurt head office of a German bank is considering opening an office in London to carry out corporate finance, investment research, commodities and derivatives activities in the United Kingdom. You are asked to advise on each of the following questions:

(a) (i) Describe the procedure that would apply for a German bank to make use of the single European passport provided under EU financial directives to establish a branch office in the UK. **(3 marks)**

(ii) Briefly discuss whether any top up permission might be needed and outline the relevant procedure and timeframe for obtaining a topup permission. **(3 marks)**

(b) Outline the division of responsibilities between the home and host state regulators in supervising the activities of the London branch office. **(3 marks)**

It is intended that the London branch office staff occasionally will travel to Paris to carry business with French customers and also that the London office staff will deal by telephone with customers based in France.

(c) What notifications need to be given before the London office can act in this way? **(2 marks)**

The German bank also has a Tokyo subsidiary which wishes to perform investment services with and for customers in the UK.

(d) (i) Can the Tokyo company exercise passport rights to carry on business in the UK?
(1 mark)

(ii) Outline any relevant exemptions from the requirement to be authorised or the restrictions on issuing financial promotions that might be available to the Tokyo company, enabling it to carry out limited UK activities? **(4 marks)**

The Tokyo company would like to issue research and promote Japanese securities to UK based investors.

(e)   Outline any exemptions from the requirement to be authorized that may apply under the Financial Promotions regime in this case. **(4 marks)**

Section C (30 Marks)

Answer TWO questions from this section

15. Outline the specific objectives of the FSA in its current "Treating Customers Fairly" initiative and discuss how firms can demonstrate Compliance. **(15 marks)**

16. The Money Laundering Sourcebook has been removed from the FSA handbook. Explain the reasons for this and discuss its intended impact. **(15 marks)**

17. Given recent events involving the activities of various hedge funds in the UK and abroad, there have been increased calls for closer regulation in this sector. Discuss the need for this and its possible consequences. **(15 marks)**

18. Assess the effectiveness of the current requirements imposed under the FSMA and the FSA Handbook (or elsewhere) with regard to the maintenance of high ethical standards in the financial services industry in the UK. **(15 marks)**

Summer 2006

Section A (30 Marks)

ALL questions in this section are to be answered.

Financial Services and Markets Act (FSMA) Financial Services Authority (FSA)

1. Specify the statutory objectives imposed on the FSA under the FSMA. **(2 marks)**

2. Under S19 of FSMA, what are the two requirements of persons carrying on a regulated activity in the United Kingdom, or purporting to do so. **(2 marks)**

3. List eight of the Principles for business detailed within PRIN of the FSA Handbook. **(4 marks)**

4. Identify the three main criteria for determining the Fitness and Propriety of Approved persons under APER in the FSA handbook. **(3 marks)**

5. List six means through which the FSA is held accountable in the exercise of its duties and functions under the FSMA. **(3 marks)**

6. List three conditions that need to be satisfied before a UK firm can exercise its passport rights to establish a branch in the EEA. **(3 marks)**

7. List three exceptions to the requirement to provide a customer with written terms of business. **(3 marks)**

8. Identify six exceptions under the Financial Promotions Order (FPO) for breach of the restriction on the issuance of financial promotions under S21 of the FSMA. **(3 marks)**

9. Identify the main compensation amounts available under COMP in the event of the collapse of a regulated firm. **(4 marks)**

10. When handling complaints under DISP a firm is required to undertake various actions within a specific timetable.

    (a) State the number of days for each of the following actions.

        (i)   Acknowledgement of receipt

        (ii) Provision of response

    (b) List two other documents which firms are required to provide when responding. **(3 marks)**

Section B (40 Marks)

Answer QUESTION 11 and ONE other.

All questions carry 20 marks each.

11.   Andy, Head of Equities Trading, is holding his weekly team meeting. The team is not performing well and Andy's boss has made it clear that he expects Andy to turn things around.

   Andy: 'OK - main point for our team meeting today – we must come up with some bright revenue generating ideas and quickly. Any thoughts?'

   Bob (Head of Proprietary Trading): 'We need to get more insight into the market and capitalise on that. Why don't we get Premises to re-locate us so that we are more in the swim of client order flow? Right next to the market makers would make best business sense. And we could arrange to see the list of client indications of interest – they're not confirmed orders at that stage and the clients would value the additional liquidity that would be provided in the market.'

   Charles (Deputy Head of Prop Trading and formerly a Research analyst): 'Better still, get us all access to all the pending research recommendation changes and take advantage of the window after they have been approved by the Research Committee, but before they have been released to clients. Don't let on, but I still have systems access to the draft reports being prepared in the Utilities sector from my time there as an analyst, and I intend to keep it that way!'

   Dave (Head of Sales): 'I'm on the board of one of our best clients - maybe I could exercise some influence there to bring more business to us?'

   Ed (Head of Syndication, Capital Markets): 'Personally, I think we should allow personal account shareholdings in the shares of our clients – that way we align our objectives with those of our clients. Anyway, these are all good ideas guys, they could really help the firm. Andy, why don't you give a prize for the best idea – a week's skiing for the winner and his best customer, would incentivise us most – we should use the classiest resort in the US, with travel, accommodation and all incidental expenses paid?'

   Fred (aside to George): 'I'm not entirely comfortable with some of this, are you? I think we should run it by Compliance and definitely escalate Charles's continuing access to draft research, if Andy won't take it up with him.'

   George (aside to Fred): 'Fred, listen, you are a long-standing close personal friend of Charles. 20 years working together and he's given you a lot of support in your career. How could you even think of putting him in a difficult position and potentially jeopardising his job? Have a heart for him and his family and don't go there. And remember, the rest of the team's jobs will be on the line if you block our route to improved performance. What's more, if previous experience is anything to go by, you'll very likely be disadvantaged or sidelined if you rock the boat right now.'

   From the above scenario:

   (a)   Identify four potential conflicts of interest, explain their regulatory and ethical nature and indicate appropriate tools for their management and control.   **(12 marks)**

   (b)   Why is appropriate management of conflicts important to firms?   **(4 marks)**

   (c)   Comment on George's and the firm's apparent attitude to whistle blowing. What provisions to facilitate whistle blowing would you expect within a firm?   **(4 marks)**

12.   You work for a large UK stockbroking firm in the City of London. The firm is reviewing its client lists and asks for your advice in connection with the following:

   (a)   Explain the general categories into which the clients of the firm should be divided. **(4 marks)**

   (b)   Explain the factors that should be taken into account in determining the extent of an individual client's experience and understanding in assigning any particular classification.
(4 marks)

   (c)   Explain the documentation that must be provided or entered into before a discretionary or advisory relationship can be established. **(4 marks)**

   (d)   Where another financial institution has introduced or referred a client, what criteria should be taken into account when determining who is the client of your firm? **(4 marks)**

   (e)   Where you carry on regulated activities for a regulated or unregulated collective investment scheme, how would you classify the client for regulatory purposes? **(4 marks)**

13.   You provide compliance advice on a part time basis to Stockwell Corporate Finance Ltd (SCFL) a small corporate finance firm with permission to advise and arrange deals in investments. Its business has always consisted solely of giving corporate finance advice and arranging corporate finance deals. SCFL does not deal in investments directly and has no dealing or settlement systems. Its three account executives all hold Controlled Function 23 (Corporate Finance Adviser).

   SCFL recently arranged the flotation of a business (Smallco) for a long-standing client, realising £40 million in cash for its 4 directors. The grateful directors of Smallco want to entrust the money to SCFL to invest for the long term in whatever way it thinks most appropriate. They offer to pay an annual fee of 1% of the value of the amount invested. Tim Robbins, the Managing Director of SCFL thinks that this is an excellent opportunity to earn income, diversify the business of the firm and support a good client relationship. He appears unconcerned about the regulatory implications, saying that the firm must 'strike while the iron is hot' and that he is not prepared to await your return from holiday which was long delayed while the flotation of Smallco took place.

   (a)   What are the regulatory implications of accepting the offer from the directors of Smallco to place their cash with SCFL? **(6 marks)**

   Although you learn, in due course, that it was suggested to Robbins at an executive meeting that there might be regulatory problems if the firm started to carry out this new business without changing the way it operates, he decided that the opportunity was too good to miss and that the firm must go ahead immediately, in view of the risk that another firm will get the business if SCFL delayed 'just to conform with yet more red tape.'

   Robbins emphasised the importance of providing a first rate service to the client, which he is confident of providing, because one of the account executives has past experience in investing funds for clients. He also instructed all members of staff to ensure that no-one outside SCFL and Smallco find out that the business is being done.

   (b)   What regulatory issues could result from this proposed course of action? **(4 marks)**

   When you return to the office on Monday you are called in immediately to Robbins' office where he tells you what has been going on whilst you were away and he says that although he was reluctant to do so, he had been persuaded by the other executives not to take any precipitate action but to await your return.

   Robbins tells you that he is determined that the firm must undertake this new business from the directors of Smallco, as he sees it being the start of important new opportunities for SCFL but, before being irrevocably committed he must know the regulatory implications of doing so, in particular what the likely requirements of the FSA would be.

   (c)   What do you tell Robbins? **(10 marks)**

14. Slide is Executive Chairman of Ruritania Goldfields, a company listed on the London Stock Exchange two years ago by Megabank, the large integrated investment bank. The shares were floated at 150p, but the market is just not interested in them – the price has been as high as 170p, but it usually trades below the issue price. They are currently trading at 140p.

Slide is desperate to get the share price up. His non-Executive Directors, who constitute his Remuneration Committee, have been very accommodating, and fully support his proposal that if the share price goes to 200p within three years of the float, Slide will receive a hefty bonus. Ruritania's year end results are due out next month and Slide knows that they are 'in line with expectations' and not at all likely to have any dramatic impact on the share price.

In order to get the price moving, Slide takes the following action over several days:

(a) He employs the services of a PR Consultancy and an Investor Relations Consultancy (both on large retainers) and instructs them to get to work in raising the profile of his company with the press and leading financial institutions.

(b) He telephones Bill, the Corporate Broker at Megabank responsible for the Ruritania account and tells Bill that

(1) he is useless and

(2) Slide will move the account from Megabank unless they get the price up.

(c) He telephones Harry, the Mining Analyst at Megabank, and tells Harry that

(1) he is useless and

(2) demands to see Harry's draft Research Note, so that he can 'polish it up a bit.'

(d) When he gets hold of Harry's Research Note, he tells him to

(1) increase the figure for the volume of ore to be extracted next year by 50% and

(2) to change the recommendation from 'Buy' to 'Outperform'.

(e) He telephones the Sales Traders at Megabank, to tell them that

(1) they are all useless and

(2) 'there is a drink in it for you' if they can get the Ruritanian price up.

(f) He convenes a meeting of all of London's Mining Analysts at a leading West End hotel and after a quick summary of the fortunes of the company, he invites them to the casino next door so that they can enjoy an all-expenses-paid evening out. They are accompanied by various young lady friends of Slide, whom he assures them are 'freelance consultants' although their knowledge of the mining industry seems somewhat slight.

(g) He contacts Rupert, the Head of the Private Client Department at Megabank, with whom he has had dealings in the past and tells Rupert that he is going to give him £25 million to manage, on a very specific mandate: Rupert is to use the money solely to buy and sell shares in Ruritanian Goldfields on Slide's behalf. Slide tells Rupert that he realises that the purchases will cause the price to rise in the short term, but that is not a problem – Rupert is to buy only when the price is soft and have the money fully invested within six months.

(h) Slide knows that Megabank's Private Client Department bought a large tranche of the shares when the company was floated and he suggests to Rupert that it might be an appropriate time for his Fund Managers to get some more stock for their clients.

Briefly explain for each of the above what circumstances would be relevant in determining whether any of the individuals might have committed Market Abuse under the FSMA? **(16 marks)**

What additional corporate governance issues and COB issues might arise as a result of Slide's conduct? **(4 marks)**

Section C (30 Marks)

Answer TWO questions in this section.

15.   Explain the main changes to the FSA enforcement process introduced after the recent review of enforcement practices (the Strachan review) and why this review was deemed necessary.

(15 marks)

16.   Comment on the value and effectiveness of the recent work undertaken by the European Commission in completing the Financial Services Action Plan (FSAP) and its proposed follow-up work during the period 2005-10.

(15 marks)

17.   Compare the various rights of redress available to consumers against financial firms and to financial institutions against the FSA commenting, in particular, on the complaints regimes set up under the FSMA as well as compensation entitlements and other common law remedies.

(15 marks)

18.   Discuss the main regulatory requirements imposed on the issuance, sale, purchase, use or holding of financial derivatives in the UK.

(15 marks)

Winter 2005

Section A (30 Marks)

Answer ALL questions in this section.

1. Specify the consequences of a breach of the general prohibition under s 19 of the Financial Services and Markets Act 2000 (FSMA). **(3 marks)**

2. List six of the supervisory principles set out in s 2(3) of the FSMA. **(3 marks)**

3. Identify the Threshold Conditions set out in Schedule 6 of the FSMA. **(3 marks)**

4. Explain the difference between a review conducted under s 12 of the FSMA and an inquiry under s 14. **(4 marks)**

5. Identify four of the specialist sourcebooks set out in Block 5 of the Financial Services Authority's (FSA) Handbook of Rules and Guidance. **(2 marks)**

6. Explain the options available to EU firms to carry on business in the UK under the FSMA. **(3 marks)**

7. List four types of collective investment scheme covered by Part XVII of the FSMA. **(4 marks)**

8. Explain the functions of the FSA as the competent authority for the listing of securities (the UKLA) under the FSMA. **(3 marks)**

9. Identify four enforcement powers that the FSA can exercise against firms acting in breach of the FSMA or the Handbook. **(2 marks)**

10. Briefly explain the different roles of the Financial Services Ombudsman and the Financial Services Compensation Scheme under the FSMA. **(3 marks)**

Section B (30 Marks)

Answer TWO questions from this section.

(NB from Summer 2006 sitting onwards, one of the four case study questions will be compulsory)

All questions carry 20 marks.

11.   The pension's office of a large European blue chip company contacts an Edinburgh fund management company with a view to having the firm manage a proportion of its global investment funds.

  (a)   How should the management company classify the prospective client for compliance purposes and what information would be required?   **(4 marks)**

  (b)   If the prospective client is assigned one status initially, in what cases can this be adjusted subsequently?   **(4 marks)**

  (c)   What documents have to be issued or entered into before the firm can begin to conduct any regulated activities on behalf of the client?   **(4 marks)**

  (d)   Explain the client reporting obligations and record keeping requirements that the firm has to comply with under FSA Conduct of Business (COB) rules.   **(4 marks)**

  (e)   If the prospective client is interested in investing in high risk products on a discretionary basis, what further action is required?   **(4 marks)**

12.   Omega Investment Bank is corporate broker to Theta Mining plc and financial adviser to Iota Mining plc. Theta Mining plc approaches Omega explaining that it wants to launch a bid for Iota and will pay Omega a significant fee if its bid is successful. 70% of the consideration for the purchase is intended to take the form of shares in Theta plc. Omega knows that Iota Mining is interested in the possibility of allying itself with a steel-maker possibly by means of a separate merger.

  (a)   What conflicts of interest may arise in this case? Which regulatory issues arise immediately?   **(5 marks)**

  Omega's mining research analyst takes a 'bearish' view of Theta Mining and wants to publish a research note to that effect. He advises the corporate broker that Theta Mining plc may have difficulty issuing the required share capital at the target price. The corporate broker asks the analyst to change his planned research note to a 'buy' recommendation. The research analyst then receives a telephone call from a large pension fund asking for his advice on suitable mining stocks to buy and sell.

  (b)   What are the principle regulatory issues that arise concerning the analyst's conduct so far? How should he handle the call from the pension fund?   **(5 marks)**

  Omega's proprietary trading desk currently holds a long position in Iota Mining and the corporate broker asks it to sell this holding to Theta Mining today at the current market price. The head of the trading desk is unaware of the proposed bid but prefers to increase the firm's holding in Iota Mining as he believes that its price will rise.

  (c)   What further regulatory issues should the head of the trading desk consider? How should he handle the position in Iota Mining?   **(5 marks)**

  In the meantime, Omega is approached by another client, Zeta Steel plc (a steel producer) who is interested in entering into a merger with Iota Mining plc. Omega advises Zeta Steel that this is not advisable and does not inform Iota Mining plc of this approach.

  (d)   What additional regulatory issues are created by Zeta Steel's approach?   **(4 marks)**

13.   You have taken on a new client at your investment bank in the City of London. The client has been introduced by a friend who was a junior analyst at a large US house. The new client is a UK based FSA regulated hedge fund manager.

      (a)   What checks must be conducted in relation to the new client to comply with relevant FSA Rules and UK money laundering requirements? **(4 marks)**

      (b)   When must these checks be carried out? **(2 marks)**

      During the first year of the relationship, a low but regular level of agency trading takes place. One day, your friend calls you up. Having originally asked funds to be routed through a prime broker account in London, your friend now asks for funds to be sent to an account in the Cayman Islands for 'tax reasons'. Shortly after this, you are asked to carry out a series of trades which are significantly larger than those that have previously been executed.

      You meet with your friend to discuss the expansion of the business and the rationale for the new payment arrangements. Your friend tells you that the trades are actually being carried out on behalf of a 'group company' but that the deals are being routed through the fund for 'tax reasons'. You are unhappy with your friend's explanation concerning the new payment arrangements. Over the next few days, your friend calls repeatedly to enquire whether you have put the new arrangements in place.

      (c)   What steps should you take to ensure that the relevant FSA Rules and UK money laundering controls are not breached? **(8 marks)**

      (d)   Explain the potential money laundering offences, defence and penalties that may otherwise apply under UK law. **(6 marks)**

14.   You are the Compliance Officer of the London branch of a European investment bank. You are investigating possible market abuse arising from a series of trades conducted by a trader in your European Equities department in shares in Boursat, a company listed on Euronext Paris.

      You speak to the trader who carried out the trades. He explains that, on the day that he placed the trade, while having a cigarette break outside the offices of the bank, he had overheard the line manager having a conversation with somebody on a mobile phone about a company which was the subject of a yet unannounced takeover bid.

      The trader informs you that, on returning to his desk he was instructed by one of the group's best clients to buy a sizable stake in Boursat. He tells you that he had a nasty feeling at the time but was not certain that the telephone call which he overheard the line manager make, was with this client. He also tells you that he raised his concerns with the Head of European Equities but was told 'in no uncertain terms' that he should place the trade as soon as possible. Shortly after the trade was placed, the takeover bid was publicly announced.

      You also interview the line manager who admits having made the call to one of his friends who worked for the client. He tells you that he had shared a carriage on the Eurostar from Paris with a man whom he recognised as a director of Boursat and had heard him talking in 'hushed tones' about certain 'possible developments' in relation to the company. However, he also explains that he had been hearing 'market rumours' about Boursat for some time and had expected a takeover bid in any event.

      (a)   Consider the potential criminal and civil liability of each of the following:

            (i)   The trader. **(4 marks)**

            (ii)   The line manager. **(4 marks)**

            (iii)   The Head of European Equitites. **(2 marks)**

            (iv)   The director of Boursat. **(2 marks)**

            (v)   The client. **(2 marks)**

      (b)   Explain the criminal and civil sanctions or penalties that may be imposed in each case from the behaviour described above. **(6 marks)**

Section C (30 Marks)

Answer TWO questions from this section.

All questions carry 15 marks.

15. Comment on the effectiveness of the regime set up to govern financial promotions under the FSMA and especially in the light of modern forms of communication. **(15 marks)**

16. Discuss the extent to which the wide ranging and substantial enforcement powers conferred on the FSA are balanced against the statutory accountability regime set up under the FSMA. **(15 marks)**

17. Explain the role and function of the Takeover Panel in the UK and the main principles and rules in accordance with which it acts. **(15 marks)**

18. 'Until the European Markets in Financial Instruments Directive (MIFID) and the Capital Requirements Directive (CRD) have come to effect, there will be a vacuum in the regulation of senior management systems and controls within UK financial institutions.' Discuss. **(15 marks)**

Summer 2005

Section A (30 Marks)

Answer ALL questions in this section.

1. Explain the difference between authorisation, permission and approval under Section 19, 20 and 59 of the Financial Services and Markets Act 2000 (FSMA). **(4 marks)**

2. Specify the consequences of carrying on activities outside the scope of permission granted to a firm by the Financial Services Authority (FSA) under S 20 of the FSMA. **(3 marks)**

3. List four categories of exempt person under the FSMA. **(2 marks)**

4. Identify four ways of managing conflicts of interest under the Conduct of Business (COB) section of the FSA Handbook of Rules and Guidance. **(2 marks)**

5. List three of the customer functions within the twenty seven controlled functions for approved persons as set out in the FSA's Supervision Manual (SUP) and briefly explain the activities covered by your examples. **(3 marks)**

6. Specify four conditions contained in COB with regard to the issuance of unsolicited real time financial promotions. **(4 marks)**

7. Identify the four process manuals contained within the Regulatory Processes block of the FSA Handbook of Rules and Guidance. **(2 marks)**

8. Specify the three types of behaviour prohibited under the UK Market Abuse regime as set out in the FSMA and explain the function of the Regular User test. **(4 marks)**

9. List three requirements as set out in COB in relation to a firm's Personal Account Dealings policy. **(3 marks)**

10. Explain the role and function of the Financial Services and Markets Tribunal under Part IX of the FSMA. **(3 marks)**

Section B

Answer TWO questions in this section.

11. The Treasury Department of a leading Australian high tech company approaches your firm with a view to utilising your advisory and portfolio management services in London. The person who would usually meet prospective clients is unavailable and you are asked to conduct the interview.

    Consider each of the following:

    (a) How would you classify the prospective client for compliance purposes and what information would you require to make any proper determination? **(4 marks)**

    (b) What identification and KYC checks should you conduct in order to comply with UK anti-money laundering regulation? **(4 marks)**

    (c) In addition to the money laundering checks, what are the main documentation requirements that apply under the COB before you can begin to conduct any designated investment business on behalf of the client? Outline the main contents of these documents. **(4 marks)**

    (d) If the prospective client is interested in investing in financial derivatives on either a discretionary or non-discretionary managed basis, describe any further requirements that would have to be complied with and outline their key contents. **(4 marks)**

    (e) If you hold client money or assets on behalf of the company, what are the main requirements that would apply under CASS? **(4 marks)**

12. You are the head of a division within a London investment bank, which covers a broad range of activities including Merger and Acquisition ('M&A') business and a separately incorporated Private Equity ('PE') operation.

    You are aware of the current high level of regulatory scrutiny attached to conflicts of interest by the FSA, especially in the area of investment banking, and some of the recent scandals that have occurred. You have also recently participated in a training video, which emphasised the ethical culture of the bank and reminded colleagues of the need for trust and integrity in dealing with clients whose interests must always be considered of paramount importance.

    (a) Explain the importance of the need to maintain high standards of behaviour and integrity under the FSA Handbook and how this is generally secured in practice. **(4 marks)**

    You become aware that your M&A team are advising client X on the acquisition of ABC Limited, which is the subject of an auction process. You are also aware through the conflict management escalation process that your PE colleagues are also participating in the auction process. The potential conflict has been managed on the basis of Chinese walls and independence policies and you have satisfied yourself on the reputational issues through disclosure.

    (b) Explain the COB requirements that apply with regard to independence policies and disclosure of conflicts of interest. **(4 marks)**

    (c) Explain what action should be taken to ensure the integrity of the Chinese walls in place and that they are effectively monitored and maintained. **(4 marks)**

    The M&A director responsible for advising client X comes to see you to provide an update on the transaction and confirms that his client is through to the final round of the auction process with one other bidder which is believed to be the affiliated PE operation. During the discussion you learn that following a review of the information made available to all potential bidders in the data room, the M&A team conducted its own comprehensive due diligence exercise which resulted in an assessment that the value of ABC Limited is significantly less than generally believed. The M&A director questions whether this will affect the bid strategy of his PE colleagues. You are also concerned to know whether PE have picked up on the over-valuation of ABC Limited and are not about to commit the Group and its Fund Investors to an investment of several hundred million dollars on the basis of erroneous information.

(d)   What courses of action are open to you and what factors would you take into account in deciding how to act?   **(4 marks)**

The next day, the M&A director responsible for advising client X comes to you in a state of excitement and informs you that their due diligence has uncovered certain accounting irregularities at ABC Limited.

(e)   What are your responsibilities to report such issues?   **(4 marks)**

13.   A private client of a leading UK 'boutique' investment bank has become increasingly dissatisfied with the quality of the service provided and has made a complaint to the firm. Your director has asked for advice on the following.

(a)   The client considers that she has been given the wrong advice with regard to some of the investments made as a result of which a significant amount of money has been lost especially in Asian equity and derivatives holdings. Outline the action that must be taken under DISP in relation to complaints   **(6 marks)**

(b)   What further redress options are available if the firm cannot satisfactorily resolve the complaint?   **(4 marks)**

(c)   What issues should be taken into account in determining whether the customer's complaint is justified?   **(4 marks)**

(d)   Following a separate investigation into the activities of the office manager, the FSA becomes aware of the extent of the loss. Can the FSA provide the client any assistance with regard to the losses suffered?   **(2 marks)**

(e)   In the event of the firm's subsequent collapse and closure, does the client have any separate right of claim apart from against the firm directly which is now in insolvency?   **(4 marks)**

14.   You are the FSA member of staff responsible for supervising General Research and Advisory Brokers Ltd (GRAB). The Financial Promotions Unit has drawn your attention to an advertisement published by GRAB in a major national newspaper about the shares in an unlisted oil services company. The promotion states that

(i)   The shares have grown by 10% more than the shares of listed companies in the same industry.

(ii)   The company has total assets of £128 million, and sales in the last year were £514 million.

(iii)   GRAB will provide a commission-free dealing service in the company's shares.

(iv)   Investors can expect to make a 25% return on the shares within 12 months.

(a)   Explain what issues the advertisement raises concerning compliance with relevant FSA rules and with relevant statutory provisions.   **(5 marks)**

(b)   In view of your findings in (a) above, describe the measures which you will now take to address the issues which you have discovered. Refer to the powers available to the FSA under statute and to the tools and policies referred to in the Regulatory Processes Block of the FSA Handbook. Also explain how your proposed course of action complies with the duties of FSA as described in S2 of FSMA and the regulatory objectives set out in S3-6 of FSMA.   **(5 marks)**

You subsequently find out that GRAB

     (v)   Has no records of who confirmed that the promotion could be issued, when or why.

     (vi)   Was dealing in the shares as principal at a bid-offer spread of 20% of the bid price.

     (vii)   Did not have permission to deal as principal in any type of investment.

The firm's chief executive believes that it was issued on the approval of an account executive who specialised in the sale of life assurance and collective investment schemes. This person has since been asked to leave the firm, because he has provided a poor standard of service to clients, giving rise to frequent complaints.

You also find out that

     (viii)   The oil services company has liabilities of £350 million.

     (ix)   GRAB has invested £22 million from clients' discretionary portfolios in the company's shares, and looks unlikely to recover more than 20% of their investments.

     (x)   The chief executive of GRAB is also a director of the oil services company.

(c)   Describe the regulatory issues arising from your new findings.   **(5 marks)**

(d)   Explain your views on the powers, tools and policies to be used on GRAB in view of the wider range of regulatory issues that you are aware of as a result of the information set out in (c). Also set out your views on the measures to be taken in respect of key approved persons at the firm and state whether you would take more stringent measures than in your answer to (b). Explain the reasons for your decision.   **(5 marks)**

Section C (30 Marks)

Answer TWO questions in this section.

15. Comment on the extent and manner in which senior managers are held accountable and responsible for regulatory breaches under the FSMA and the FSA's Handbook of Rules and Guidance. **(15 marks)**

16. Compare the effectiveness of various responses currently in place to deal with market abuse at the UK and European levels. **(15 marks)**

17. Assess the value and effectiveness of the current arrangements in place to combat money laundering and terrorist financing. **(15 marks)**

18. Identify the principal types of risk that financial intermediaries have to manage and the main requirements or standards that apply with regard to their control. **(15 marks)**

Winter 2004

Section A (30 Marks)

Answer ALL questions in this section.

1. Explain the content and purpose of the general prohibition under the Financial Services and Markets Act 2000 (FSMA). **(2 marks)**

2. List the four categories of authorised person under the FSMA. **(4 marks)**

3. List any three of the Financial Services Authority's (FSA) general functions under the FSMA. **(3 marks)**

4. List three of the consequences of breaching the restriction on the issuance of unlawful communications under S21(1) of the FSMA. **(3 marks)**

5. Specify any six of the general exceptions on the issuance of unlawful communications under the Financial Promotions Order (FPO). **(3 marks)**

6. Explain the purpose of the 'know your customer' (KYC) requirement under the Conduct of Business Sourcebook (COB). **(3 marks)**

7. Identify the three elements of the fit and proper test (FIT) for approved persons. **(3 marks)**

8. List any three general principles set out in the City Takeover Code. **(3 marks)**

9. List four of the core requirements set out in the FSA's Training and Competence Sourcebook (TC). **(2 marks)**

10. Explain the purposes of a warning notice, a decision notice, a final notice and a supervisory notice under the Decision Making Manual (DEC). **(4 marks)**

Section B

Answer TWO questions in this section.

(Please note: from June 2006 candidates are given one compulsory question and have to choose one other).

11.   You work for a medium-sized investment bank in London and are approached by the Head of Finance of a large fish processing company in Peterhead. The company purchases newly landed fish stocks which it sells on through Billingsgate Market in London. The company also deals with a number of restaurants and food suppliers on the European Continent who purchase stock directly and have it shipped using their own freight services. The company has heard about the possible value of using futures contracts to hedge commodity and foreign exchange risk. The company would either like to use existing possible exchange-traded futures contracts through Euronext.liffe or possibly develop new over the counter (OTC) products with the assistance of your firm.

You are asked to advise on each of the following

(a)   Explain the extent to which the proposed operations of the proposed customer and your firm may fall within the scope of FSMA.   **(4 marks)**

(b)   Outline the main classification and documentation requirements that would have to be complied with by your firm.   **(4 marks)**

(c)   Explain the separate requirements that will apply if your firm is to become responsible for managing the client's portfolio of investment contracts developed under the proposed arrangements.   **(4 marks)**

(d)   Identify any additional requirements that would apply under FSMA if either your company or the client wishes to promote the newly designed OTC fish futures contracts to third parties in the UK.   **(4 marks)**

(e)   Comment on any additional European issues that may arise if the new OTC products developed are to be marketed either to existing clients of the company or other third parties on the Continent.   **(4 marks)**

12.   The owner of a small specialist investment management company decides to purchase a holiday home in Thailand. While on vacation, someone suggests that he should settle in the Far East and provide his services over the internet using a local service provider. The owner of the business has some website design work carried out through a merchant in Pantib in Bangkok and the site opens for business one month later. This promises 'best cut-price virtual investment management services for all prospective investors anywhere in the globe'. Someone at the FSA in London notices the advertisement and refers it to the Financial Promotions Task Group, where you work.

You are asked to advise on the following:

(a)   Explain the extent to which the services offered may be covered by FSMA.   **(4 marks)**

(b)   Identify the nature of the type of advertisement issued and the relevant provisions that would apply under the FSA's Conduct of Business Sourcebook (COB).   **(4 marks)**

(c)   Explain the action that the owner may take to avoid breaching the UK restrictions on issuing financial promotions.   **(4 marks)**

(d)   Identify the potential enforcement action that the FSA may be able to take in the event that the new business breaches any of the provisions of the FSMA.   **(4 marks)**

(e)   Explain the remedies that may be available to potential recipients in the UK of the management services offered in the event that there is a significant or total loss of their funds.   **(4 marks)**

13. You are the compliance officer of an investment bank, which has just taken on as a client, Crimpleton Bains plc, a company whose shares are admitted to trading on the London Stock Exchange. The company is generally beset by scandal. Some concern has been expressed in relation to the manner in which Crimpleton Bains plc's officers, employees and advisers have conducted themselves in the past.

You are asked to consider whether any market abuse issues, or indeed other regulatory or legal issues, arise from the following circumstances.

(a) Crimpleton Bains plc makes widgets. It has recently been disclosed that your client may have sold widgets in breach of UN Sanctions against Iraq. As a result of this disclosure and the possibility of prosecution, the share price has slumped. It turns out that, one week before this information was made public, an employee of Crimpleton Bains plc sold all his shares, and then resigned. He tells you that he sold the shares as soon as he found out what his employers were up to and that his behaviour had nothing to do with a desire to avoid loss and everything to do with his personal morality. **(4 marks)**

(b) On two occasions, Crimpleton Bains plc gave an informal preview of a profit warning – which it was shortly going to announce to the market – to a journalist who had previously written favourable articles about the company. On the second occasion, the journalist was asked to sign a confidentiality agreement and was given a warning to the effect that he should not deal on the basis of that information until it had been announced to the market. On neither occasion did the journalist deal in the securities of the company. **(4 marks)**

(c) You review the text of announcements submitted by Crimpleton Bains plc to its previous corporate finance advisers and in comparing the text which, ultimately, was published by the regulatory information services, it is clear that some significant inaccuracies have arisen. You conclude that the error was that of the previous corporate finance advisers.
(4 marks)

(d) Crimpleton Bains plc's profitability is closely related to the price of fuel on the world markets, which has generally affected the share value of most similar manufacturing companies, including your client. It is clear to you that earlier statements relating to the sales growth of the company are no longer accurate. However, an internal revision of Crimpleton Bains plc's sales growth forecasts has not been announced to the market.
(4 marks)

(e) Crimpleton Bains plc has in the past held breakfast briefings with selected analysts. They have discontinued them, but can't remember whose idea it was to stop. They would like to start hosting them again. **(4 marks)**

14. A medium-sized banking group in the north of England takes over an equivalent sized group in Greece with the new Head Office of the combined entity being in London. It is agreed that many of the client relation services provided will be managed out of the head office of the Greek firm in Athens although telephone enquiries will be dealt with through a reception centre outsourced to Delhi. This may include dealing with existing UK and overseas clients of both groups as well as possibly accepting new clients for a range of telephone banking services to be developed. One of the concerns raised as part of the due diligence investigations undertaken is whether the new combined operations will be able to comply with the UK money laundering provisions. You have recently been appointed the Head of Compliance for the new group.

(a) Comment on the extent to which the existing UK money laundering requirements would apply with regard to the services to be provided in Athens and/or Delhi. **(4 marks)**

(b) Identify the main money laundering offences that might arise and defences that would apply to the extent that the services provided were covered under (a) above. **(4 marks)**

(c)   Outline the main customer identification, documentation and record requirements that would generally apply. **(4 marks)**

(d)   What action should be taken in the event that money laundering suspicions are raised by one of the call centre operators in Delhi? **(4 marks)**

(e)   Comment on the extent to which the new senior management of the combined group would be responsible and may be held liable for any breaches of the money laundering requirements applicable. **(4 marks)**

Section C (30 Marks)

Answer any TWO questions.

Each question carries 15 marks

15. Explain the structure and objectives of the High Level Standards as set out in the FSA's Handbook of Rules and Guidance. **(15 marks)**

16. Comment on the extent to which the new market abuse offences created under FSMA are more effective and responsive than the earlier provisions governing insider trading in the UK as set out in the Criminal Justice Act 1993. **(15 marks)**

17. Assess the extent to which the carrying on of financial derivatives related activities is regulated in the UK (including both exchange traded and over the counter (OTC) products). **(15 marks)**

18. Compare the main rights available to securities firms wishing to carry on financial business in the UK coming from within the EEA, the USA or Asia. **(15 marks)**

Summer 2004

Section A (30 Marks)

Answer ALL questions in this section.

1. Explain the difference between authorisation and permission under the Financial Services and Markets Act 2000 (FSMA). **(2 marks)**

2. List any eight of the statutory objectives or statutory principles with which the Financial Services Authority (FSA) has to comply under FSMA. **(4 marks)**

3. Specify four of the threshold conditions which a regulated firm has to meet to obtain a Part IV permission under FSMA. **(2 marks)**

4. Explain the purpose of the Regulated Activities Order (RAO). **(2 marks)**

5. Explain the purpose and content of the aggregation and allocation rule under the Conduct of Business (COB) section of the FSA Handbook of Rules and Guidance. **(4 marks)**

6. Identify three market abuse offences and three market abuse defences. **(6 marks)**

7. Explain the difference between a 'real time' and a 'non-real time' financial promotion. **(3 marks)**

8. What is a penny share and what risk warnings should be provided to potential investors in such instruments under the COB? **(2 marks)**

9. Identify the main content of a key features document under the COB. **(3 marks)**

10. Explain the difference between the Ombudsman Scheme and the Financial Services Compensation Scheme under FSMA. **(2 marks)**

Section B (40 Marks)

Answer TWO questions from this section.

(Please note: from June 2006 candidates are given one compulsory question and have to choose one other).

Each question carries 20 marks.

11. The head of a large firm of Independent Financial Advisers contacts your firm asking you to provide them with various portfolio investment management services for individuals known to them. Your firm is regulated by the FSA in the conduct of such services.

    Consider and discuss each of the following.

    (a) Identify your potential client, or clients, and the relevant client classifications that would apply under COB. **(4 marks)**

    (b) Outline the main documentation requirements that should be complied with by your firm. **(4 marks)**

    (c) Explain the main rules that would apply with regard to the safe custody of any securities held with your firm. **(4 marks)**

    (d) Identify the main client money rules that have to be complied with by your firm. **(4 marks)**

    (e) Explain any additional requirements that would apply if stock lending, margin trading or other collateral arrangements were to be permitted. **(4 marks)**

12. A small group of fund managers within an investment bank based in Hong Kong are instructed to set up a private equity fund, structured as a limited partnership, to raise money in the London markets. The fund will be an unregulated collective investment scheme. The fund management team has not decided where it will be based or the structure of the fund. They are, in particular, concerned about the regulatory implications of attempting to launch such a fund in the UK. You are asked to provide advice on each of the following.

    (a) One possibility is that the fund manager will be based in Jersey. A team based in London would source deals in the UK and provide investment reports to the Jersey manager who would take the ultimate decisions on whether or not to invest. The team in London will then play a prominent role in negotiating the terms on which the fund will invest. The London team will also be involved in marketing fund interests to potential investors.

    Explain which regulated activities will have to be included within any Part IV Permission of the London team. **(4 marks)**

    (b) Identify any additional permissions that the London team will require if investment and other day-to-day decisions are made on behalf of the fund in London rather than by the Jersey manager. **(2 marks)**

    (c) Explain the general restrictions that would apply with regard to promoting such a fund in the UK. **(4 marks)**

    (d) The London team are interested in tapping investment opportunities and marketing the fund to investors in the European Economic Area. Advise the firm on any additional regulatory obligations that may apply if they take this course of action. **(4 marks)**

    (e) The London team are about to meet with a website designer. They are proposing to put their draft private placement memorandum on to their new website. Advise the team as to the most efficient way of achieving this without creating any significant additional regulatory problems. **(2 marks)**

    (f) In the event that investors are concerned with the performance or conduct of the fund, explain what rights or remedies may be available to them under the FSMA or FSA Handbook. **(2 marks)**

    (g) Explain any further remedies or rights of action that may be available in the event of the subsequent collapse of the fund. **(2 marks)**

13.   A German publishing company proposes acquiring a majority stake in a leading newspaper group that publishes a range of titles in the UK. Both companies and their major subsidiaries are listed in their respective markets.

A number of meetings are arranged, to be held in the UK and in Germany, between the senior managers of the two companies. The Company Secretary of the UK group is informed that certain parties are considering purchasing or disposing of shares in one or both companies and approaches you as head of compliance for the UK group. You are asked to advise on the following.

(a)   The Managing Director of the German group has placed an order through his broker for the purchase of a block of shares in a number of subsidiary companies within the UK group (but not the holding company directly).   **(10 marks)**

(b)   One of the senior managers of the UK group has instructed an investment adviser in Hong Kong to purchase shares in the German company through Hong Kong to be held in the name of a nominee company.   **(2 marks)**

(c)   A group of senior managers in the German company instructs the management company responsible for the German group's pension fund to purchase an additional block of shares in both companies.   **(2 marks)**

(d)   The cousin of the wife of one of the senior managers in the UK holding company decides to purchase as many shares as he can afford in the UK company after the prospective bid was mentioned by the manager's wife to his friend.   **(2 marks)**

(e)   One of the staff employed by the cleaning company which services the offices of the UK parent company finds a copy of the proposed bid announcement on the floor while cleaning up and decides to purchase shares in the company using that month's salary.   **(4 marks)**

14.   A bureau de change opens in the shopping mall under Canary Wharf in London. The office puts a promotional advertisement in its windows, advising that, for a limited period only, it will offer currency exchange services into sterling or euros at exceptionally low rates of commission with 'no questions asked'. The manager of the bureau de change approaches you to discuss any potential liability under UK money laundering laws. You are asked to explain the following.

(a)   The meaning of money laundering for the purposes of the relevant UK requirements.

                                                                                                                             (4 marks)

(b)   The main offences and defences that may apply in the event that the office is considered to have engaged in money laundering.   **(6 marks)**

(c)   The nature of any customer identification or record requirements.   **(4 marks)**

(d)   The extent to which the office may avoid asking any difficult questions of customers with regard to the source of funds and the extent to which it has to report any information where this is voluntarily tendered by customers.   **(4 marks)**

(e)   Any potential liability that may be attached to the content of the advertisement alone and, in particular, with the reference to 'no questions asked'.   **(2 marks)**

Section C (30 Marks)

Answer TWO questions from this section.

Each question carries 15 marks.

15. Explain the purpose and nature of the approved persons regime established under FSMA and the FSA Handbook of rules and guidance. **(15 marks)**

16. Outline the means by which conflicts of interest in research departments can be managed under the FSA Handbook. **(15 marks)**

17. Discuss the extent to which eurobond activity and the eurobond markets are regulated under FSMA. **(15 marks)**

18. Comment on the progress made to date in the creation of a single capital market within the European Union. **(15 marks)**

Winter 2003

Section A (30 Marks)

Answer ALL questions in this section.

1. Identify the main sanctions imposed for breach of the general prohibition against carrying on regulated activities without being authorised or exempt under the Financial Services and Markets Act (FSMA). **(4 marks)**

2. List the four categories of authorised person set out in FSMA. **(4 marks)**

3. Identify four of the threshold conditions set out in Schedule 6 of FSMA. **(2 marks)**

4. Explain the best execution rule under the Financial Services Authority (FSA) Handbook of Rules and Guidance and identify two situations in which the obligation may not apply. **(3 marks)**

5. Specify the main requirements imposed under the FSA Conduct of Business (COB) rules with regard to suitability. **(3 marks)**

6. Describe the main requirements that apply to becoming an exempt appointed representative of an authorised person. **(3 marks)**

7. Describe three of the main requirements that apply to a firm authorised to provide custody services. **(3 marks)**

8. Specify the main financial limits on compensation that may be payable to customers in connection with deposit taking and investment business. **(4 marks)**

9. State four means through which the FSA is held accountable for the discharge of its functions under FSMA. **(2 marks)**

10. Identify the circumstances in which the FSA will not be immune from liability in damages to investors or depositors for loss suffered under FSMA. **(2 marks)**

Section B (40 Marks)

Answer TWO questions from this section.

11.   A rich far eastern domiciled individual approaches a small private securities firm in London to discuss possible investment opportunities. The individual claims to be a sophisticated investor.

Consider each of the following.

(a)   How would you classify the prospective client for FSA Conduct of Business (COB) purposes? Under which types of headings may the client be categorised and what information would you require to make any proper determination?   **(4 marks)**

(b)   If the prospective client is assigned one status initially, in what circumstances may this be adjusted subsequently? Comment, in particular, on the possibility that the prospective client may wish to have either more, or less, protection than that already provided.   **(4 marks)**

(c)   What documentation requirements generally apply under the COB rules before you can begin to conduct any regulated activities on behalf of the client?   **(4 marks)**

(d)   If the prospective client is interested in investing in financial derivatives on either a discretionary or non-discretionary managed basis, do any further requirements have to be complied with?   **(4 marks)**

(e)   With what continuing classification or documentation obligations under the COB must the firm comply, in carrying out business on behalf of the individual?   **(4 marks)**

12.   A US investment management company wants to set up an operation in London to launch a new pooled investment product under the terms of which investors will own a proportionate share in a portfolio of business property holdings across Europe. You are asked to advise on each of the following.

(a)   Explain the main requirements that apply with regard to the setting up of a new financial business in the UK under FSMA.   **(4 marks)**

(b)   Comment on the extent to which the proposed arrangements might fall within the definition of a collective investment scheme under FSMA.   **(4 marks)**

(c)   Identify any other investment activities that may be involved.   **(4 marks)**

(d)   Explain the main restrictions that apply with regard to the sale and promotion of such schemes in the UK.   **(4 marks)**

(e)   Assuming that the investment management company is a European firm, comment on any additional issues that may arise under European legislation and the FSMA.   **(4 marks)**

13.   You work for a private bank that provides specialist investment services for wealthy individuals. A rather large US gentleman carrying a cowboy hat and wearing cowboy boots comes into your office in the city. He explains that he is involved with the 'oil business' (with no further information being provided with regard to the source of the funds involved). The gentleman advises that he would like to open a portfolio of high-risk investments through the London markets. He is particularly interested in oil and energy-related futures and other derivative contracts.

Advise on each of the following.

(a)   Explain any initial concerns that may arise from a compliance perspective and what action you would take, specifically with regard to money laundering checks and internal notifications within your firm.   **(4 marks)**

(b)   Confirm the potential money laundering offences, defences and penalties that may apply under UK law.   **(6 marks)**

(c)   Explain any additional measures that may be relevant from an international, European or US perspective.   **(4 marks)**

The gentleman leaves after your initial meeting. He telephones the following week to discuss progress and the reason for any delay.

(d)   What would you advise?   **(2 marks)**

You are subsequently informed (during the course of the identity checks undertaken) that the gentleman has links with a known right-wing organisation that has been connected with terrorist sympathy groups in certain parts of the world.

(e)   Advise on any additional potential areas of liability that may arise.   **(4 marks)**

14.   You are the Compliance Officer of Wealth Services International (UK) Limited, a newly established London based subsidiary of Wealth Services International Inc, a US based financial advisory firm aimed at affluent individuals. You have been asked to provide your views on the feasibility of setting up a global website for the group. The website will be hosted in the US with its content managed by Wealth Services International Inc.

Your opinion is sought on each of the following matters.

(a)   The website will advertise Wealth Services International's personal wealth advisory and management services. You are asked to advise on anything required to ensure that the website does not 'raise any UK compliance issues'.   **(4 marks)**

(b)   The advisory and management services are to be provided primarily to UK customers by Wealth Services International (UK) Limited. The CEO of Wealth Services International Inc would, however, like to offer some advisory and management services using staff based in the US. The website designers have also proposed introducing a 'live chat' facility that will allow Wealth Services International Inc staff (based in the US) to provide advice to UK based customers and potential customers of the group through an online chatroom.
                                                                                    (4 marks)

(c)   The website will also advertise details of mutual funds – all of which are unregulated collective investment schemes – managed by Wealth Services International Inc. Individuals will be able to apply for these funds online.   **(4 marks)**

(d)   Webworld Inc is to design and host Wealth Services International Inc's website and has asked for an indemnity from Wealth Services International Inc in the event that the project results in Webworld Inc breaching any relevant laws or legislation including 'the UK Financial Services and Markets Act 2000'. Before providing this indemnity, Wealth Services International Inc is anxious to know what risks Webworld Inc may be incurring under UK regulatory laws.   **(4 marks)**

(e)   The Head of Sales at Wealth Services International Inc has been in discussions with Topwealth.com, a company located in the UK which operates an online website based on 'concierge' service. Topwealth.com arranges for the provision of a range of services to its 'members' who are all affluent individuals located in various jurisdictions including the UK.

        The intention is that Topwealth.com will run an 'advertorial' listing which will praise the products and services of the Wealth Services International group and be accompanied by a hypertext link to Wealth Services International website. There is also talk of 'branding' the service in Topwealth.com's name. Topwealth.com will be paid a 'success fee' based on the number of customers signed up by the Wealth Services International group.   **(4 marks)**

Section C (30 Marks)

Answer TWO questions from this section.

All questions carry 15 marks each.

15. Comment on the extent to which the High Level Standards set out in Block 1 of the FSA Handbook of Rules and Guidance control conflicts of interest or how these are otherwise dealt with under the Handbook. **(15 marks)**

16. Outline the main enforcement powers conferred on the FSA under FSMA and how these are developed or expanded under its Handbook. **(15 marks)**

17. Discuss the manner in which market abuse is controlled under current or proposed UK and European legislation. **(15 marks)**

18. Explain the purpose and content of the current laws, rules and regulations that apply with regard to the disclosure of interests in shares and the substantial acquisition of shares in the UK. **(15 marks)**

Summer 2003

Section A (30 Marks)

Answer ALL questions in this section.

1. Identify the general functions of the FSA under FSMA. **(4 marks)**

2. List four of the Principles for Businesses set out in PRIN. **(4 marks)**

3. The Financial Promotion rules on the communication of unsolicited real time financial promotions contain a number of requirements that must be complied with. List three of these requirements. **(3 marks)**

4. The FSA's client money and assets rules require that client money is segregated from a firm's assets. Provide three exceptions to this general rule. **(3 marks)**

5. The FSA approved persons rules set out 27 Controlled Functions. Name four of the Significant Influence functions and four of the Customer Functions. **(4 marks)**

6. Identify three of the functions in which a Senior Executive Officer (SEO) in a regulated firm must comply with SYSC. **(3 marks)**

7. List three ways in which the FSA can be held accountable under FSMA. **(3 marks)**

8. The FSMA provides for two sets of statutory exemptions against an action for market abuse. Explain each of these. **(2 marks)**

9. Identify two circumstances in which a customer may exercise cancellation rights under the FSA's cancellation or withdrawal rules. **(2 marks)**

10. The FSMA includes revised provisions with regard to RIEs and RCHs. Provide three examples of an RIE and one example of an RCH. **(2 marks)**

Section B (40 Marks)

Answer TWO questions in this section.

(Please note: from June 2006 candidates are given one compulsory question and have to choose one other).

All questions carry 20 marks.

11. You are the newly appointed Compliance Officer of an old established securities firm in the City of London. You are asked to advise on the relevant customer classification of the following parties including any rights to opt up or down and the nature of the customer agreement or terms of business that should be entered into.

(a)   A non-regulated Cayman incorporated hedge fund.   **(4 marks)**

(b)   An unregulated collective investment scheme.   **(4 marks)**

(c)   Megabank – a UK authorised clearing bank.   **(4 marks)**

(d)   The Treasury department of an FTSE listed company.   **(4 marks)**

(e)   An individual based in the Middle East with one year's experience of trading in equities.

                                                                                          (4 marks)

12. A Spanish bank, operating through a branch in London, decides to offer custody services to its private and professional customers in the UK. You are asked to advise on each of the following matters.

(a)   The general implications of providing a new financial activity under FSMA in the UK.

                                                                                          (4 marks)

(b)   The extent to which this activity may be covered by an existing European licence and FSMA implications of this.   **(4 marks)**

(c)   The main prudential and regulatory provisions that would govern the provision of the service and the relationship between the bank and its customers.   **(4 marks)**

(d)   The obligations that would apply with regard, in particular, to any stock lending of investments of a private customer.   **(4 marks)**

(e)   The main additional requirements that would apply in connection with the sales and promotion of such services in the UK.   **(4 marks)**

13. You are the Head of Compliance at Megabank, a large integrated securities house. Megabank has recently appointed Roy 'Brass' Neck to re-invigorate its Equities Division, which includes both Equity Research and Equity Sales. Neck's reputation is as a practical, hands-on manager, with aggressive ideas about the ways to generate business and motivate staff.

After two weeks in the post, he comes to you with the following proposals, which he wants implemented without delay.

(a)   Whenever the Corporate Finance Department goes to 'pitch' for a new client, they must be accompanied by an analyst from the Equities Department. He explains that this will show the potential client that Megabank has a strong team of experts; it will also enable the analysts to provide a 'reality check' to control over-enthusiastic Corporate Financiers and turn down unsuitable new clients.

(b)   The specialised dealers who currently work in the Private Client Department must be redeployed within the Equity Department, and report to Neck. This is so that he can control the dealers' activities and ensure that all the order flow in equities is retained within the firm. At present, too many trades are being executed with other houses via SETS and Retail Service Providers. He will also be able to give the dealers large lines of stock, which they can then place with private clients.

(c)   If a corporate client is going to make an announcement, the Corporate Finance Department must brief the Equity Division well before the announcement is made, in order for them to be prepared for the inevitable questions from clients, which will arise when the announcement is made.

(d)   The Nominee and Safe Custody Department must notify all Equities Division staff of every 'S212 Notice' they receive. (S212 of the Companies Act gives companies the power to demand details of the identity of underlying shareholders within a reasonable time. Company secretaries usually write to nominee companies to find out who the beneficial owners are.)

What advice would you provide Mr Neck with regard to each of the arrangements that he wants to put in place?   **(20 marks)**

14.   You are the Money Laundering Reporting Officer of Poundwise Wealth International Limited, an FSA regulated firm that specialises in managing the investments of some of the wealthiest sports personalities in the world. Your firm has recently been approached by Esteban Morrisse, a famous bullfighter who retired at the top of his profession four years ago and has sinced moved to London. He now wants your firm to take him on as a client.

You meet Esteban Morrisse who tells you that he has been a bullfighter all his life and owes all of his wealth to his sport. He speaks in glowing terms of his affection for the English and his plans to settle in London permanently. While making small talk with him, he tells you that he would have loved to have been able to share with the English his love of bullfighting and indeed once tried to stage a bullfight in the Millenium Dome. He tells you his plans collapsed when a 'busybody lawyer' told him that he would have been locked up if he tried.

'Sometimes you English amaze me,' he says. 'In your country, it would be quite all right for me to stab a bull if I did it in a slaughterhouse. But if I were to do it in the bullring, with hundreds of people cheering, I'd be locked up as a common criminal!'

If you take on Esteban Morrisse as a client, what obligations do you and your firm have under the Proceeds of Crime Act 2002 and the FSA Rules?   **(18 marks)**

While you are considering your legal obligations you receive a call from Esteban Morrissee. 'What's with the delay?' he asks. 'Is there a problem? If there is, I want you to tell me all about it and I will help to sort things out.'

What will you tell him?   **(2 marks)**

Section C (30 Marks)

Answer TWO questions in this section.

All questions carry 15 marks.

15. 'The FSMA establishes a separate but parallel statutory regime for financial promotions (under S21) in addition to the dual authorisation and permission system created (under S19(1) and S20(1)).' Discuss. **(15 marks)**

16. 'The new regulatory regime established under FSMA is, to a significant extent, based on internal management accountability and liability rather than external supervision and sanction.' Discuss. **(15 marks)**

17. Explain the main provisions and principles that apply with regard to the conduct of takeovers and other corporate acquisitions in the UK. **(15 marks)**

18. Outline the main markets and trading systems on the London Stock Exchange, together with the main dealing and reporting requirements that apply to each. **(15 marks)**

Winter 2002

Section A (30 Marks)

Answer ALL questions in this section.

1. Identify the four statutory objectives of the Financial Services Authority (FSA) under the Financial Services and Markets Act 2000 (FSMA) and four of the statutory principles of good regulation.
    (4 marks)

2. Explain the nature and significance of an 'authorised person' and an 'exempt person' under FSMA 2000.
    (4 marks)

3. Identify four of the five threshold conditions set out in the FSMA 2000.
    (2 marks)

4. List four of the regulated activities and four of the investments covered by FSMA 2000.   **(4 marks)**

5. In what circumstances would a firm be entitled to classify a client as a private client who would otherwise be an intermediate customer under the FSA Handbook of Rules and Guidance (the Handbook)?
    (4 marks)

6. Name two of the sections within the Handbook that set out the key obligations in relation to management functions.
    (2 marks)

7. Identify and explain the main regulatory requirements that apply with regard to financial promotions under FSMA 2000 and FSA Handbook and the source of the main exceptions available.
    (3 marks)

8. Explain the purpose of the 'Regular Market User Test' with regard to market abuse.   **(2 marks)**

9. Name four types of administrative sanction against a firm available to the FSA under FSMA 2000.
    (2 marks)

10. Identify the three forms of redress available under the Redress block of the Handbook.   **(3 marks)**

Section B (40 Marks)

Answer any TWO questions in this section.

(Please note: from June 2006 candidates are given one compulsory question and have to choose one other).

All questions carry 20 marks.

11. A newly established Italian financial services company is considering offering financial services over the internet. It is concerned about the possible implications of FSMA 2000 on its activities. It asks for your advice on:

    (a) Whether any proposed selling arrangements could fall under the provisions of FSMA 2000.
    (4 marks)

    (b) The regulatory consequences for the firm, if this was considered to constitute the carrying on of a regulated activity in the United Kingdom. **(4 marks)**

    (c) The different means of becoming an authorised person available to the firm under FSMA 2000.
    (4 marks)

    (d) The general nature of the requirements imposed with regard to the promotion of financial services on the internet. **(4 marks)**

    (e) The general nature of the customer classification and consequent customer agreement or terms of business obligations that would apply. **(4 marks)**

12. (a) You are the Compliance Officer of an FSA regulated firm which markets unregulated collective investment schemes. You have been asked to advise on whether such financial products will be covered by FSMA 2000. **(2 marks)**

    (b) Explain the main restrictions that will apply with regard to the marketing and sale of such products. **(4 marks)**

    (c) The firm then decides to market the schemes to individuals who fall within the Certified High Net Worth Individuals exemption. Advise on the action that the firm must take in this case. **(4 marks)**

    (d) In addition to persons who fall within the Certified High Net Worth Individuals exemption, you are also asked to outline four other categories of person to whom unregulated collective investment schemes may be marketed. **(6 marks)**

    (e) Mary Cherry, one of the firm's fund managers, subsequently proposes that the Offering Memorandum which contains details of these unregulated investment schemes be displayed on your firm's website. The website is to allow investors to apply for interests in these unregulated collective investment schemes using an application form displayed on your firm's site. Explain the action that may be taken to ensure that the restriction on promoting unregulated collective investment schemes contained in S238 of FSMA 2000 is not breached. **(4 marks)**

13. You are the Compliance Officer of Dumbarton Bank which is regulated by the FSA. Your monitoring system has uncovered what appears to be an unusual trading pattern in the shares of Popcat plc, which was listed on the London Stock Exchange exactly one week ago. A research report into Popcat plc has recently been written by one of your firm's analysts, Basil Bengo, and has been published this morning. The report contains a SELL recommendation in relation to Popcat plc. Popcat plc manufactures self-heating cans of coffee.

    You interview Basil Bengo about the circumstances in which the report was written. Basil Bengo informs you that the main reason that the report contained a SELL recommendation was that he had visited an old friend, Norbert Wiener, who runs a large cash and carry. Basil tells you that he arrived at Norbert's warehouse to find it under an inch of warm coffee. Norbert had told Basil that, twice in the last month, individual self-heating cans of coffee had spontaneously begun to heat up, resulting in a chain reaction that had destroyed thousands of pounds worth of stock. Norbert told Basil that he had heard similar stories from other operators of cash and carry businesses and that a number of them were planning to sue Popcat plc.

(a)   Explain your initial concerns at this stage.   **(6 marks)**

Basil Bengo also tells you that, prior to the publication of his report, he had met with Max Brooklynshaw, the CEO of Popcat plc, to discuss his research. Basil told Max that he was planning to publish a SELL recommendation. Basil tells you that during the course of the meeting, Max had mentioned to him that although there had been certain problems with the self-heating coffee cans, they were about to launch a bond issue that would considerably strengthen their financial position. The bond issue was not yet public knowledge.

As an afterthought, Max tells Basil:

'I'm afraid that this information is rather price sensitive: you're an insider now and so you can't use it.'

(b)   Explain your concerns about Max's behaviour.   **(6 marks)**

(c)   Having received the information relating to the bond issue, what should Basil have done?
                                                                                (2 marks)

You then ask Basil Bengo whether he had mentioned his intentions to publish a SELL recommendation to anybody prior to publication. Basil tells you that he may have mentioned his intentions to a friend and colleague in sales, Dallas Hickerson. You interview Dallas Hickerson who advises you that the only person with whom he had spoken was a client at a fund manager, Stan Roscoe Ltd, which held 2% of Popcat plc. He admits that he mentioned the 'general thrust' of his conversation with Basil Bengo. However, Dallas tells you that Stan Roscoe had informed him that they were increasingly unimpressed with the management at Popcat plc and were therefore planning to sell their stake in the company in any event. Stan Roscoe Ltd then placed a sell order with Dallas Hickerson, selling their 2% stake in Popcat plc.

The research report was published the following day.

(d)   What concerns do you now have and would it have made any difference if Dallas had
       solicited the sell order but had not disclosed his knowledge?   **(6 marks)**

14.   You are the Compliance Officer within a large United Kingdom banking group. Your responsibilities include money laundering deterrence and reporting suspicious transactions to NCIS and the police authorities to the extent relevant.

      The following four cases are referred to you. Identify the suspicions and concerns, if any, that you may have and explain what action you would take in each case.

      Case 1

      A newly appointed Credit Manager at a car loan company within your Group raises concerns with you about one of his customers, Ray. Ray had recently bought a luxury sports car worth about £55,000. He obtained a five-year loan for £40,000 through the credit company and had paid the balance in cash.

      The Credit Manager undertook some checks against historical records and discovered that Ray had taken out several loans over the previous six years.

      All were for the same amount of money and all with a large proportion of cash, incurring a redemption penalty upon early repayment of the loans. Ray had seemed quickly to become bored with the new cars and sold them on to private buyers and small garages, obtaining cheques from these new owners in each case.   **(5 marks)**

Case 2

The manager of a local money exchange office recently opened a personal account in his own name at a local retail branch of your bank. The branch also maintains the account of the money exchange office.

Although the manager is well known to the staff, he was subjected to the usual verification of identity procedures which were satisfactorily completed. When asked how he intended to use the account, such as whether salary will be received into the account, he replied that the account was for his own personal use and that he wished to keep it separate from his other personal banking facilities, which he maintained with another financial institution. The account was opened without further questioning.

Within a few weeks of opening the account, the manager credited the proceeds of various currency exchanges to the account. The branch is used to various currencies being purchased and sold by the exchange house, although only with proceeds being debited (or credited) to the account of the exchange house itself.

No individual member of staff within the branch undertook any significant number of transactions for this customer mainly due to job rotation, training, holidays and sickness. Many who saw him in the branch often assumed that he was there on business for the exchange office.

Within a month, the balance on the personal account was in excess of £500,000 and the customer called into the branch to arrange a wire transfer for £450,000 to a third party in Switzerland. He asked your bank to quote the name of the exchange office as the remitter. The instructions were followed by the branch.

After a further two months, the customer has asked for a second wire transfer for £450,000 to be made to the same third party's account in Switzerland. He has again requested that the bank show the remitter as the money exchange office. The Branch Manager refers the matter to you for advice.

(5 marks)

Case 3

Robert Morgan has approached a branch within your Group to establish an account relationship for his new company, which has already opened accounts in the Cayman Islands and Spain (with non-Group companies).

The company has a website and Morgan has handed to the officer dealing with the account opening a glossy professional brochure that sets out the company's history and Morgan's own background.

It appeared from this that the business was involved in setting up home building schemes in areas with deprived housing and it encouraged wealthy investors to invest funds in the schemes covered.

Morgan and the other signatory (a member of Lloyd's of London) were properly identified and all of the correct company documentation was provided. The account was duly opened.

Within a short period of time, a number of substantial wire transfers were made into the account and a balance in excess of £5m was accumulated. Some payments of around £100k were paid away to accounts in the name of the companies in the Cayman Islands and Spain. Some smaller amounts were also withdrawn in cash.

When your Group office received a request to send £5m to an account of a law firm in Switzerland, the office became suspicious and reported the matter to you. The balance on the account is currently in excess of £5.1m. **(5 marks)**

Case 4

Midas has maintained both personal and company accounts with your bank for just over one year and he appears to be involved in a legitimate business that deals in precious metals mainly involving the export of gold bullion.

Midas has purchased gold bullion from your bank, paid for by funds held on the company account. In the last year, he has purchased more than 800kg to the value of more than £5m. On each occasion, Midas has collected the gold bullion from the bank in person.

The bank's records show that the funds transferred into the company account were from a third party company based abroad. This business seems profitable for Midas who has generated a substantial income from this comparatively simple and straightforward operation in a short period of time. **(5 marks)**

Section C (30 Marks)

Answer any TWO questions in this section.

All questions carry 15 marks.

15.   Explain the mechanisms through which the FSA is made accountable for its activities under the new regulatory regime set up under the FSMA 2000.   **(15 marks)**

16.   Explain the purpose of the Approved Persons regime and the main obligations that are imposed upon firms and management under the FSMA and the Handbook.   **(15 marks)**

17.   Explain the mechanisms through which the FSA supervises compliance by firms with their regulatory obligations on a day-to-day basis. You should comment, in particular, on the main powers available to the FSA under the FSMA 2000 and the content of the Supervision manual (SUP) as well as any other relevant sections of the Handbook.   **(15 marks)**

18.   Comment upon the progress that has been made in the creation of a single financial services market place within Europe and the nature and content of the further work currently being undertaken in the completion of this initiative.   **(15 marks)**

REGULATION AND COMPLIANCE
Answers

Winter 2007

Section A – Answers

1. An insider is a person who has inside information (unpublished, price sensitive, specific or precise, relating to an issuer(s) or security(ies) from an inside source (by virtue of being a director, shareholder, employee or having access by virtue of office or employment or the direct or indirect source being one of the above).

2. Under COBS 3 an authorised firm would, ordinarily, be categorised as a per se professional client. However, where the firm is conducting eligible counterparty business it can be categorised as a per se Eligible Counterparty. The firm could elect up to elective Eligible Counterparty status and for MiFID business must give "express confirmation" to the recategorisation.

3. Section 19 of the Financial Services and Markets Act 2000 (also known as the general prohibition) states that a person may not carry out regulated activities by way of business in, or into, the UK unless they are authorised, exempt or excluded. The list of regulated activities is set out in the Regulated Activities Order published by HM Treasury. Breach of S19 is a criminal offence resulting in a maximum penalty of two years' imprisonment and/or an unlimited fine.

4. The market abuse regime set out in S118 FSMA applies to all persons, businesses or corporate entities, wherever they are located, who engage in behaviour relating to qualifying investments traded on a prescribed market (UK RIE, PLUS & regulated markets, except S118(4)&(8)). The behaviour must fall into one or more of the seven 'heads' of market abuse which are S118(2) Insider Dealing, S118(3) Improper Disclosure, S118(4) Misuse of Information, S118(5) Manipulating Transactions, S118(6) Manipulating Devices, S118(7) Dissemination & S118(8) Misleading Behaviour and Distortion.

5. Under COBS 9.3.2 churning describes a circumstance where a firm overtrades in investments generally to generate commissions. This would contravene the "Client's best interest" rule (COBS 2.1.1) which is applied to designated investment business carried on for a retail client and also to a professional client in relation to MiFID or equivalent third country business.

6. Individual offences under the Proceeds of Crime Act 2002

    ▦   S327-329: Assisting a person to launder, e.g. retain, conceal, transfer, use, disguise etc. the proceeds of criminal conduct: 14 years imprisonment and/or unlimited fine.

    ▦   S330-332: Failure to report knowledge, suspicion or reasonable grounds for suspicion of laundering: five years imprisonment and/or unlimited fine.

    ▦   S333: Tipping Off, i.e. disclosures which may prejudice an investigation into the laundering of criminal proceeds where the person knows or suspects that an investigation is or may commence: five years imprisonment and/or unlimited fine.

Institutional liability under the Money Laundering Regulations 2007

    ▦   Failure of financial businesses to implement appropriate systems, i.e. reporting and recognising suspicions and training: two years imprisonment and unlimited fine.

Institutional liability under the Anti Money Laundering requirements in the FSA's

SYSC Sourcebook

    ▦   Failure of an authorised firm to implement and monitor appropriate systems, e.g. appropriate training, there are no criminal sanctions but the FSA may impose fines and censures.

7.   The FSA rules governing the issue of confirmation notes (COBS 16.2)) and periodic statements (COBS 16.3) link to Principle 7 which requires firms to pay due regard to the information needs of their clients.

Confirmation notes must be sent to retail & professional clients promptly after each trade. In the case of retail clients "promptly" means as soon as possible and no later than the business day following the date of the transaction (T+1). If a transaction is conducted after normal market hours, it will be treated as a trade executed the next day. Aggregated orders will be treated as executed on allocation.

Periodic statements must be provided, regarding the managing of investments on behalf of a client, in a durable medium. For retail clients statements have to be prepared and sent out for securities six monthly unless a retail client requests it on a three monthly basis. If the client elects to receive information on a transaction by transaction basis, then the periodic statement must be sent 12 monthly. Where the managing of investments authorises a leveraged portfolio, the periodic statement must be provided at least once a month.

8.   The Market in Financial Instruments Directive allows investment firms to passport throughout the EEA. Under MiFID the home state retains responsibility for organisational matters including authorisation, systems and controls, conflicts of interest, client assets and certain Conduct of Business rules such as Personal Account Dealing and Investment Research. The host state is responsible for operational matters such as Conduct of Business in the host country and other specified provisions. For example, a firm passporting into the UK would need to comply with FSA principles, approved persons, Training and Competence and complaints rules.

9.   A DPB is a Designated Professional Body. Such bodies (e.g. The Law Society) regulate professionals (accountants, lawyers and actuaries). The professionals are exempt from the requirement to seek authorisation where a regulated activity is carried out ancillary to their profession. This is set out in the FSMA (Exemption) Order 2001. The FSA will monitor their DPB to ensure that they are being properly regulated. The FSA rules regarding professional firms are contained in the Professional Firms (PROF) source book in the Specialist Sourcebooks section of the FSA Handbook.

10.   Under CASS 7 Client Money: MiFID Business, firms must carry out regular reconciliations between. its own client money records and those of third parties, such as a bank, holding client money as regularly as necessary and as soon as possible after the date to which the reconciliation relates. If a firm fails to comply with this rule in any material respect, then it must inform the FSA without delay.

Section B

11. (a)   The question concerns the offence of insider dealing.

(i)   Criminal and other legal consequences

Tim is an insider under the Criminal Justice Act 1993, as he has inside information (unpublished, price sensitive, specific/precise, relating to a particular issuer/security) from an inside source. The news at the board meeting is obtained by virtue of his position as a non-executive director. Although he does not deal himself, he discloses the information to Bob. He may be able to argue the defence that he did not know Bob owned shares personally and, therefore, did not expect that dealing would take place. However, he did know that Bob managed a fund with a significant holding of shares in Banks-r-us and therefore was likely to deal.

Bob has the information from an inside source as he receives the information from a director. If Tim has passed all his knowledge to Bob, Bob has inside information. This makes Bob an insider. He deals on a regulated market and is therefore likely to be prosecuted for insider dealing. None of the defences appear to apply.

If found guilty of insider dealing, the maximum penalty that can be imposed on Bob and Tim is a seven-year prison sentence and an unlimited fine. As an alternative to a criminal prosecution, the FSA may seek to prosecute Tim and Bob for market abuse under S118(3)FSMA 'Improper Disclosure' & S118(2)FSMA 'Insider Dealing' respectively as their behaviour related to qualifying investments traded on a prescribed market. The FSA would be able to fine them for committing market abuse, but could not impose a prison sentence.

(ii)   Consequences for regulatory status and ethical considerations

Tim and Bob may also be in breach of Statement of Principle (APER) 1 (integrity) and 3 (market conduct) for their activities.

If Banks-r-us is failing the capital adequacy tests laid down by the FSA, this should be reported to the FSA under Principle (PRIN) 11 of the Principles for Business. If Bob fails to do so, he could be breaching APER 4 and 7.

For Tim, it appears he is favouring his own positions over those of his customers that may breach PRIN 6. There is also concern that the PA dealing rules in COBS 11.7 have not been complied with which would require him to comply with his firm's procedures and notify details of trades done.

Penalties that could be imposed by FSA against Tim and Bob for breach of the Statements of Principle include censures, fines and possible withdrawal of approval.

It is also possible that Tim and Bob are members of the Securities and Investments Institute. As such they will be in breach of principles 2 (integrity) and 4 (proper market conduct) of the SII's Code of Conduct. These would constitute material breaches of the Code and so would be incompatible with continued membership of the SII for Tim and Bob.

(b)   (i)   This question concerns the Money Laundering Regulations 2007 (MLR), the Proceeds of Crime Act 2002 (POCA) and the FSA's SYSC rules on money laundering.

POCA creates three main offences for individuals.

−   Assisting another person to launder proceeds obtained from criminal conduct – this covers actions such as concealing, removing, using, disguising and transferring funds - maximum penalty 14 years' imprisonment and/or an unlimited fine.

– Failure to report knowledge, suspicion or the reasonable grounds for suspicion of the laundering of the proceeds of crime – maximum penalty five years' imprisonment and/or an unlimited fine.

– Providing information to another person which is likely to prejudice an investigation into criminal conduct i.e. tipping off – maximum penalty five years' imprisonment and/or an unlimited fine.

Under the MLR, each firm must appoint a Money Laundering Reporting Officer. It is unclear whether this has been done here. Senior management may be found guilty of a criminal offence if they fail to ensure that proper training and procedures to combat money laundering are in place within the firm. The maximum penalty is two years imprisonment and/or an unlimited fine.

In addition, the MLR imposes a number of obligations in respect of identification of clients, record keeping, internal reporting and internal procedures.

The firm may have breached Principle 3 of the Principles for Businesses and Senior Management Arrangements, Systems and Controls, (SYSC) for failure to have adequate internal procedures and controls – it is not acceptable for the compliance officer to go on a course without cover for situations of this kind and unclear if the firm has a MLRO. In addition, the firm should have ensured that Irving attended the training courses that have been held for the past three years. Failure to comply with training requirements will breach the FSA Training and Competence Sourcebook.

Ginger was right to be suspicious of the instructions that she received and to report the incident to a senior member of staff. However, Ginger should have reported to the Money Laundering Reporting Officer or other person designated to take such reports. The lack of clear procedures suggest that no such procedures exist which would be a clear breach of the Money Laundering Regulations and/or SYSC rules on money laundering.

Irving should not have gone ahead with the transaction until he had received confirmation from the compliance officer/MLRO that he was authorised to do so. The suspicious nature of the transaction may lead to criminal charges for failure to report and even assistance as the transaction has now gone ahead. In addition, he will have broken the regulations on client identification. Clearly, if Irving were to delay, he would have to ensure that it did not constitute tipping off.

(ii) The review of management controls should start with checking the apportionment of senior management responsibility under SYSC2. The firm should have a clear structure or responsibility for identifying and recording who is responsible for ensuring the firm complies with its senior management compliance oversight for anti-money laundering.

The SYSC money laundering requirements (set out in SYSC6) require senior management to have a risk management system that is comprehensive and proportionate to the nature, scale and complexity of its activities. I would recommend that senior management commission a review of how well the firm is meeting these obligations. This would be most sensible to co-ordinate with the MLRO's duty to report annually to senior management on the effectiveness of the firm's anti-money laundering systems.

12. (a) My advice to Agatha concerning breaches of rules is as follows.

■ The original transaction is an execution-only designated investment business trade in shares (i.e. non-complex products) and this under COBS rule 8.1 requires Brown Jones to enter into a basic agreement with Agatha.

▨   Under COBS rule 16.2 trade confirmations are required to be sent out as soon as possible and no later than the first business day following the execution. This has not occurred. The confirmation note should contain a number of important disclosures, including the fact that a part of the deal has been conducted as principal. Regardless of the nature of the deal, agency or principal, the firm should ensure under COBS rule 11.5 that Agatha obtains best execution.

▨   Under the Client Assets Sourcebook (CASS) and Principle 10 of the Principles for Businesses (PRIN) client money should be segregated and Agatha is entitled to interest (unless advised to the contrary). The cheque which has been despatched to Agatha should not have been drawn on the company's own account but from the client account where the funds should be held. Agatha should have received the money without having to enquire herself.

▨   The suitability of the advice to invest into options seems prima facie to be wrong. Brown Jones has a duty under COBS 9 and PRIN 9 to ensure the suitability of personal recommendations given to certain customers. In order to assess the suitability of this advice, the firm should have complied with 'know your customer' requirements under COBS 9.2 by undertaking a fact-find on Agatha to establish her investment objectives, attitude to risk, and ability to financially bear the consequences of the trade.

▨   Prior to giving any advice on the merits of options, Agatha, as a retail client investing in contingent liability transactions should have received a basic client agreement under COBS 8.1. This should include any relevant risk warnings. In any event, the discretionary management of her funds by Brown Jones requires a formal client agreement to be entered into.

▨   Under CASS the gilts must normally be registered either in the name of Agatha or an appropriate nominee. It is unclear whether this has occurred, although the use of the gilts by the firm tends to indicate they are not properly registered.

▨   A firm is not allowed to use a client's assets as collateral for its own purposes without consent – this would be a breach of the CASS custody rules and PRIN 10 (as well as possibly PRIN 1 and 2).

▨   The employee who spoke to Agatha is obliged under S59 of FSMA to be an approved person. It is the responsibility of the firm to ensure this has occurred.

(b)   Complaints and Compensation Procedures

Under the FSA Sourcebook 'Dispute Resolution: Complaints' (DISP), Agatha would normally complain to the firm first and if they do not properly respond, she can use the Financial Ombudsman Service who can recommend compensation up to £100,000 plus costs. If this is not successful, Agatha could pursue her claim for compensation through the courts. As she is a Private Person, has suffered loss and the firm has breached certain rules she will be able to bring these actions under S150 FSMA to recover her losses. The use of S150 tends to be cheaper and easier as she will not have to prove negligence on the part of the firm.

However, since the firm has been declared insolvent, it seems unlikely that this will be of much use unless her funds are properly segregated. As an individual retail client, Agatha will also be an Eligible Claimant under the Financial Services Compensation Scheme and can seek redress. Under this scheme her maximum payout will be £48,000 as her loss relates to investments.

13. As Target plc is a UK plc the Takeover Code and Companies Act restrictions will apply. In addition, this scenario raises issues relating to the UKLA Listing Rules and Model Code. There are also concerns relating to criminal and civil offences regarding misuse of information and manipulation.

(a) Monday, 4 June – Transaction

The FSA's Disclosure and Transparency Rules requires disclosure to the company within two business days (for a UK issuer) because Swift Move has gone through the 3% Material Interest threshold for holdings of shares to which voting rights are attached. In addition, because Target is listed, the Listing Rules require them to announce this to the market via a Regulatory Information Service by the end of the following day.

(b) Tuesday, 5 June and purchases 6 and 7 June

The parties may be a Companies Act concert party and thus disclosures may need to be made to the company. In addition, the agreement to provide free use of Target's research may be a breach of their directors' duties and consequently, Principle 3 of the Takeover Directive Principles.

(c) 11 June – Purchase by Megapocket

This contravenes the law on insider dealing contained in the Criminal Justice Act 1993 as Megapocket is an Insider (he has inside information from an inside source). It therefore also breaches S118(2) FSMA the 'Insider Dealing' head of Market Abuse. This covers behaviour in relation to qualifying investments trading on a prescribed market (UK RIE, PLUS & regulated markets). The penalty for breach includes unlimited fines.

It also breaches Rule 4.1 of the Takeover Code, which prohibits insider dealing, and the Model Code on directors' dealings that would require Megapocket to have obtained permission to deal from a senior member of the board. All dealings by directors of listed companies in the shares of their own company must be registered and then disclosed to the market via a Regulatory Information Service.

(d) 12 June – Offer

The artificial price support for the paper offer breaches the criminal offence of S397 FSMA, which is punishable by seven years imprisonment and unlimited fines. In particular, the conduct creates a false or misleading impression about the price of Swift Move shares.

It also breaches the market abuse provisions in S118(5) FSMA 'Manipulating Transactions'.

The conduct also contravenes Principle 4, no false markets, of the Takeover

Directive Principles and so the parties could be disciplined by the Takeover Panel.

{Note that none of the parties concerned are working in an authorised firm and so it would NOT be appropriate to have discussed breaches of PRIN or APER)

14. (a) The following points are of concern.

Regarding Mr Popocros

▪ How do we categorise Mr Popocros under COBS 3.1? He appears to be a retail client, although it is unclear if he is execution only or advisory. He should be categorised before we act for him and be informed as to his categorisation..

▪ Have we done money laundering checks and KYC? These are required under the Money Laundering Regulations 2007. Mr Popocros is an existing customer of the Shipping Department, but shipping is a separate legal entity from Treasury so we should also undertake these checks.

▦   Are sugar futures the right product for Mr Popocros to hedge his risk? Will this hedge against loss of business to a rival firm? Suitability and appropriateness need to be addressed under COBS 9 and 10.

▦   To what extent can a service be provided without consideration towards suitability? If he is a retail non-advised client the Conduct of Business Rules (COBS) on suitability will not apply. However, Principle 9 of the Principles for Businesses (customers relationships of trust) will apply to a wider range of customers and a duty is owed to assess the appropriateness of non-advised trades in complex products.To do this the firm would need to ask the client to provide information on his knowledge and experience in the relevant field and thereby determine whether the client has the requisite experience and knowledge to understand the risks involved.

▦   Do the commission arrangements agreed between Shipping and Treasury need to be disclosed in customer documentation? COBS rule 6.1.9 requires disclosure of commission to retail clients in connection with designated investment business.

▦   What documentation requirements can be waived if Mr Popocros does not wish to sign anything? As a retail client entering into contingent liability transactions on a non-advised basis he will need a basic written client agreement under COBS 8.1 and a two-way derivative risk warning. Certain overseas customers can waive this requirement where the firm has taken reasonable steps to ensure the customer does not wish to receive the agreement. It is unclear whether Mr Popocros is resident overseas. In any event, the firm must ensure retail clients understand the risks of their transactions in complex products under COBS rule 10.2. The firm will have problems proving this if there are language problems.

▦   What are Mr Popocros' investment objectives in buying Eurobonds? Have the firm considered KYC issues under COBS rule 9.2? This should have been established during the fact-find.

Regarding Mr Wotolos

▦   Mr Wotolos is unapproved. What activities can he perform? Under S59 FSMA and the Supervision Sourcebook, he must be approved to perform controlled functions, which include customer functions. If he is not the firm could be disciplined and Mr Popocros as a 'Private Person' could sue the firm for losses under S71 FSMA.

▦   With how many other customers is Mr Wotolos discussing investment business?

▦   Is Mr Wotolos properly trained and competent for the role he is doing? Under the Competent Employees' Rule the Training and Competence Sourcebook requires employees to competent to carry on an activity and to have passed an appropriate examination before carrying on the activity.

▦   To what extent can Mr Wotolos act as an agent for Treasury, and what should he or Treasury ensure is disclosed to Mr Popocros, prior to dealing? There is a conflict having Mr Wotolos acting for Mr Popocros as Mr Wotolos is receiving commissions. The firm must apply PRIN 2 (skill, care and diligence) PRIN 6 (customer's interests) and PRIN 8 (conflicts). Under SYSC 10 common platform firms must take all reasonable steps to identify conflicts of interest between the firm and its clients, and to maintain and operate effective organisational and administrative arrangements to prevent conflicts giving rise to damage to a client's interests. It is unlikely that it will be appropriate for Mr Wotolos to be involved in the way he envisages.

Regarding the Firm

▪ Do its commission arrangements breach PRIN 3? In addition, where commission and remuneration arrangements present conflicts, the firm must manage these conflicts under Senior Management Arrangements, Systems and Controls (SYSC 10).

▪ Are the systems and controls adequate? If Mr Wotolos is advising other people without the requisite approval, then the firm is breaching SYSC (employees and agents, organisation).

▪ Has the firm dealt appropriately with the conflicts which have arisen here?

(b) The possible courses of action are to allow Mr Wotolos to 'help' the client, or to deal with Mr Popocros directly.

The suggested best course of action would be to meet with Mr Wotolos and explain that we need to regularise the situation. This means that Mr Popocros must become a client of the Treasury business and that Mr Wotolos will no longer be able to discuss investment issues with any clients. We must ensure we comply with COBS and PRIN in dealing with Mr Popocros. If we cannot ensure he understands the risks and procedures as a result of language difficulties, then we should consider whether we can act for him at all.

Section C

Remember with Section C answers, these are often subjective and as such the following does not intend to be a 'model' answer. The following represent possible answers to each question to consider your own answers against.

15. The growth of the internet has broadened the opportunities for marketing investment business, but has also created many challenges for the regulators. The internet raises new challenges which could fundamentally change the way financial services are regulated.

    Perhaps the most familiar challenge is the difficulty of regulating transactions which are not done in a formal market place. The internet allows consumers to enter into products in an environment which is difficult for the regulator to police. The internet contains so much information that regulators do not easily have the resources required to monitor sites in detail.

    Jurisdictional problems also exist in that internet sites may both originate from a country which is outside the regulator's legal or practical jurisdiction. The E-Commerce Directive has helped to clarify this so that e-commerce promotions (i.e. those from a distance electronically delivered, e.g. on a website) are subject to home state rules in the EEA. However, confusion exists as host state rules still apply for non-electronic promotions and for unsolicited real-time promotions. This creates a major challenge for firms in deciphering and applying the correct rules.

    A further challenge is the potential for money laundering. In many respects, the rise in internet business and the truly cross-border nature of the internet have made money laundering much easier due to the anonymity which it can create. Whilst the Money Laundering Regulations 2007 and FSA SYSC Sourcebook contain identification requirements including non-face to face contact with new clients, these can be difficult to apply in practice and arguably do not address the issue of funds which have already been placed into the system.

    Whilst the above are familiar challenges, the internet does present completely novel challenges. Financial services regulation has always been primarily focused, not on the supplier of a product, but the middleman – the person who sells the product. The internet removes this person from the transaction, allowing the supplier to sell directly to the general public. A common technique used by the regulator to ensure that telesales are adequately regulated is to require, under COBS chapter 5, that physical documentation is given to the customer to confirm the discussion by way of client agreement or key features documents. Upon receipt of such documentation, the customer has a cancellation period or withdrawal rights.

    The conduct of business rules have needed to undergo a shift in focus in order to cope with e-commerce. Some argue that the COBS rules still do not go far enough. The Conduct of Business Rules are arguably still rooted in traditional ways of physical documents and have not yet caught up with the internet revolution. Whilst they do make provision for electronic delivery of documents and broaden the scope of financial promotions, some say there is very little innovation in any other respects in terms of ensuring that customers have read and understood the contents of the information. Having said that, COBS rules are now largely media neutral which is a major improvement on the pre-N2 regime.

    If electronic documents are going to be used, many question marks that still surround electronic signatures must be addressed. There are still concerns over their security and enforceability that must be dealt with if they are to provide any certainty for consumers or product providers.

    One of the advantages of physical documentation is that it, hopefully, brings home to a consumer the consequences of their actions. People will agree to things over the internet, but when they are asked to sign a document agreeing the same things, will approach this with more caution. Internet documentation poses a threat as a culture has developed whereby dialogue boxes are ticked without thought and warnings are scrolled past. The advantage of the internet is quick and easy information. Consumers may, therefore, be placing themselves more at risk. FSA must develop some way of dealing with the potential consequence that the protections that they try to provide by way of risk warnings and agreement are ineffective if they are to achieve their regulatory objectives of Consumer Protection (S5 FSMA) and Promoting Public Awareness (S4 FSMA).

The internet also allows large amounts of information to be presented to consumers in an environment difficult to monitor. Therefore, companies can give performance figures, advertising and comparative tables which may only come to the attention of FSA in the event of misselling. FSA clearly has an obligation to educate consumers to ensure that they are not misled by such information. In addition, the FSA have implemented new rules on the presentation of past performance data which should address some of these concerns, e.g. no data can be included where less than 12 months of data is available.

The internet, therefore, presents some familiar challenges and some novel challenges. The regulators and governments must try to tame the internet as it is clear that even familiar challenges are on a much larger scale when dealing with the internet. The culmination suggests that an ongoing assessment of law and regulation is required to cope with the possibilities and opportunities presented by the internet.

16.   It is hardly surprising to observe that FSA and other regulators are placing increasing emphasis on the responsibilities of managers and directors. This emphasis springs, in part, from a recognition that the most recent scandals and frauds have arisen because of failures in the control systems within investment business. Barings, Daiwa, Sumitomo and Kidder Peabody are all examples of such scandals, in which there was dishonest behaviour by individuals (Leeson et al.), but also of management failure. By placing responsibility for control with the Chief Executive Officer, the regulators are clearly seeking to prevent recurrences of such problems and to make the accountability obvious. Another dynamic is that the regulators are seeking to avoid the problems that arose in the aftermath of the Barings collapse in February 1995. Whilst Nick Leeson was imprisoned, the lasting public remembrance of the disciplinary process was that the directors and managers 'escaped' largely unscathed. Whilst such a depiction does scant justice to the factors of the individual cases, there can be little doubt that regulator's public relations were poorly handled and did little to develop credibility and trust in the regulatory system.

In the post-N2 environment, the FSA places a heavy burden on senior managers. Under S59 FSMA, all persons who govern the firm or perform significant influence functions must be approved, as these are controlled functions. In order to obtain such approval, the person must show (under FIT) fitness and propriety (e.g. competence, capability, integrity etc). Once approved, such persons must comply with seven Statements of Principle set out in the FSA Handbook (APER). The first four of these are applicable to all approved persons within an authorised firm and are therefore fairly general.

▓   They must act with integrity when performing their function.

▓   They must act with skill, care and diligence when performing their function.

▓   They must observe proper standards of market conduct when performing their function.

▓   They must deal with the regulator in an open and cooperative way.

The final three principles specifically apply to significant influence functions and shall be looked at in more detail.

▓   Senior managers must take responsible steps to ensure that the business of the firm for which they are responsible is organised properly.

      This requires senior management to ensure proper reporting lines and apportionment of responsibility.

▓   Senior managers must exercise skill, care and diligence in their management role.

This seeks to ensure that senior management understand the areas they manage and therefore are able to properly assess the risks to the business of their decisions. Suitable and responsible delegation is also key in delivering against this requirement.

▓   Senior managers must take reasonable care to ensure that the business of the firm for which they are responsible complies with the regulatory requirements.

Clearly, this seeks to ensure that compliance is not left to the Compliance Department, but is seen as a shared responsibility throughout the management.

In addition to these principles, the FSA have produced a Sourcebook, Senior Management Arrangements, Systems and Controls (SYSC) to flesh out these principles. SYSC covers areas such as apportionment, organisation, remuneration policies, risk management and compliance functions. Firms can be disciplined for failing to implement these in conjunction with the principles. Examples of such disciplinary action include the £500,000 fine against Carr Sheppards in May 2004, the £63,000 fine against Langtons (IFA) Ltd in September 2006 and the fine of £350,000 against BNP Private Bank in May 2007.

There are concerns in the industry that the increased burden on senior managers and the firm in compliance with the principles and SYSC will not only be unnecessarily time consuming, but will also hurt the investor by increasing compliance costs. On the other hand the FSA must apply the principles of good regulation (set out at S2(3) FSMA) in introducing and enforcing rules that required them, inter alia, to be proportionate and facilitate innovation. In view of this, SYSC makes clear procedures required will depend on the nature, scale and complexity of the firm.

Overall, the regulator's approach is sound and sensible and correctly attributes responsibility to the 'captain of the ship'. We must hope that the implementation of the policy is fair and reasonable in practice and that authorised firms heed these requirements. Concerns still remain as to the effect in practice that these rules will have. This is evidenced by the FSA's letter to 300 banks and building societies in September 2003 concerning their treasury operations and the lack of proper systems and controls in place. This suggests that many firms have still not learnt the lessons of the past.

The importance of competent senior management is even more important in a 'More Principles Based Regulations' world. As the FSA moves away from prescriptive detailed rules and allows senior management to apply princples based regulation, this requires the skills of senior management to identify and manage the risks in their business.

17.   The introduction of criminal offences such as insider dealing (Criminal Justice Act 1993) and misleading statements and practices (formerly in the Financial Services Act 1986 and now under S397 FSMA), together with the FSA Principles and Conduct of Business Rules, went some way to producing a more regulated and open market. However, critics have argued that the 1986 Act did not produce the open, transparent and fair market that was intended. Evidence to back their claims comes in the form of the poor record of successful insider dealing convictions since the introduction of the CJA.

In May 1997, the government announced important changes to the UK regulatory system and, on 30 November 2001 'N2', the Financial Services and Markets Act came into force. The Act sets out a number of statutory objectives for financial regulation under Section 2(2) FSMA – maintaining confidence in the financial system, promoting public awareness of the financial system, securing the appropriate degree of protection for consumers and reducing financial crime. The reduction of market abuse is essential to ensuring confidence in the financial markets to ensure reputational strength and liquidity.

Section 118 FSMA gave the FSA new powers to prosecute for market abuse at 'N2' which were updated on 1 July 2005 as a result of implementation of the Market Abuse Directive. FSA drafted a Code of Market Conduct in the Business Standards block of the FSA Handbook setting out guidance as to how they will interpret and enforce the offences contained in S118 FSMA. Breach of the Code will be evidence towards a breach of S118 FSMA and the FSA will be able to impose financial penalties, whilst injured parties will be able to seek compensation.

Market abuse includes

- S118(2) – Market Abuse (Insider Dealing)

- S118(3) – Market Abuse (Improper Disclosure)

- S118(4) – Market Abuse (Misuse of Information)

- S118(5) – Market Abuse (Manipulating Transactions)

- S118(6) – Market Abuse (Manipulating Devices)

- S118(7) – Market Abuse (Dissemination)

- S118(8) – Market Abuse (Misleading Behaviour) and Market Abuse (Distortion)

The rules apply to all persons (including unauthorised persons). The scope is any behaviour (which covers action and inaction) which occurs in relation to a qualifying investment trading on a prescribed market (UK RIE, PLUS & regulated markets except S118(4) & (8)).

The FSA hope that, in particular, the Code will reassure legitimate market users that many existing practices are acceptable to the regulator. This is to counteract the usual criticism that market regulation inhibits professionals from being innovative or risk taking. However, the wide scope of the FSA's Code (and in particular the insistence by Treasury that the regime will allow the FSA to fine on the civil standard of proof) has led to some practitioners becoming fearful that the FSA will use its powers in an uneven and capricious manner. Ironically, this may actually damage the market if there is a feeling that the UK is overregulated. In order to calm fears, the FSA has been very vocal about their desire to use their enhanced powers proportionately.

The powers for the FSA to tackle market abuse have promoted widespread comment and, whilst most seem to support the idea in principle, there are a number of concerns about how the new regime will fit in with the existing criminal offences. For example, concerns exist over the interrelation of the proposed offence with the Human Rights Act 1998. A civil offence with the threat of unlimited fines may be unworkable if it can be successfully argued that the Human Rights Act requires such penalties to have a criminal burden of proof.

In addition the regime applies to those outside the UK but in practice extra-territorial legislation is very difficult and costly to enforce.

There is much sensitivity in the industry regarding the market abuse regime. Whilst there has been an acceptance that the current criminal regime has not done enough to prevent financial crime, there may be a general feeling that the new regime seeks to give the FSA too much power. The FSA has used the provisions in S118 FSMA on a number of occasions e.g. £17 million fine against Shell in August 2004, £13.9 million fine against Citigroup in June 2005 and a £6.3m fine against Deutsche Bank in April 2006.

Some have criticised the size of the fines for insider dealing as being too low to cause a deterrent effect but, on the counter argument, the FSA's principles of good regulation require proportionate action.

More recently, the whole structure of market abuse as a 'civil' offence with its lower burden of proof has been questioned by the Davidson case. It was found on appeal, that where the punishment for market abuse is so severe (eg large fine for an individual) that it is felt to be criminal in nature, then the burden of proof is that of the 'heightened civil standard' which is almost the same as 'beyond reasonable doubt' that is required under CJA93.

Perhaps, one major benefit has been that concern over the new offence within firms has raised awareness of the need to train staff on good market practices which has to be a benefit to the fair operation of the markets.

18. The Market in Financial Instruments Directive was implemented by the UK on 1st November 2007.

The directive is a maximum harmonisation directive and therefore aims to be a complete set of conduct of business rules for each country to transpose into their national legislation framework. This will help achieve the Financial Services Action Plan objective of creating a common market in financial services across the EEA by removing barriers to the free movement of financial services around Europe.

The FSA had to justify to the European Commission the additional rules over and above the requirements of MiFID. As MiFID is a maximum harmonisation directive, any national regulator that adds additional rules must justify this 'gold plating' in reference to the risks posed to investor protection or market integrity. The UK had four areas of 'gold plating' and justified them on the following basis:

- Apportionment of senior manager responsibility – wish to retain high standards of accountability of senior management set out in SYSC2

- Content of confirmation and periodic statements – more detailed disclosures thought necessary especially in derivative transactions

- Packaged product market requirements – the UK has significantly more investment for personal retirement and home ownership than other EU member states and this has been an area of previous misselling with both private pension and endowments. With some packaged products being MiFID business (unit trusts, OEICs and investment trust schemes) and some non-MiFID (life policies and pensions) the FSA is concerned that there will be distortion to the markets in these products if rules are not harmonised. This will in particular relate to disclosure of independent or tied status (Initial Disclosure Document), information about the products and menu of charges and their disclosure

- Use of dealing commission – the FSA addressed specific market failings in restricting soft commissions to execution of trades and research. This goes beyond the general limit on inducements set out in MiFID

The harmonisation of the COB rules throughout the EEA should be a significant step towards achieving the Lamfalussy Committee's goal of a unified European financial market. The goal should allow the EU to become as important a capital market as the US. The implementation of MiFID will facilitate trading of EU securities in other places than their domestic market. This should be a good move for London which is already a major world market for securities. The recent surge of listings of overseas companies in the UK, partly to avoid the onerous rule bound regulations in the US, is proof that an effective regulatory system that balances a light touch regulatory approach through principles based regulation can be very good for the UK's status as a leading world financial centre.

Summer 2007

Section A – Answers

1. An insider is a person who has inside information (unpublished, price sensitive, specific or precise, relating to an issuer(s) or security(ies) from an inside source (by virtue of being a director, shareholder, employee or having access by virtue of office or employment or the direct or indirect source being one of the above).

2. Under COB 4 an authorised firm would, ordinarily, be classified as a market counterparty. However, where the firm has underlying customers, it may opt down to intermediate status if the parties agree. Furthermore, a long-term insurer acting on behalf of a life fund would automatically be treated as an intermediate customer.

3. Section 19 of the Financial Services and Markets Act 2000 (also known as the general prohibition) states that a person may not carry out regulated activities by way of business in, or into, the UK unless they are authorised, exempt or excluded. The list of regulated activities is set out in the Regulated Activities Order published by HM Treasury. Breach of S19 is a criminal offence resulting in a maximum penalty of two years' imprisonment and/or an unlimited fine.

4. The market abuse regime set out in S118 FSMA applies to all persons, businesses or corporate entities, wherever they are located, who engage in behaviour relating to qualifying investments traded on a prescribed market (UK RIE, PLUS & regulated markets, except S118(4)&(8)). The behaviour must fall into one or more of the seven 'heads' of market abuse which are S118(2) Insider Dealing, S118(3) Improper Disclosure, S118(4) Misuse of Information, S118(5) Manipulating Transactions, S118(6) Manipulating Devices, S118(7) Dissemination & S118(8) Misleading Behaviour and Distortion.

5. Churning describes a circumstance where a firm overtrades in investments generally to generate commissions. It is prohibited under COB rule 7.2. The rule protects all discretionary customers and private advisory customers.

6. Individual offences under the Proceeds of Crime Act 2002

    ▪   S327-329: Assisting a person to launder, e.g. retain, conceal, transfer, use, disguise etc. the proceeds of criminal conduct: 14 years imprisonment and/or unlimited fine.

    ▪   S330-332: Failure to report knowledge, suspicion or reasonable grounds for suspicion of laundering: five years imprisonment and/or unlimited fine.

    ▪   S333: Tipping Off, i.e. disclosures which may prejudice an investigation into the laundering of criminal proceeds where the person knows or suspects that an investigation is or may commence: five years imprisonment and/or unlimited fine.

    ▪   Institutional liability under the Money Laundering Regulations 2003

    ▪   Failure of financial businesses to implement appropriate systems, i.e. reporting and recognising suspicions and training: two years imprisonment and unlimited fine.

    ▪   Institutional liability under the Anti Money Laundering requirements in the FSA's SYSC Sourcebook

    ▪   Failure of an authorised firm to implement and monitor appropriate systems, e.g. appropriate training, there are no criminal sanctions but the FSA may impose fines and censures.

7.   The FSA rules governing the issue of confirmation notes (COB 8.1) and periodic statements (COB 8.2) link to Principle 7 which requires firms to pay due regard to the information needs of their clients.

Confirmation notes must be sent to all customers (private and intermediate) promptly after each trade. Promptly means no later than the business day following the date of the transaction (T+1) or within any period agreed in writing by the customer. If a transaction is conducted after normal market hours, it will be treated as a trade executed the next day. Aggregated orders will be treated as executed on allocation.

Periodic statements provide information about the value and composition of an account or portfolio. They must be sent where a firm acts as investment manager, administers an account containing designated investments or uncovered derivatives or where a firm sells, advises or manages structured capital at risk products (SCARPS). Statements have to be prepared and sent out for securities six monthly (dispatched within 25 business days of the valuation date) and for derivatives monthly (dispatched within 10 business days of the valuation date).

8.   The ISD is the Investment Services Directive that allows investment firms to passport throughout the EEA. Under the ISD the home state retains responsibility for authorisation, fit and properness, capital adequacy, client money, compensation and the Conduct of Business within the home state. The host state is responsible for Conduct of Business in the host country and other specified provisions. For example, a firm passporting into the UK would need to comply with FSA principles, approved persons, Training and Competence, systems and controls and complaints rules.

Under MiFID, the Conduct of Business rules will be harmonised so that there should be no significant differences in the rules between each member state. New client classifications will be introduced that will be standardised across the EEA for retail client, professional client and eligible counterparty. Transaction reporting requirements will be to the home state regulator and may therefore reduce the ability of national regulators to see monitor the transactions happening on their own domestic market. Transposition measures were due to be completed by the end of January 2007 although many EU states are still completing this process. The start date for MiFID is scheduled for 1 November 2007.

9.   A DPB is a Designated Professional Body. Such bodies (e.g. The Law Society) regulate professionals (accountants, lawyers and actuaries). The professionals are exempt from the requirement to seek authorisation where a regulated activity is done ancillary to their profession. This is set out in the FSMA (Exemption) Order 2001. FSA will monitor their DPB to ensure that they are being properly regulated.

10. Under FSA client money rules found in the Client Assets Sourcebook (CASS), the following bank accounts are envisaged.

     ▪   General Client Account (risks pooled).

     ▪   Designated Client Account.

Section B – Answers

11. (a) The question concerns the offence of insider dealing.

(i) **Criminal and other legal consequences**

Tim is an insider under the Criminal Justice Act 1993, as he has inside information (unpublished, price sensitive, specific/precise, relating to a particular issuer/security) from an inside source. The news at the board meeting is obtained by virtue of his position as a non-executive director. Although he does not deal himself, he discloses the information to Bob. He may be able to argue the defence that he did not know Bob owned shares personally and, therefore, did not expect that dealing would take place. However, he did know that Bob managed a fund with a significant holding of shares in Banks-r-us and therefore was likely to deal.

Bob has the information from an inside source as he receives the information from a director. If Tim has passed all his knowledge to Bob, Bob has inside information. This makes Bob an insider. He deals on a regulated market and is therefore likely to be prosecuted for insider dealing. None of the defences appear to apply.

If found guilty of insider dealing, the maximum penalty that can be imposed on Bob and Tim is a seven-year prison sentence and an unlimited fine. As an alternative to a criminal prosecution, the FSA may seek to prosecute Tim and Bob for market abuse under S118(3)FSMA 'Improper Disclosure' & S118(2)FSMA 'Insider Dealing' respectively as their behaviour related to qualifying investments traded on a prescribed market. The FSA would be able to fine them for committing market abuse, but could not impose a prison sentence.

(ii) **Consequences for regulatory status and ethical considerations**

Tim and Bob may also be in breach of Statement of Principle (APER) 1 (integrity) and 3 (market conduct) for their activities.

If Banks-r-us is failing the capital adequacy tests laid down by the FSA, this should be reported to the FSA under Principle (PRIN) 11 of the Principles for Business. If Bob fails to do so, he could be breaching APER 4 and 7.

For Tim, it appears he is favouring his own positions over those of his customers that may breach PRIN 6. There is also concern that the PA dealing rules in COB 7.13 have not been complied with which would require him to comply with his firm's procedures and notify details of trades done.

Penalties that could be imposed by FSA against Tim and Bob for breach of the Statements of Principle include censures, fines and possible withdrawal of approval.

It is also possible that Tim and Bob are members of the Securities and Investments Institute. As such they will be in breach of principles 2 (integrity) and 4 (proper market conduct) of the SII's Code of Conduct. These would constitute material breaches of the Code and so would be incompatible with continued membership of the SII for Tim and Bob.

(b) (i) This question concerns the Money Laundering Regulations 2003 (MLR), the Proceeds of Crime Act 2002 (POCA) and the FSA's SYSC rules on money laundering.

POCA creates three main offences for individuals.

▪ Assisting another person to launder proceeds obtained from criminal conduct – this covers actions such as concealing, removing, using, disguising and transferring funds – maximum penalty 14 years' imprisonment and/or an unlimited fine.

▪ Failure to report knowledge, suspicion or the reasonable grounds for suspicion of the laundering of the proceeds of crime – maximum penalty five years' imprisonment and/or an unlimited fine.

■ Providing information to another person which is likely to prejudice an investigation into criminal conduct i.e. tipping off – maximum penalty five years' imprisonment and/or an unlimited fine.

Under the MLR, each firm must appoint a Money Laundering Reporting Officer. It is unclear whether this has been done here. Senior management may be found guilty of a criminal offence if they fail to ensure that proper training and procedures to combat money laundering are in place within the firm. The maximum penalty is two years imprisonment and/or an unlimited fine.

In addition, the MLR imposes a number of obligations in respect of identification of clients, record keeping, internal reporting and internal procedures.

The firm may breached Principle 3 of the Principles for Businesses and Senior Management Arrangements, Systems and Controls, (SYSC) for failure to have adequate internal procedures and controls – it is not acceptable for the compliance officer to go on a course without cover for situations of this kind and unclear if the firm has a MLRO. In addition, the firm should have ensured that Irving attended the training courses that have been held for the past three years. Failure to comply with training requirements will breach the FSA Training and Competence Sourcebook.

Ginger was right to be suspicious of the instructions that she received and to report the incident to a senior member of staff. However, Ginger should have reported to the Money Laundering Reporting Officer or other person designated to take such reports. The lack of clear procedures suggest that no such procedures exist which would be a clear breach of the Money Laundering Regulations and/or SYSC rules on money laundering.

Irving should not have gone ahead with the transaction until he had received confirmation from the compliance officer/MLRO that he was authorised to do so. The suspicious nature of the transaction may lead to criminal charges for failure to report and even assistance as the transaction has now gone ahead. In addition, he will have broken the regulations on client identification. Clearly, if Irving were to delay, he would have to ensure that it did not constitute tipping off.

(ii)   The review of management controls should start with checking the apportionment of senior management responsibility under SYSC2. The firm should have a clear structure or responsibility for identifying and recording who is responsible for ensuring the firm complies with its senior management compliance oversight for anti-money laundering.

The SYSC money laundering requirements (set out in SYSC3) require senior management to have a risk management system that is comprehensive and proportionate to the nature, scale and complexity of its activities. I would recommend that senior management commission a review of how well the firm is meeting these obligations. This would be most sensible to co-ordinate with the MLRO's duty to report annually to senior management on the effectiveness of the firm's anti-money laundering systems.

12.   (i)   **My advice to Agatha concerning breaches of rules is as follows.**

■ The original transaction is an execution-only one in shares and this under COB rule 4.2 does not require Brown Jones to enter into an agreement with Agatha at this stage.

■ Under COB rule 8.1 confirmations are required to be sent out promptly (i.e. T + 1). This has not occurred. The confirmation note should contain a number of important disclosures, including the fact that a part of the deal has been conducted as principal. Regardless of the nature of the deal, agency or principal, the firm should ensure under COB rule 7.5 that Agatha obtains best execution.

■ Under the Client Assets Sourcebook (CASS) and Principle 10 of the Principles for Businesses (PRIN) client money should be segregated and Agatha is entitled to interest (unless advised to the contrary). The cheque which has been despatched to Agatha should not have been drawn on the company's own account but from the client account where the funds should be held. Agatha should have received the money without having to enquire herself.

■ The suitability of the advice to invest into options seems prima facie to be wrong. Brown Jones has a duty under COB rule 5.3 and PRIN 9 to ensure the suitability of advice given to certain customers. In order to assess the suitability of this advice, the firm should have complied with 'know your customer' requirements under COB rule 5.2 by undertaking a fact-find on Agatha to establish her investment objectives, attitude to risk etc.

■ Prior to giving any advice on the merits of options, Agatha, as a private customer investing in contingent liability transactions should have received a two-way client agreement under COB 4.2. This should include the derivative risk warning and she should have signed and returned this after an opportunity to consider it. In any event, the discretionary management of her funds by Brown Jones requires a formal two-way client agreement to be entered into.

■ Under CASS the gilts must normally be registered either in the name of Agatha or an appropriate nominee. It is unclear whether this has occurred, although the use of the gilts by the firm tends to indicate they are not properly registered.

■ A firm is not allowed to use a client's assets as collateral for its own purposes without consent – this would be a breach of the CASS custody rules and PRIN 10 (as well as possibly PRIN 1 and 2).

■ The employee who spoke to Agatha is obliged under S59 of FSMA to be an approved person. It is the responsibility of the firm to ensure this has occurred.

(ii) **Complaints and Compensation Procedures**

Under the FSA Sourcebook 'Dispute Resolution: Complaints' (DISP), Agatha would normally complain to the firm first and if they do not properly respond, she can use the Financial Ombudsman Service who can recommend compensation up to £100,000 plus costs. If this is not successful, Agatha could pursue her claim for compensation through the courts. As she is a Private Person, has suffered loss and the firm has breached certain rules she will be able to bring these actions under S150 FSMA to recover her losses. The use of S150 tends to be cheaper and easier as she will not have to prove negligence on the part of the firm.

However, since the firm has been declared insolvent, it seems unlikely that this will be of much use unless her funds are properly segregated. As an individual private customer, Agatha will also be an Eligible Claimant under the Financial Services Compensation Scheme and can seek redress. Under this scheme her maximum payout will be £48,000 as her loss relates to investments.

13. As Target plc is a UK plc the Takeover Code and Companies Act restrictions will apply. In addition, this scenario raises issues relating to the UKLA Listing Rules and Model Code. There are also concerns relating to criminal and civil offences regarding misuse of information and manipulation.

(a) Monday, 4 June – Transaction

S198 of the Companies Act 1985 requires disclosure to the company within two business days because Swift Move has gone through the 3% Material Interest threshold. In addition, because Target is listed, the Listing Rules require them to announce this to the market via a Regulatory Information Service by the end of the following day. Following the implementation of the Companies Act 2006, the requirements are now contained in the Disclosure and Transparency Rules (DTR) in the FSA's Handbook.

(b)   Tuesday, 5 June and purchases 6 and 7 June

The parties may be a Companies Act concert party and thus disclosures may need to be made to the company. In addition, the agreement to provide free use of Target's research may be a breach of their directors' duties and consequently, Principle 3 of the Takeover Directive Principles.

(d)   11 June – Purchase by Megapocket

This contravenes the law on insider dealing contained in the Criminal Justice Act 1993 as Megapocket is an Insider (he has inside information from an inside source). It therefore also breaches S118(2) FSMA the 'Insider Dealing' head of Market Abuse. This covers behaviour in relation to qualifying investments trading on a prescribed market (UK RIE, PLUS & regulated markets). The penalty for breach includes unlimited fines.

It also breaches Rule 4.1 of the Takeover Code, which prohibits insider dealing, and the Model Code on directors' dealings that would require Megapocket to have obtained permission to deal from a senior member of the board. All dealings by directors of listed companies in the shares of their own company must be registered and then disclosed to the market via a Regulatory Information Service.

(e)   12 June – Offer

The artificial price support for the paper offer breaches the criminal offence of S397 FSMA, which is punishable by seven years imprisonment and unlimited fines. In particular, the conduct creates a false or misleading impression about the price of Swift Move shares.

It also breaches the market abuse provisions in S118(5) FSMA 'Manipulating Transactions'.

The conduct also contravenes Principle 4, no false markets, of the Takeover

Directive Principles and so the parties could be disciplined by the Takeover Panel.

{Note that none of the parties concerned are working in an authorised firm and so it would NOT be appropriate to have discussed breaches of PRIN or APER)

14.   (i)   The following points are of concern.

Regarding Mr Popocros

1.   How do we classify Mr Popocros under COB rule 4.1? He appears to be a private customer, although it is unclear if he is execution only or advisory. He should be classified before we act for him.

2.   Have we done money laundering checks and KYC? These are required under the Money Laundering Regulations 2003. Mr Popocros is an existing customer of the Shipping Department, but shipping is a separate legal entity from Treasury so we should also undertake these checks.

3.   Are sugar futures the right product for Mr Popocros to hedge his risk? Will this hedge against loss of business to a rival firm? Suitability and understanding of risk need to be addressed under COB rules 5.3 and 5.4.

4.   To what extent can a service be provided without consideration towards suitability? If he is a private execution-only customer the Conduct of Business Rules (COB) on suitability will not apply. However, Principle 9 of the Principles for Businesses (customers relationships of trust) will apply to a wider range of customers. Even if a duty is not owed, the firm should consider the reputational damage of dealing where it is not really suitable for the customer.

5. Do the commission arrangements agreed between Shipping and Treasury need to be disclosed in customer documentation? COB rule 5.7 requires disclosure of commission to private customers.

6. What documentation requirements can be waived if Mr Popocros does not wish to sign anything? As a private customer entering into contingent liability transactions he will need a two-way client agreement under COB 4.2 and a two-way derivative risk warning. Certain overseas customers can waive this requirement where the firm has taken reasonable steps to ensure the customer does not wish to receive the agreement. It is unclear whether Mr Popocros is resident overseas. In any event, the firm must ensure private advisory customers understand the risks of their transactions under COB rule 5.4. The firm will have problems proving this if he has had no warnings and there are language problems.

7. What are Mr Popocros' investment objectives in buying Eurobonds? Have the firm considered KYC issues under COB rule 5.2? This should have been established during the fact-find.

Regarding Mr Wotolos

1. Mr Wotolos is unapproved. What activities can he perform? Under S59 FSMA and the Supervision Sourcebook, he must be approved to perform controlled functions, which include customer functions. If he is not the firm could be disciplined and Mr Popocros as a 'Private Person' could sue the firm for losses under S71 FSMA.

2. With how many other customers is Mr Wotolos discussing investment business?

3. Is Mr Wotolos properly trained and competent for the role he is doing? The Training and Competence Sourcebook requires training to be timely, planned, structured and evaluated and that relevant examinations are passed.

4. To what extent can Mr Wotolos act as an agent for Treasury, and what should he or Treasury ensure is disclosed to Mr Popocros, prior to dealing? There is a conflict having Mr Wotolos acting for Mr Popocros as Mr Wotolos is receiving commissions. The firm must apply PRIN 2 (skill, care and diligence) PRIN 6 (customer's interests) and PRIN 8 (conflicts). Any conflicts should be disclosed or otherwise dealt with. It is unlikely that it will be appropriate for Mr Wotolos to be involved in the way he envisages.

Regarding the Firm

1. Do its commission arrangements breach PRIN 3? In addition, where commission and remuneration arrangements present conflicts, the firm must manage these conflicts under Senior Management Arrangements, Systems and Controls (SYSC) and COB rule 7.1.

2. Are the systems and controls adequate? If Mr Wotolos is advising other people without the requisite approval, then the firm is breaching SYSC (employees and agents, organisation).

3. Has the firm dealt appropriately with the conflicts which have arisen here?

(ii) The possible courses of action are to allow Mr Wotolos to 'help' the client, or to deal with Mr Popocros directly.

The suggested best course of action would be to meet with Mr Wotolos and explain that we need to regularise the situation. This means that Mr Popocros must become a client of the Treasury business and that Mr Wotolos will no longer be able to discuss investment issues with any clients. We must ensure we comply with COB and PRIN in dealing with Mr Popocros. If we cannot ensure he understands the risks and procedures as a result of language difficulties, then we should consider whether we can act for him at all.

Section C – Answers

Remember with Section C answers, these are often subjective and as such the following does not intend to be a 'model' answer. The following represent possible answers to each question to consider your own answers against.

15.   The growth of the internet has broadened the opportunities for marketing investment business, but has also created many challenges for the regulators. The internet raises new challenges which could fundamentally change the way financial services is regulated.

Perhaps the most familiar challenge is the difficulty of regulating transactions which are not done in a formal market place. The internet allows consumers to enter into products in an environment which is difficult for the regulator to police. The internet contains so much information that regulators do not easily have the resources required to monitor sites in detail.

Jurisdictional problems also exist in that internet sites may both originate from a country which is outside the regulator's legal or practical jurisdiction. The E-Commerce Directive has helped to clarify this so that e-commerce promotions (i.e. those from a distance electronically delivered, e.g. on a website) are subject to home state rules in the EEA. However, confusion exists as host state rules still apply for non-electronic promotions and for unsolicited real-time promotions. This creates a major challenge for firms in deciphering and applying the correct rules.

A further challenge is the potential for money laundering. In many respects, the rise in internet business and the truly cross-border nature of the internet have made money laundering much easier due to the anonymity which it can create. Whilst the Money Laundering Regulations 2003 and FSA Money Laundering Sourcebook (until 31/8/06) contain identification requirement including non-face to face contact with new clients, these can be difficult to apply in practice and arguably do not address the issue of funds which have already been placed into the system.

Whilst the above are familiar challenges, the internet does present completely novel challenges. Financial services regulation has always been primarily focused, not on the supplier of a product, but the middleman – the person who sells the product. The internet removes this person from the transaction, allowing the supplier to sell directly to the general public. A common technique used by the regulator to ensure that telesales are adequately regulated is to require, under COB chapters 4 and 6, that physical documentation is given to the customer to confirm the discussion by way of client agreement or key features documents. Upon receipt of such documentation, the customer has a cancellation period or withdrawal rights.

The conduct of business rules have needed to undergo a shift in focus in order to cope with e-commerce. Some argue that the COB rules still do not go far enough. The Conduct of Business Rules are arguably still rooted in traditional ways of physical documents and have not yet caught up with the internet revolution. Whilst they do make provision for electronic delivery of documents and broaden the scope of financial promotions, some say there is very little innovation in any other respects in terms of ensuring that customers have read and understood the contents of the information. Having said that, COB rules are now largely media neutral which is a major improvement on the pre-N2 regime.

If electronic documents are going to be used, many question marks that still surround electronic signatures must be addressed. There are still concerns over their security and enforceability that must be dealt with if they are to provide any certainty for consumers or product providers.

One of the advantages of physical documentation is that it, hopefully, brings home to a consumer the consequences of their actions. People will agree to things over the internet, but when they are asked to sign a document agreeing the same things, will approach this with more caution. Internet documentation poses a threat as a culture has developed whereby dialogue boxes are ticked without thought and warnings are scrolled past. The advantage of the internet is quick and easy information. Consumers may, therefore, be placing themselves more at risk. FSA must develop some way of dealing with the potential consequence that the protections that they try to provide by way of risk warnings and agreement are ineffective if they are to achieve their regulatory objectives of Consumer Protection (S5 FSMA) and Promoting Public Awareness (S4 FSMA).

The internet also allows large amounts of information to be presented to consumers in an environment difficult to monitor. Therefore, companies can give performance figures, advertising and comparative tables which may only come to the attention of FSA in the event of misselling. FSA clearly has an obligation to educate consumers to ensure that they are not mislead by such information. In addition, the FSA have implemented new rules on the presentation of past performance data which should address some of these concerns, e.g. no data can be included where less than 12 months of data is available.

The internet, therefore, presents some familiar challenges and some novel challenges. The regulators and governments must try to tame the internet as it is clear that even familiar challenges are on a much larger scale when dealing with the internet. The culmination suggests that an ongoing assessment of law and regulation is required to cope with the possibilities and opportunities presented by the internet.

16. It is hardly surprising to observe that FSA and other regulators are placing increasing emphasis on the responsibilities of managers and directors. This emphasis springs, in part, from a recognition that the most recent scandals and frauds have arisen because of failures in the control systems within investment business. Barings, Daiwa, Sumitomo and Kidder Peabody are all examples of such scandals, in which there was dishonest behaviour by individuals (Leeson et al.), but also of management failure. By placing responsibility for control with the Senior Executive Officer, the regulators are clearly seeking to prevent recurrences of such problems and to make the accountability obvious. Another dynamic is that the regulators are seeking to avoid the problems that arose in the aftermath of the Barings collapse in February 1995. Whilst Nick Leeson was imprisoned, the lasting public remembrance of the disciplinary process was that the directors and managers 'escaped' largely unscathed. Whilst such a depiction does scant justice to the factors of the individual cases, there can be little doubt that regulator's public relations were poorly handled and did little to develop credibility and trust in the regulatory system.

In the post-N2 environment, the FSA places a heavy burden on senior managers. Under S59 FSMA, all persons who govern the firm or perform significant influence functions must be approved, as these are controlled functions. In order to obtain such approval, the person must show (under FIT) fitness and propriety (e.g. competence, capability, integrity etc). Once approved, such persons must comply with seven Statements of Principle set out in the FSA Handbook (APER). The first four of these are applicable to all approved persons within an authorised firm and are therefore fairly general.

1. They must act with integrity when performing their function.

2. They must act with skill, care and diligence when performing their function.

3. They must observe proper standards of market conduct when performing their function.

4. They must deal with the regulator in an open and cooperative way.

The final three principles specifically apply to significant influence functions and shall be looked at in more detail.

5. Senior managers must take responsible steps to ensure that the business of the firm for which they are responsible is organised properly.

   This requires senior management to ensure proper reporting lines and apportionment of responsibility.

6.   Senior managers must exercise skill, care and diligence in their management role.

      This seeks to ensure that senior management understand the areas they manage and therefore are able to properly assess the risks to the business of their decisions. Suitable and responsible delegation is also key in delivering against this requirement.

7.   Senior managers must take reasonable care to ensure that the business of the firm for which they are responsible complies with the regulatory requirements.

      Clearly, this seeks to ensure that compliance is not left to the Compliance Department, but is seen as a shared responsibility throughout the management.

In addition to these principles, the FSA have produced a Sourcebook, Senior Management Arrangements, Systems and Controls (SYSC) to flesh out these principles. SYSC covers areas such as apportionment, organisation, remuneration policies, risk management and compliance functions. Firms can be disciplined for failing to implement these in conjunction with the principles. Examples of such disciplinary action include the £500,000 fine against Carr Sheppards in May 2004, the £63,000 fine against Langtons (IFA) Ltd in September 2006 and the fine of £350,000 against BNP Private Bank in May 2007.

There are concerns in the industry that the increased burden on senior managers and the firm in compliance with the principles and SYSC will not only be unnecessarily time consuming, but will also hurt the investor by increasing compliance costs. On the other hand the FSA must apply the principles of good regulation (set out at S2(3) FSMA) in introducing and enforcing rules that required them, inter alia, to be proportionate and facilitate innovation. In view of this, SYSC makes clear procedures required will depend on the nature, scale and complexity of the firm.

Overall, the regulator's approach is sound and sensible and correctly attributes responsibility to the 'captain of the ship'. We must hope that the implementation of the policy is fair and reasonable in practice and that authorised firms heed these requirements. Concerns still remain as to the effect in practice that these rules will have. This is evidenced by the FSA's letter to 300 banks and building societies in September 2003 concerning their treasury operations and the lack of proper systems and controls in place. This suggests that many firms have still not learnt the lessons of the past.

The importance of competent senior management is even more important in a 'More Principles Based Regulations' world. As the FSA moves away from prescriptive detailed rules and allows senior management to apply princples based regulation, this requires the skills of senior management to identify and manage the risks in their business.

17.   The introduction of criminal offences such as insider dealing (Criminal Justice Act 1993) and misleading statements and practices (formerly in the Financial Services Act 1986 and now under S397 FSMA), together with the FSA Principles and Conduct of Business Rules, went some way to producing a more regulated and open market. However, critics have argued that the 1986 Act did not produce the open, transparent and fair market that was intended. Evidence to back their claims comes in the form of the poor record of successful insider dealing convictions since the introduction of the CJA.

      In May 1997, the government announced important changes to the UK regulatory system and, on 30 November 2001 'N2', the Financial Services and Markets Act came into force. The Act sets out a number of statutory objectives for financial regulation under Section 2(2) FSMA – maintaining confidence in the financial system, promoting public awareness of the financial system, securing the appropriate degree of protection for consumers and reducing financial crime. The reduction of market abuse is essential to ensuring confidence in the financial markets to ensure reputational strength and liquidity.

      Section 118 FSMA gave the FSA new powers to prosecute for market abuse at 'N2' which were updated on 1 July 2005 as a result of implementation of the Market Abuse Directive. FSA drafted a Code of Market Conduct in the Business Standards block of the FSA Handbook setting out guidance as to how they will interpret and enforce the offences contained in S118 FSMA. Breach of the Code will be evidence towards a breach of S118 FSMA and the FSA will be able to impose financial penalties, whilst injured parties will be able to seek compensation.

Market abuse includes

- S118(2) – Market Abuse (Insider Dealing)
- S118(3) – Market Abuse (Improper Disclosure)
- S118(4) – Market Abuse (Misuse of Information)
- S118(5) – Market Abuse (Manipulating Transactions)
- S118(6) – Market Abuse (Manipulating Devices)
- S118(7) – Market Abuse (Dissemination)
- S118(8) – Market Abuse (Misleading Behaviour) and Market Abuse (Distortion)

The rules apply to all persons (including unauthorised persons). The scope is any behaviour (which covers action and inaction) which occurs in relation to a qualifying investment trading on a prescribed market (UK RIE, PLUS & regulated markets except S118(4) & (8)).

The FSA hope that, in particular, the Code will reassure legitimate market users that many existing practices are acceptable to the regulator. This is to counteract the usual criticism that market regulation inhibits professionals from being innovative or risk taking. However, the wide scope of the FSA's Code (and in particular the insistence by Treasury that the regime will allow the FSA to fine on the civil standard of proof) has led to some practitioners becoming fearful that the FSA will use its powers in an uneven and capricious manner. Ironically, this may actually damage the market if there is a feeling that the UK is overregulated. In order to calm fears, the FSA has been very vocal about their desire to use their enhanced powers proportionately.

The powers for the FSA to tackle market abuse have promoted widespread comment and, whilst most seem to support the idea in principle, there are a number of concerns about how the new regime will fit in with the existing criminal offences. For example, concerns exist over the interrelation of the proposed offence with the Human Rights Act 1998. A civil offence with the threat of unlimited fines may be unworkable if it can be successfully argued that the Human Rights Act requires such penalties to have a criminal burden of proof.

In addition the regime applies to those outside the UK but in practice extra-territorial legislation is very difficult and costly to enforce.

There is much sensitivity in the industry regarding the market abuse regime. Whilst there has been an acceptance that the current criminal regime has not done enough to prevent financial crime, there may be a general feeling that the new regime seeks to give the FSA too much power. The FSA has used the provisions in S118 FSMA on a number of occasions e.g. £17 million fine against Shell in August 2004, £13.9 million fine against Citigroup in June 2005 and a £6.3m fine against Deutsche Bank in April 2006.

Some have criticised the size of the fines for insider dealing as being too low to cause a deterrent effect but, on the counter argument, the FSA's principles of good regulation require proportionate action.

More recently, the whole structure of market abuse as a 'civil' offence with its lower burden of proof has been questioned by the Davidson case. It was found on appeal, that where the punishment for market abuse is so severe (eg large fine for an individual) that it is felt to be criminal in nature, then the burden of proof is that of the 'heightened civil standard' which is almost the same as 'beyond reasonable doubt' that is required under CJA93.

Perhaps, one major benefit has been that concern over the new offence within firms has raised awareness of the need to train staff on good market practices which has to be a benefit to the fair operation of the markets.

18.   The FSA issued PS07/2 Implementing the Markets in Financial Instruments Directive (MiFID) in January 2007. This set out the FSA's transposition of MiFID into UK regulations in time for the 31 January deadline. Only the UK and Romania fully achieved this deadline out of the EU states. Most other countries were expected to make the transposition arrangements by the end of March but some other countries are going to be later. However, all countries still claim they will be implementing MiFID on time.

The directive is a maximum harmonisation directive and therefore aims to be a complete set of conduct of business rules for each country to transpose into their national legislation framework. This will help achieve the Financial Services Action Plan of creating a common market in financial services across the EEA by removing barriers to the free movement of financial services around Europe.

The FSA had to justify to the European Commission the additional rules over and above the requirements of MiFID. As MiFID is a maximum harmonisation directive, any national regulator that adds additional rules must justify this 'gold plating' in reference to the risks posed to investor protection or market integrity. The UK had four areas of 'gold plating'and justified them on the following basis

1.   Apportionment of senior manager responsibility – wish to retain high standards of accountability of senior management set out in SYSC2

2.   Content of confirmation and periodic statements – more detailed disclosures thought necessary especially in derivative transactions

3.   Packaged product market requirements – the UK has significantly more investment for personal retirement and home ownership than other EU member states and this has been an area of previous misselling with both private pension and endowments. With some packaged products being MiFID business (unit trusts, OEICs and investment trust schemes) and some non-MiFID (life policies and pensions) the FSA is concerned that there will be distortion to the markets in these products if rules are not harmonised. This will in particular relate to disclosure of independent or tied status (Initial Disclosure Document), information about the products and menu of charges and their disclosure

4.   Use of dealing commission – the FSA addressed specific market failings in restricting soft commissions to execution of trades and research. This goes beyond the general limit on inducements set out in MiFID

The harmonisation of the COB rules throughout the EEA should be a significant step towards achieving the Lamfalussy Committee's goal of a unified European financial market. The goal should allow the EU to become as important a capital market as the US. The implementation of MiFID will facilitate trading of EU securities in other places than their domestic market. This should be a good move for London which is already a major world market for securities. The recent surge of listings of overseas companies in the UK, partly to avoid the onerous rule bound regulations in the US, is proof that an effective regulatorly system that balances a light touch regulatory approach through principles based regulation can be very good for the UK's status as a leading world financial centre.

Winter 2006

Please note: the answers given have not been updated to reflect technical changes since the date of the exam and therefore this document is only intended to provide guidance on the suggested content of your answers. In particular, we have used bullet points throughout to highlight the areas you could have discussed or considered. In the examination, particularly with Section C questions, it may often be more appropriate to set out certain answers in paragraph form. To see the examiner's report on this exam, please go to www.sii.org.uk.

Section A

1. A person who breaches the general prohibition commits an offence under S 23(1) FSMA and is liable to six months imprisonment or a fine (not exceeding the statutory maximum) on summary conviction or two years imprisonment and an unlimited fine or both (S 23(1)).

    Agreements entered into by a person in breach of the general prohibition are also unenforceable (S 23(1)). The other party is entitled to any money or property paid or transferred and compensation for any loss sustained.

2. An individual may be treated as an intermediate customer where they have opted up to intermediate status. The following four conditions must be complied with:

    (a) The firm must take reasonable care to determine that the customer has sufficient experience and understanding (having regard to knowledge and understanding, length of time active in the market, frequency of dealings, reliance on advice, size and nature of transactions and financial standing);

    (b) The firm has given written warning to the customer of the protections lost;

    (c) The firm has given the customer sufficient time to consider the implications of opting up; and

    (d) The customer has given written consent or the firm has otherwise been able to demonstrate that informed consent has been given.

3. Exempt persons are set out in the Exemption Order issued by each Treasury under S 38(1) FSMA. This includes:

    (a) Government organisations and related bodies (including the Bank of England and National Savings Bank);

    (b) Other central banks;

    (c) Super-national organisations (such as the International Monetary Fund and World Bank);

    (d) Municipal banks and local authorities;

    (e) Charities;

    (f) Members of the professions;

    (g) Members of Lloyd's;

    (h) Appointed representatives;

    (i) Recognised Investment Exchanges (RIEs), Recognised Overseas Investment Exchanges (ROIEs) and Recognised Clearing Houses (RCHs).

4.   The regulated activities listed in Schedule 2 FSMA include:

(a)   Dealing in investments;

(b)   Arranging deals in investments;

(c)   Deposit-taking;

(d)   Safe-keeping and administration of assets;

(e)   Managing investments;

(f)   Investment advice;

(g)   Establishing collective investment schemes;

(h)   Using computer-based systems for providing investment instructions.

Specified investment include:

(a)   Securities;

(b)   Instruments creating or acknowledging indebtedness;

(c)   Government and public securities;

(d)   Instruments entitling to investments;

(e)   Certificates representing securities;

(f)   Units and collective investment schemes;

(g)   Options;

(h)   Futures;

(i)   Contracts for differences;

(j)   Contracts of insurance;

(k)   Participation in Lloyd's syndicates;

(l)   Deposits;

(m)   Loans secured on land;

(n)   Rights in investments.

5.   The FSA Handbook specifies seven principles applicable to approved persons carrying out controlled functions. Only three of these nevertheless apply with regard to significant influence functions. These consist of:

(5)   Proper organisation of business;

(6)   Skill, care and diligence in management;

(7)   Comply with regulatory requirements.

6.   The purpose of the KYC requirement is to ensure that a firm has sufficient up-to-date information to determine whether the recommendations made are suitable for the particular customer concerned.

The rule requires that a firm advising a private customer or acting as an investment manager for a private customer (or arranging a pension opt-out or transfer for a private customer) must take reasonable steps to ensure that it is in possession of sufficient personal and financial information relevant for the services that the firm has agreed to provide.

Firms must keep the information obtained under regular review where they are acting in a discretionary capacity or advising on a continuous basis.

Where the private customer declines to provide relevant personal and financial information, the firm should not proceed without promptly advising the customer that the lack of such information may adversely affect the quality of the services provided.

7.   Part XXVII FSMA applies with regard to:

(a)   Authorised or unauthorised unit trust schemes;

(b)   Open-ended investment companies;

(c)   Recognised overseas schemes including:

(i)   Other EEA constituted schemes;

(ii)   Designated country or territory schemes; and

(iii)   Individually recognised overseas schemes.

8.   Disciplinary powers include:

(a)   Fines;

(b)   Private or public censure;

(c)   Injunction;

(d)   Varying or withdrawing approval;

(e)   Varying or cancelling permission;

(f)   Information gathering;

(g)   Investigations;

(h)   Reports by skilled persons;

(i)   Restitution;

(j)   Bankruptcy or insolvency.

9.   Market abuse as defined in s118(2) applies with regard to:

(a)   Insider (not-public) information;

(b)   False or misleading impressions;

(c)   Market distortion.

10.   Confirmations must include the following:

(a)   The firm's name and address;

(b)   The fact that the firm is regulated by the FSA;

(c)   Confirm that the firm has acted as principal where relevant;

(d)   The customer's name (but not necessarily address);

(e)   Transaction details (including investment, sale or purchase, price, date and time and consideration);

(f)   Remuneration;

(g)   Any fees, taxes or duties (including Stamp Duty).

Section B

11. **Conflicts of Interest**

Question 11 was concerned with the management of conflicts of interest in connection with the provision of investment research by independent and trading firms and breach of relevant regulatory and statutory provisions including PRIN, SYSC, APER and CGA 1993 and SS 118 and 397 FSMA.

(a) Tony has been provided with two sets of information with Brian's refusal to comment on the FDA approval and Brian's subsequent general comment on escorting Tony to his car. This creates immediate problems with regard to conflicts of interest and how they should be managed as well as possible offences of insider dealing (CJA 1993) and market abuse and market manipulation (SS 118 and 397 FSMA). Specific obligations on the management of conflicts of interest are dealt with in COB 7.1 and COB 7.16 (investment research) and 7.17 (research recommendations) as well as under PRIN 1 (integrity), 2 (skill, care and diligence), 3 (management and control), 6 (customers' interest) and 8 (conflicts of interest) as well as SYSC and APER. Reference may also have been made to the SII Code of Conduct.

As the question is concerned only with the action that Tony should take to preserve his own reputation at this stage, many of these issues can be referred to in general terms and then developed in further detail in subsequent parts of the question.

At this stage, the immediate and main action that Tony should have taken was to refer the matter to Compliance and take advice. A more complete answer may then have referred one or more of the following:

(i) Disclose the relevant facts to Compliance and not publish until consent is given;

(ii) Ensure that the matter is properly recorded by Compliance;

(iii) Make a separate record of the information supporting the original downgrade decision and reasons for not altering that position;

(iv) Not disclose the warnings received from Brian to anyone else within the investment bank;

(v) Possibly ask a separate analyst to assume responsibility for the report although this decision will probably be taken by Compliance.

The point may also be made that it is not clear whether Tony is an approved person and therefore subject to APER. The firm will still be subject to the requirements under COB even if Tony is not an approved person.

It is also questionable whether Tony should have attended such a selective briefing in the first case.

(b) The equivalent issues have to be considered with regard to Johnson including, in particular, possible breach of APER (assuming that he is an approved person) and the offences of insider dealing, market abuse and market manipulation. Johnson should not have asked for information concerning the drugs' approval as this would have constituted an inside disclosure.

As the question is allocated five marks, appropriate detail should have been provided on the constituent elements of each of the principal offences. It is, in particular, unlikely that the comment made by Brian would be considered specific or precise enough under both the CJA and S 118. Johnson is nevertheless still considering changing his position on the basis of the concerns raised. Failure to disclose is also relevant in considering the application of S 397.

Johnson should again notify Compliance and take advice. Other more specific issues that could have been referred to include:

(i)   Report to Compliance and take instructions;

(ii)   Ensure that appropriate records are kept;

(iii)   Consider possible conflicts of interest rules under COB 7.1 and 7.16/7.17;

(iv)   Confirm application of each of the statutory offences;

(v)   Confirm possible breach of APER while Compliance considers relevance of PRIN and SYSC;

(vi)   Include disclosure of bank's brokerage position in report as required under COB 7.17;

(vii)   Disclose any major shareholdings or other interests;

(viii) Disclose any individual dealing ('spinning');

(ix)   Include other required disclosures as specified in COB 7.17 (offer, regulation, facts and separate interpretations, estimates or opinions, sources, projections and forecasts, substances, valuation summaries; key definitions, date and any recent corrections);

(x)   Comply with any more general firm policy governing management of conflicts of interests under COB 7.1 (disclosure, Chinese walls, independence or decline to act);

(xi)   Avoid other disclosure within firm;

(xii)   Avoid dealing ahead of investment (front-running under COB 7.3);

(xiii) Avoid breach of personal account dealing (PAD under COB 7.13);

(xiv)   Consider request to have stop placed on restricted or watch lists and to have Johnson placed on an insider list.

(c)   Compliance will possibly advice Tony to continue with his original report as this was not affected by the two disclosures made and it is unlikely that these would be considered precise or specific enough to constitute statutory offences. The constituent elements of each offence would nevertheless have to be considered separately and an opinion taken.

All of the issues referred to in (a) above would apply with regard to Tony's individual conduct (including possible breach of APER, COB 7.1, 16 and 17 as well as the bank's conflicts of interest policy). It would also look for any breaches of other particular obligations (such as COB 7.3 or 7.13). Compliance would then also consider possible breach by the firm of PRIN and SYSC.

More specific points made include:

(i)   Advise Tony that he may have been an insider although no breach has been committed due to the lack of specificity;

(ii)   Possibly include Tony on the insider list to avoid subsequent conflict;

(iii)   Advise Tony not to deal or encourage any others to deal or disclose the information;

(iv)   Ask that the report is issued by a separate independent analyst if any residual concerns are considered to arise;

(v)   Not allow Tony to attend any subsequent selective briefings or meetings with the company;

(vi)   Place the stop on a watch list or possibly restricted list later;

(vii)   Confirm with the company when the FDA approval is expected and possibly advise them to consider making a public disclosure;

(viii) Disclosure should also be made of the company's conduct to the FSA for regulatory and listing purposes.

(d)   The main further issues raised are concerned with Johnson's possible breach of s 397 for failing to disclose and the breach of relevant regulatory and listing provisions by senior management and the company in pushing for the release of a positive report.

Johnson should initially disclose the matter to Compliance, failing which the FSA directly. He would be protected from disclosure under the 'whistle-blowing procedures' in SYSC 4 and the Public Interest Disclosure Act 1998. Equivalent disclosure is also provided for under the SII Code.

Relevant breaches of PRIN, SYSC and APER should also be considered. The specific rules applicable to the conduct of the research published should also be complied under COB 7.16 and 17 (above).

Johnson may breach ss 118 and 397 in failing to disclosure. Senior management within the investment bank and the company may also be considered to have breached ss 118 and 397 in pressurising the publication of a positive report. Relevant constituent elements may have been referred.

Possible breach of director's duties and listing rules more generally by the company may be referred to.

The nature of possible sanctions that may imposed by the FSMA should have been referred to, including censure (private or public), financial penalties and withdrawal or restriction of authorisation (permission) or approval.

Compliance will separately consider any necessary internal action that should be taken (as above). This may include internal disciplinary action as well as placing the stock on a watch or stop list. Internal compliance procedures will be reviewed and adjusted as necessary. Appropriate reports should be made to the FSA. The bank should co-operate fully with the FSA to avoid additional sanction and benefit from the early settlement procedure.

12.   **Financial Promotions**

The question was concerned with the issuance of financial promotions and commencement of business by a newly established hedge fund management company in London.

(a)   The nature of the activities carried on by the fund manager (including dealing, arranging deals and possible investment advice) could initially have been distinguished from the nature of the fund itself as an unregulated collective investment scheme. While the management activities will be carried on in the UK, the fund (or funds themselves) would generally be established elsewhere (such as the Cayman Islands).

The particular issue raised is concerned with possible breach of the restrictions on financial promotion imposed under s 21 FSMA and relevant provisions within COB 3. The relevant statutory sections should have been referred to (including offence, defence and penalty) as well as exemptions under the FPO and CBO 3.

Cold-calling itself would constitute an unsolicited real-time financial promotion under COB 3. Promotions must be clear, fair and not misleading and, in particular, include no untrue claims, make clear the purpose of the call, confirm that the customer is willing to proceed (and stop if not), provide a contact point and do not approach the customer at an unsociable hour or use any unlisted numbers.

Unsolicited real-time promotions may also only be made to certain types of customer under the FPO or CBO. These principally consist of market counter parties, intermediate customers or certified sophisticated investors. (A number of the FPO exceptions do not apply to unsolicited calls.) Other exemptions are available where calls are 'envisaged' or they relate to marketable ungeared packaged products or readily realisable securities (other than warrants). None of these will apply in the particular case.

Further specific restrictions apply with regard to the promotion of unregulated collective investment schemes under s 238 FSMA and the supporting Promotion of Collective Investment Schemes (Perceptions) Order 2001 (as amended). These again include market counter parties and intermediate customers as well as certain FPO exceptions (including certified sophisticated investors). Other contactees must either have been participants (within the last 30 months) or the firm must have taken reasonable steps to ensure that the investment is suitable.

(b)   Clients must either be classified as market counter parties or customers (intermediate or private). Candidates may either have discussed all of the main classification categories or focused on the specific types of client that may have been permitted under the exceptions referred to in (a) above. As much detail as possible should have been provided to obtain the full five marks.

(c)   Relevant documentation would have included:

(i)   Relevant Terms of Business or Client Agreements (COB 4.2), with detailed information being provided with regard to the content of each and signing or timing requirements;

(ii)   Separate disclosure of services, fees and commissions (including an Initial Disclosure Document under COB 4.3 in connection with any packaged products);

(iii)   KYC Questionnaire or "fact-find" under COB 5.2 if relevant;

(iv)   Provision of a suitability letter (COB 5.3) if relevant;

(v)   A K Features document if a packaged product was concerned (COB 6.1, 6.2 and 6.5);

(vi)   Identity checks and Know Your Customer (KYC) confirmation for money laundering purposes.

As much detail as possible should have been provided to obtain the full five marks.

(d)   Reference should have been made to the additional requirements imposed with regard to the use of Client Agreements (COB 4.2) where discretionary investment management may be relevant as well as the additional risk warnings that should be provided (COB 5.4) that should have provided with particular products including warrant and derivatives, non-readily realisable investments, penny shares, stabilisation, stock lending structured capital at risk products (SCARPs) or highly geared products. As much detail as possible should again have been provided to obtain full marks.

13.   **Market Abuse**

The question is concerned with 'wall-crossing' and supporting restrictions in connection with the short selling of internationally traded stock and potential breach of PRIN and APER as well as the commission of insider trading and market abuse (CJA and s118 FSMA). This parallels the decision issued by the Financial Services and Markets Tribunal in the case of Philippe Jabre and the FSA on 27 July 2006. The FSMT rejected the appeal by Philippe Jabre and held, in particular, that the FSA could ask that the issue of suitability was reconsidered at the appeal stage and that short selling of equivalent stock listed in London constituted market abuse under s 118 FSMA.

(a)   Rapier has 'wall-crossed' (or become restricted) with the pre-marketing (pre-sounding) discussions conducted with the salesman from the investment bank. The relevant issue is accordingly coded:

(i)   The consequences of wall-crossing and restriction in prohibiting subsequent dealing;

(ii)   The passing of inside information (specific and precise, price sensitive, unpublished and relevant);

(iii)   Whether the stock was listed on a prescribed market in London;

(iv)   Whether the stock was on an existing watch or restricted list;

(v)   Whether Rapier was already on an insider list;

(vi)   Whether and when the forthcoming issue would be announced to the public;

(vii)   Market abuse and relevant conditions (as defined in s118 FSMA);

(viii) Whether Rapier has already disclosed or discussed any of this with Compliance;

(ix)   Whether existing reporting procedures were adequate;

(x)   Whether the firm's existing conflicts of interest, policy and, in particular, Chinese walls procedures were operating effectively;

(xi)   Whether there had been any breach of PRIN by the firm or APER by Rapier.

As much detail as possible should have been provided within the time available.

The more general issue that arises is whether the firm can be held liable for any offences committed by a senior manager. Vicarious liability was confirmed in the case of Jabre where the seniority and authority of the individual concerned was sufficient. This could either be raised under sub-section (a) or (d) below.

(b)   The completion of pre-existing orders would not constitute insider trading or market abuse under relevant defences. The entering into any new transactions to borrow or short sell would nevertheless be prohibited. No new contracts or orders should be entered into following the initial contact and discussion. All relevant offence conditions and defences could have been discussed in as much detail as possible.

Reference may also have been to the due diligence and reasonable precaution defence in s123 FSMA.

Reference may also have been to breach of PRIN and APER.

(c)   The issue relates to the territorial scope of application of the insider trading and market abuse offences. If Rapier is not trading in the particular securities to which the information relates, there may be no offence of insider trading under the CJA 93. The scope of application of s 188 FSMA is nevertheless wider as this applies to any dealing in shares dealt with on a 'prescribed market'. If the shares in the Brazilian bank are already dealt with on any UK prescribed market, any dealing in shares in the bank in any other market across the market will constitute market abuse as confirmed by the FSMT in the Jabre decision. It was stated that it would otherwise have been absurd for traders to misuse information by trading on any non-UK market where this would otherwise constitute market abuse under S 188. The scope of application of the offence has since been clarified under the revisions made in the implementation of EU Market Abuse Directive (MAD).

Reference may also have been to breach of PRIN and APER.

(d)   As Rapier has already traded and booked a substantial profit for the firm, Compliance will now be concerned with the effects of this on the operation of its internal systems and controls, the need to report the breach to the FSA (under PRIN (11)) and the internal regulatory action and external (FSA) penalties that will be imposed.

Relevant issues include:

(i)   The nature of any internal sanction to be imposed on Rapier;

(ii)   The need to review reporting and conflicts of interest policy management practice within the firm;

(iii)   Any more general corrective action to be taken to prevent substantial FSA sanction;

(iv)   The facts should be reported immediately to the FSA under PRIN (11);

(v)   Applicable sanctions for breach of s118 FSMA against Rapier (unlimited fine);

(vi)   Sanction against firm for vicarious liability of Rapier under s118)as confirmed in Jabre);

(vii)   Possible penalties for breach of CJA 93 in the event that insider dealing may have been established (although unlikely);

(viii) Penalties for breach by Rapier of APER 2 (due skill, care and diligence) and 3 (market conduct);

(ix)   Possible breach by Rapier of APER 1 (integrity) (not confirmed Jabre);

(x)   Possible breach by the firm of PRIN 5 (market conduct);

(xi)   Possible related breaches of PRIN or SYSC as well as implications on COND and FIT;

(xii)   Possibility of public or private censure and consequent reputational damage.

Reference may also have been to difficulty for Rapier in subsequently reapplying for approved persons status under FIT in the event of previous restriction or cancellation. Even if earlier approval was not formally withdrawn, Rapier may have significant difficulties in retaining this status subsequently. If approval had been cancelled, Rapier would have the responsibility of establishing fit and properness again. The issue was left open in the Jabre case.

Reference could also have been made to breach of the SII Principles as well as the more general need to maintain ethical standards in financial markets.

14.   European Banking

The question was concerned with the scope of passport of Treaty rights available to EEA authorised institutions.

(a)   The relevant procedures provided for the exercise of establishment rights by an EEA bank coming to the UK provided for under s 31 and Schedule 3 FSMA and AUTH should have been explained. As much detail as possible should have been provided for the full three marks.

The scope of the rights conferred would be restricted to the activities either listed in the Banking Consolidation Directive (BCD) or the Investment Services Directive (ISD) (to be replaced by the MIFID) and as already authorised in the home country. Passport rights would not then be available for commodity derivative business and corporate finance and investment advice would only be covered as non-core activities under the ISD. The bank would accordingly have to conduct at least core activity to which the non-core activities could be attached.

Commodity derivatives should be covered by the MIFID when it comes into effect in November 2007. Failing this, the bank may consider exercising Treaty rights under Schedule 4 FSMA although the scope of the possible rights available would have to be confirmed with the FSA as Schedule 4 does not have the same full scope of application as the underlying Treaty rights on which the passport rights are based.

(b) The division of responsibility between the home and host state regulators should have been explained in as much detail as possible. The home authority would be responsible for authorisation, suitability, capital adequacy, client assets, home COB (including compensation) and any other core provisions (including training, systems and controls and money laundering). The FSA as the host state would be responsible for COB and approved persons, training and competence, PRIN, systems and controls, market conduct, enforcement and decision-making and complaints, as well as any other provisions applicable in the general good. Revised provisions will apply under the MIFID and NewCOB.

(c) If the bank wishes to exercise service rights, the home regulator in Germany would have to be approached under the separate procedures provided under Schedule 3 in connection with the right of establishment. The relevant procedures and timing should have been explained. Telephone approaches will be covered by the Distance Marketing Directive.

(d) As a non-EEA firm, a Tokyo subsidiary would not be able to exercise passport rights. Limited exceptions may nevertheless be available under the FPO for non-authorised promotions under s 21 FSMA. These include generic promotions, investment professionals, overseas recipients, deposits and insurance, one-off communications, certified high net worth individuals, associations of certified high net worth individuals, certified sophisticated investors and high net worth companies. The London subsidiary may also become the representative office for the Tokyo company.

Reference may be made to the distinction between non-real-time and real-time promotions and the different effects that this would have on the ability of the Tokyo subsidiary to promote its activities in the UK.

The Tokyo company would not require separate authorisation or permission where it was only carrying on dealing or arranging deals in Tokyo. It could also act for UK customers on an execution-only basis provided that there was no breach of the financial promotion rules.

(e) Whether the provision of investment research would constitute as regulated activity would initially have to be considered. If this was generic and public without constituting the provision of investment advice, no specific authorisation or permission would be required in the UK.

The promotions could also be approved by the London subsidiary, which would be an authorised person for the purposes of s 21. The firm may then be able to rely on the additional exception provided under the COB. These include financial promotions made to or directed at market counter parties or intermediate customers, one-off non-real-time or one-off solicited real-time promotions, general image advertising, personal quotations or illustrations or separate takeover promotions inter alia.

The need for exemption would be dependent upon the extent to which either activity constituted a regulated activity in the UK for the purposes of the FSMA. The issuing of generic research would not be covered by the RTO insofar as it did not constitute the provision of investment advice with regard to a particular investment.

The promotion of Japanese securities generally may also not constitute a regulated activity for the purposes of the FSMA. Even to the extent that it may, the generic promotions exception available under the FSMA 2000 (Financial Promotion) Order 2005 may apply both regard to Japanese securities and to investment research.

Other FPO exceptions may also be available. These would include investment professionals, overseas recipients, one-off communications, certified high net worth individuals (net income of £100,000 or more or net assets of £250,000 or more), associations of certified high net worth individuals, certified sophisticated investors and high net worth companies.

The COB exceptions would not apply except to the extent that the promotions were to be approved by a UK authorised person.

Section C

15. **Customer Relations**

References should have been made to the main 'treating customers fairly' documents where this information was available. This includes the September 2005 discussion paper on 'TFC – Building on Progress' and the FSA CBO letter in 2004. TFC was also referred to in recent Annual Reports and Business Plans.

TFC is linked to the FSA's consumer protection and consumer education objectives (FSMA S 2 (2)(b) and (c)). Reference may also have been made to relevant supervisory principles (FSMA S 2(3)).

The general objective is to highlight the treatment of consumers especially in the retail area within firm's compliance functions. Senior management should be closely involved and TFC built in to firms' general internal business and compliance structure.

TFC requirements are to come into effect by March 2007. A 'principles based approach' is to be adopted. As many of the specific requirements involved as possible should have been referred to. These include:

(a) Transparency and disclosure;
(b) Management involvement;
(c) Revised disputes and complaint handling procedures;
(d) Avoidance of excessive obligation;
(e) Client identification, documentation and evaluation;
(f) Revised client asset rules (CASS).

Reference may also have been made to relevant MIFID pressure and incorporation of TFC within the FSA's more generally Arrow II framework.

Candidates may have referred to and discussed relevant difficulties with the FSA's policy more generally. This may have included:

(a) Lack of clear definition;
(b) Lack of clear obligation (relevant rules) and direction;
(c) Consequent uncertainty in terms of detailed application and compliance;
(d) Possible consequent unfairness in terms of sanction and enforcement;
(e) Difficulty in securing and measuring any consequent benefit.

Despite the difficulties referred to, this is an important initiative which should be taken forward with industry support.

16. **Money Laundering**

The responsibility and involvement of the FSA in money laundering could initially have been referred. This is based on statutory objective 4 (s 2(2)(d) and 7 FSMA). This could also be considered relevant to market confidence and consumer protection and education (s 2(2)(a), (b) and (c) FSMA). The relevant supervisory principles also include efficient use of resources, proportionality and management responsibility (S2(3) FSMA).

The main reasons for the policy change include:

(a) The FSA's focus on principles based regulation;
(b) The need to focus on systems and controls and management responsibility (PRIN, FIT and SYSC);
(c) The desire to avoid duplication and overlap in terms of regulatory content and coverage;
(d) The need to integrate money laundering compliance within management and control cultures more directly;
(e) The desire to allow firms additional flexibility in terms of implementation and compliance.

All of this will also be achieved without any reduction in terms of consumer protection or the effective implementation and enforcement of the relevant criminal and civil laws as well as supporting regulatory provision.

Well structured answers should have referred to the main current body of law governing money laundering in the UK at some stage. This includes the main offences under the Proceeds of Crime Act 2002 and Terrorism Act 2000, as well as relevant Money Laundering regulations (as revised in 2003). The revised Joint Money Laundering Steering Group (JMLSG) Guidelines should have been referred to and the consolidated Third European Money Laundering Directive.

Reference may also have been made to the FSA's January 2000 theme which included money laundering and other relevant international developments including the work of the FATF and its revised Recommendations on money laundering and Anti-Terrorist financing.

As much detail as possible should have been provided.

17. **Hedge Funds**

The objective of the question was to identify the main difficulties that arise with regard to the regulation of hedge fund and the possibility regulatory response that the FSA and others may adopt.

Relevant difficulties include:

(a)   Location in off-shore financial centres (for tax and regulatory advantage);

(b)   High levels of dealing;

(c)   Complex investment strategies (often based on sophisticated and mathematical and computer modelling);

(d)   Significant use of short and long positions with possible distorting effects on markets;

(e)   Use of overlapping strategies in more than one sector or asset class (including securities, currency and commodities) with consequent effects on principal markets concerned including many of the main commodity sectors;

(f)   Use of complex supporting derivative contracts on OTC and formal markets;

(g)   Possible insider dealing and market abuse;

(h)   Possible 'spinning';

(i)   Possible systemic threats;

(j)   High levels of investment and consequently high levels of possible investor loss;

(k)   Difficulty in promoting and selling to retail or less sophisticated customers;

(l)   General lack of regulatory transparency and oversight.

Reference may have been made to recent scandals including LCTM, Amarth and Jabre or similar scandals.

Despite these difficulties, the advantages of hedge funds are generally accepted by the main regulatory authorities. These include:

(a)   Appropriate source of higher risk investment for wealthier individuals;
(b)   Increased liquidity support for main and smaller markets;
(c)   Development of more sophisticated risk management strategies and techniques;
(d)   Legitimate source of investment reward;
(e)   General contribution to financial innovation.

The current regulatory structure applicable to hedge funds should have been outlined. This includes:

(a)   Establishment only in accordance with relevant laws in particular jurisdiction (including exclusion from US securities laws);

(b)   Full regulation and supervision of investment managers in each of the main financial centres including New York State and London;

(c)   Restrictions or promotion of unregulated funds in most jurisdictions including as an unregulated collective scheme in the UK.

Some of the main official papers and reports that have been produced could have been noted. These principally include the earlier work of the Financial Stability Forum (FSF) in Basel as well as work undertaken by the New York Federal Reserve Bank and the FSA in London. The FSA did consider regulating hedge funds directly but has decided against this.

Possible regulatory responses to the continued development of hedge funds may have been referred. This could have included:

(a)   Need for direct regulation;

(b)   Imposition of portfolio composition of Rules;

(c)   Imposition of restrictions on total fund sizes;

(d)   Restriction on investment in particular sectors or assets;

(e)   Increased (or relaxed) restrictions on promotion;

(f)   Increased disclosure and transparency;

(g)   Development of market based best practice in the sector;

(h)   Increased co-operation between regulators on the cross-border supervision of relevant funds.

18.   **Ethical Standards**

Some candidates made the introductory point that the FSA has no direct or express statutory responsibility or authority for the promotion of high ethical standards in the financial area. This can nevertheless be considered as part of the construction of more effective general regulatory framework within which the FSA secures its four statutory objectives (market confidence, consumer protection, consumer education and financial crime).

Candidates could have initially discussed all of the relevant sections of the regulatory framework set up under the FSMA within which ethical standards can be promoted. These include:

(a)   The statutory objectives and supervisory principles (s 2(2) and (3) FSMA);

(b)   The duties of the FSA (s 2(5) FSMA);

(c)   The authorisation regime (ss 19 and 31 FSMA);

(d)   The permission regime (s 41 FSMA);

(e)   The financial promotion regime (s 21 FSMA, RTO, COB and NewCOB rules);

(f)   The approved persons regime (s 59 and FIT and APER);

(g)   The general principles (PRIN);

(h)   The systems and controls requirements and specific obligations imposed on senior management (SYSC and APER);

(i)   The rules based nature of the new regime (ss138 and 157 FSMA);

The main sets of regulatory provisions that apply in this area may then have been summarised. These include:

(a)   Relevant specific obligations either within COB or NewCOB (including advising (COB 5.1), know-your-customer (COB 5.2), suitability (COB 5.3), understanding risk (COB 5.4), information (COB 5.5) and charges (COB 5.6 and 5.7) as well as KFD (COB 6.1, 6.2 and 6.5), decision trees (COB 6.5), projections (COB 6.6), cancellation and withdrawal (COB 6.7) and conflicts of interest (COB 7.1), churning and switching (COB 7.1), front running (COB 7.3), order priority 9COB 7.4), best execution (COB 7.5), timely execution (COB 7.6), aggregation and allocation (COB 7.7), realisation (COB 7.8), lending (COB 7.9), PAD (COB 7.13), programme trading (COB 7.14), non-market transactions (COB 7.15), investment research (COB 7.16), research and recommendations (COB 7.17), dealing commission (COB 7.18), reporting (COB 8), client assets (CASS) and records;

(b)   Market abuse (s 118 FSMA) and misleading statements and practices (s 397 FSMA);

(c)   Listing and UKLA;

(d)   Recognition of Takeover Code and Panel work;

(e)   Enforcement and remedies more generally.

Some candidates also referred to some of the difficulties that can arise implementing with such a policy. These include:

(a)   Lack of any clear definition of ethical objective or policy;

(b)   Consequent difficulties in securing implementation and compliance;

(c)   Lack of any effective means of measuring or validating compliance with general standards set;

(d)   Unfairness in terms of sanction and penalties;

(e)   More general confusion of policy objectives and regulatory priorities.

Summer 2006

Please note: the answers given have not been updated to reflect technical changes since the date of the exam and therefore this document is only intended to provide guidance on the suggested content of your answers. In particular, we have used bullet points throughout to highlight the areas you could have discussed or considered. In the examination, particularly with Section C questions, it may often be more appropriate to set out certain answers in paragraph form. To see the examiner's report on this exam, please go to www.sii.org.uk.

Section A

1. S3   Maintaining Confidence in the Financial System
    S4   Promoting Public Understanding
    S5   Protecting Consumers
    S6   Reduction of Financial Crime

2. The two requirements set out under S19 are that a person should be either

    ▓   authorised, or.

    ▓   exempt.

3. List 8 out of any one of the following 11 Principles for Businesses

PRIN 1	Integrity	PRIN 7	Communications with Clients
PRIN 2	Skill, Care and Diligence	PRIN 8	Conflicts of Interest
PRIN 3	Management and Control	PRIN 9	Customers – Relationship of Trust
PRIN 4	Financial Prudence	PRIN 10	Clients' Assets
PRIN 5	Market Conduct	PRIN 11	Relations with Regulators
PRIN 6	Customers' Interests		

4. Honesty, integrity and good reputation

    Competency and capability

    Financial soundness

5. List any six of the following.

    ▓   HM Treasury (HMT) appoint the Board and Chairman and judge the FSA against the principles of good regulation set out in S2 (3) of FSMA. Annual report to HM Treasury on discharge of its functions and extent to which the four regulatory objectives have been met.

    ▓   Within three months of the report to HMT, the FSA holds a public meeting to facilitate open discussion of its report.

    ▓   Under FSMA S7, the FSA has its own internal mechanisms to ensure appropriate standards of corporate governance are met, such as a majority of non-executives on its board.

    ▓   An independent disciplinary hearing function in the Regulatory Decisions Committee (RDC) separate from the FSA investigatory functions.

    ▓   Under COAF, the FSA has established a scheme for dealing with complaints against the FSA.

    ▓   S160 of FSMA subjects the rules and practices of the FSA to the OFT and Competition Commission to ensure they are not anti-competitive.

    ▓   The FSA may be subject to judicial review where a court will determine whether the FSA has acted outside the scope of its powers.

■ There are practitioner and consumer groups set up under Ss8-11 of FSMA to ensure the FSA is accountable to the bodies it regulates and the consumers it seeks to protect.

■ The Financial Services and Markets Tribunal (FSMT) which as part of the Department for Constitutional Affairs provides an independent body to rehear FSA's enforcement and authorisation cases subject to appeal.

6. Notice of its intention to establish a branch must be given to the FSA identifying the relevant activities and containing any other information specified

The FSA must issue a consent notice to the host state regulator

The host regulator must have notified the firm of any applicable provisions or two months elapse since the consent notice was issued

7. List any three of

■ Execution-only transactions.

■ Direct offer financial promotions.

■ Activities relating to collective investment schemes.

■ Advice required to complete the preparation of terms of business.

■ Supplying a published recommendation.

8. List any six of

■ Generic promotions.

■ Investment professionals.

■ Overseas recipients.

■ Deposits and insurance.

■ One-off communications.

■ Certified high net worth individuals (net income of over £100,000 or net assets of over £250,000).

■ Certified sophisticated investors.

■ High net worth companies.

9. ■ Investments £48,000 (100% of £30,000 and 90% of next £20,000).

■ Deposits £31,700 (100% of £2,000 and 90% of next £33,000).

■ Long-term insurance, 90% of value attributed to policy.

■ General insurance, 100% of valid claim if compulsory and 100% of £2,000 and 90% of remainder if non-compulsory.

10. (a) (i) Acknowledgement of receipt
Five business days

(ii) Provision of response
Four weeks for holding response if no final response has been given
Eight weeks for final response or indication that final response not yet available

(b) A copy of the firm's internal complaint handling procedures

A copy of the Financial Ombudsman Service's explanatory leaflet

Section B

Question 11.

Compulsory Case Study – Conflicts of Interest

(a) A number of separate conflicts of interest were raised in this question. These were principally concerned with

▓ client and proprietary trading.

▓ use of research and front running.

▓ personal account dealing; and.

▓ board representation.

The other main issues were concerned with

▓ remuneration and inducements; and.

▓ failure to report (whistle-blowing).

Reference should have been made to all available PRIN, APER, SYSC and COB provisions. The Securities and Investments Institute's Principles could also have been noted.

As much detail as possible should have been provided with discussion of each relevant factual situation.

Separate reference may also been included to possible market abuse (s 118 FSMA), insider dealing (CJA) and misleading statements and practices offences (s 397 FSMA).

Breach of relevant duties of a fiduciary under the common law could also have been noted.

Relevant tools include general systems and controls obligations as well as specific conflicts of interest measures. This, in particular, includes disclosure, declining to act, Chinese walls or maintenance of an independence policy.

(b) Justification for the imposition of controls on conflicts of interest could have been explained principally in terms of market inefficiency and treating customers fairly (an FSA priority).

Some reference could have been included to the FSA's statutory objectives including specifically market confidence and consumer protection as well as public awareness and financial crime.

Reference may also have made to possible sources of risk (including financial risk, operational, legal and reputational risk) as well as to breach of specific regulatory provisions including FSMA and the FSA Handbook (PRIN, APER and SYSC as well as COB).

Relevant ethical issues could have been highlighted with specific reference to the SII Principles. Some candidates did refer to the nature of the penalties and sanctions imposed although this is more concerned with the consequences rather than justification for the imposition of such controls.

(c) George's failure to report should have been criticised in terms of relevant reporting and whistleblowing obligations. Specific reference should have been made to APER and SYSC.

The prohibition on the imposition of penalties on whistleblowers under the Public Interest Disclosure Act should have been noted. Additional reference may also have been made to the SII Principles.

Question 12.

Client Identification and Customer Agreements

(a)   The general categories of client classification should have been explained including specifically market counter parties and intermediate or private customers. As much detail as possible should have been provided for the full four marks.

(b)   The criteria used in determining whether a private customer should be classified as intermediate could have been referred to. These include knowledge and understanding of designated investments, markets and risks, length of time active in the market, frequency of dealings, reliance on advice, size and nature of transactions and financial standing. The other conditions for either opting up or down should also have been noted. As much detail as possible should have been provided.

(c)   The use of terms of business, customer agreements and two-way agreements should have been noted. A summary of the content of each may also have been provided with relevant exceptions being noted. Reference could also have been made to relevant KYC and suitability requirements, questionnaires and letters. Reference could also have been made to relevant money laundering obligations.

        Additional documentation may have included derivatives or other warning notices, disclosure of charges, safe custody form for discretionary clients and client money forms including any separate mandates.

(d)   Relevant agency rules and introduction requirements should have been explained. Firms may treat agents as clients if the agent is another authorised firm or an overseas financial services institution or where this is not to avoid duties that would otherwise be imposed.

(e)   Relevant agency rules and introduction requirements should have been explained. Firms may treat agents as clients if the agent is another authorised firm or an overseas financial services institution or where this is not to avoid duties that would otherwise be imposed.

Question 13.

Scope of Permission and Investment Management

(a)   The main issue raised is concerned with scope of permission and authorisation to conduct an investment management activity. SCFL's permission is restricted to arranging deals in investments and providing advice. SCFL would breach the general prohibition in s 19(1) FSMA. Relevant consequences should have been referred to including offences and enforceability (ss 23 and 26-28 FSMA).

        Reference could also have been made to relevant systems and controls and personnel requirements in the event of SCFL undertaking investment management or custody functions. Relevant SYSC and APER requirements should have been referred to.

(b)   Robbins and SCFL would breach various PRIN as well as SYSC and APER requirements by continuing with the business, failing to take proper compliance advice and failing to notify the FSA.

(c)   All relevant requirements for extending SCFL's scope of permission and related management, personnel and systems and controls obligations should have been referred to in taking on this new business. All relevant provisions within the FSMA, SYSC and APER should have been referred to. Additional obligations concerning investment management and discretionary investment management set out in COB and CASS could also have been referred to.

Question 14.

Market Abuse

(a) The objective of the question was to determine candidates' ability to identify potential market abuse situations. The relevant conditions set out in s 118 and Part VIII FSMA as well as MAR could either have been referred to initially or to the extent relevant in connection with each factual situation described. Relevant conditions, defences and penalties should have been referred to in each case with relevant guidance set out in the Code of Market Conduct. Other relevant issues raised include PRIN, APER and SYSC obligations as well as possible stabilisation and improper remuneration and inducements.

(b) Related corporate governance issues include the Companies Act framework more generally as well as the Combined Code and Directors' Model Code and Listing Rules. COB restrictions on conflicts of interest, churning and switching as well as front running and soft commissions and stop/restricted and watch lists could also have been referred to.

Section C

Question 15.

Enforcement Review

The question was concerned with the nature and structure of the FSA enforcement process and perceived difficulties and recent reform proposals.

The nature of the enforcement process could have been reviewed by way of introduction. Reference had then to be made to the recent review conducted and main recommendations issued. Difficulties included cost and delay as well as conflicts including efficient use of resources. Actions were unsuccessful with an increasing number being referred to the Financial Services Appeals Tribunal. There was also insufficient use of independent advice.

Recommendations included reducing the membership of the RDC, strengthening its independence and use of discount penalties. Cases would be subject to legal review before being taken forward with delays being cut by 30%.

Question 16.

European Financial Services

Candidates should have referred to the background and nature and content of the EU Financial Services Action Plan (FSAP) and to the Lamfalussy Report and recommendations. Reference may have been made to specific directives including the Market Abuse Directive, Prospectuses Directive, Transparency Directive, Takeover Directive and Market in Financial Instruments Directive (MIFID).

As the FSAP generally covered the period up until 2005, reference should also have been made to the December 2005 White Paper on Financial Services for the period 2005-2010. This is principally based on the idea of dynamic consolidation with only further limited legislative intervention in particular areas where this is justified on a cost benefit basis. This generally follows the better regulation agenda adopted in the UK.

Question 17.

Redress

Question 17 was generally concerned with the rights of recovery dealt with under the Redress block of the FSA Handbook of Rules and Guidance as well as other specific statutory rights of action. Candidates should have discussed DISP, COMP and COAF in as much detail as possible.

Reference could have been made to the recent action for misfeasance and public office against the Bank of England by the former depositors of BCCI. The action was abandoned last November with the Bank being awarded up to £83m in indemnity damages in January 2006. Reference may also have been made to other statutory rights of action such as under s 150 FSMA for breach of statutory duty and damages.

Question 18.

Financial Derivatives

The purpose of the question was to assess candidates' command of the relevant provisions that apply with regard to financial derivatives in the UK. Respondents were assisted with the specific reference to issuance, sale, purchase, use or holding of derivatives to suggest possible solutions.

Winter 2005 – Answers

Please note: the answers given have not been updated to reflect technical changes since the date of the exam and therefore this document is only intended to provide guidance on the suggested content of your answers. In particular, we have used bullet points throughout to highlight the areas you could have discussed or considered. In the examination, particularly with Section C questions, it may often be more appropriate to set out certain answers in paragraph form. To see the examiner's report on this exam, please go to www.sii.org.uk.

Section A

1. There are two main consequences, criminal and civil proceedings

   Criminal proceedings under S23 (1) and (2) would give rise to a penalty in the Magistrates Court of a maximum of 6 months jail and/or a maximum £5,000 fine. In the Crown Court there would be a maximum penalty of 2 years in jail and/or unlimited fine.

   Civil proceedings under S26 and S27 make agreements voidable at the discretion of the other investor. The investor may also sue for damages for any losses or recovery of assets

2. List any six (but no more) of the following

   ▪ Efficient and economic use of resources.

   ▪ Management responsibility.

   ▪ Proportionate restrictions.

   ▪ Facilitate innovation.

   ▪ Maintain competitive position of UK markets.

   ▪ Minimise adverse effects on competition.

   ▪ Facilitate industry competition.

3. ▪ Legal status (body corporate or partnership)

   ▪ Location (head and registered office must be in the UK).

   ▪ No close links that prevent effective supervision.

   ▪ Maintenance of adequate resources.

   ▪ Fit and proper (suitability).

4. Section 12 reviews are conducted by an independent person appointed by the Treasury to consider the economy, efficiency and effectiveness with which the FSA has used its resourcs in discharging its functions (S12 (1)).

   Section 14 inquiries are held where the Treasury considers that this is in the public interest in one or two sets of circumstances.

   ▪ A systems or operational failure which created a grave risk to the regulatory system set up under the FSMA.

   ▪ The listing regime set up under Part VI.

5. List any four (but not more) of the following

    - Collective Investment Schemes (CIS).
    - New Collective Investment Schemes (COLL).
    - Professional Firms (PROF).
    - Lloyd's sourcebook (LLD).
    - Recognised Investment Exchange and Recognised Clearing House sourcebook (REC).
    - Credit Unions (CRED).
    - Electronic Commerce Directive (ECO).
    - Electronic Money (ELM).

6. There are three routes available

    - Exercise the passport rights provided under any of the European financial directives by complying with the procedures set out in Schedule 3 FSMA.
    - Exercise Treaty rights by complying with the procedures set out in Schedule 4 FSMA.
    - Make a separate application for Part IV permission under s 40 FSMA.

7. - Authorised unit trusts.
    - Open-ended investment company schemes (OEICs).
    - Recognised schemes.
    - Unregulated schemes.

8. The general functions of the FSA with regard to listing are set out in s 73(2).

    - Issue rules with regard to listing under Part VI.
    - Issue general guidance with regard to listing.
    - Determine the general policy and principles governing the listing regime.

9. List any four of the following.

    - Fines.
    - Imprisonment.
    - Public or private censure.
    - Injunction.
    - Restitution.
    - Variation, cancellation or suspension of permission.

    The examiner said he would also give credit for references to information collection, premises entry or inspection powers. These are not strictly enforcement measures although they are included within the Enforcement Manual (ENF).

10. The Dispute Resolution: Complaints (DISP) sourcebook sets out the requirement for an Ombudsman scheme for resolution of disputes between investors and authorised firms. The Financial Ombudsman Service is independent of the FSA and has the power to require firms to take appropriate actions or pay compensation up to £100,000.

    Under the Compensation (COMP) sourcebook, the FSA is required to establish a scheme to protect investors when a regulated firm is no longer able to pay claims against it; e.g. the firm is insolvent. This is funded by a levy on all other authorised firms. There are various limits to the compensation that can be paid out; e.g. investment business claims received a maximum payout of £48,000.

Section B

Question 11.

(a)   Reference should have been made to the classification rules in COB 4.1.

As a pension fund of a large blue chip company we can assume it has more than £10m of assets that it manages for more than 50 members. Therefore as a minimum the pension fund would be an intermediate customer.

You could also have discussed that as this is a European company, we do not know for sure that the pension fund is a separate Occupational Pension Scheme. Therefore it may have been appropriate to evaluate the company itself with the same result of intermediate customer.

The examiner would also have given credit for reference to the new client classifications to be introduced under the MIFID (eligible counterparty, professional and retail) even though they are not in force.

Relevant information was also to be specified. This includes name and registered address, turnover, type of business, investment objectives, directors, company assets, financial accounts, balance sheet and profit & loss statements.

(b)   Eligibility for opting up or opting down and relevant conditions should have been provided in as much detail as possible.

Opting up:

▪   Expert two way agreement after sufficient opportunity to consider.

▪   Intermediate to market counterparty.

–   One way for companies over £10m of assets (€ size limits could also be given). Size test to be met at time of opting up.

–   Two way for other investors (size criteria of £10m could be given)

Opting down:

The firm may treat any client as private customer, except another authorised firm. Just because a market counterparty or intermediate customer has been treated by the firm as a private customer, it does not give that client the right of access to the Financial Ombudsman Scheme or the Financial Services Compensation Scheme.

The examiner's report says that candidates should also have stated that 'firms should also request information concerning investment objectives (understanding risk) and know your customer (KYC) compliance', although it is not clear what relevance this has to the question.

(c)   The use and content of terms of business should have been explained under a COB 4.2 and the circumstances in which two-way client agreements would be required.

Intial documentation is required to be in place before the firm can conduct regulated activities only for private customers. For intermediate customers such as the pension fund, the documentation can be in place within a reasonable period. As it appears that the pension fund will require discretionary investment management services, a one-way terms of business letter will be the appropriate documentation. If the firm has opted the penion fund down to private customer, a two way client agreement would be required.

The key contents of a client agreement or terms of business letter are

▪   Name and address of firm.

▪   Name and address of customer.

▪   Services to be provided.

▩   Investment objectives or restrictions.

▩   Fees (unless provided separately).

▩   Complaints handling.

(d)   Reporting requirements under COB 8 should have been set out.

Under COB 8.1 the firm has a duty to send a confirmation of all trades promptly (by end of next business day) unless the customer requests otherwise.

When acting as an investment manager or if the customer has uncovered derivative positions or SCARP products, the firm will need to send out six monthly (securities) or monthly (derivatives) portfolio valuation statements.

Record keeping may have been split into account opening documentation (five years for anti-money laundering), transactions (three years), complaints (three years), suitability records (three years) and pension transfers and FSAVCs (indefinitely).

(e)   The conditions in which risk warning notices are required should have been explained even though they only relate to private customers. Relative high-risk products include futures, options, warrants, contracts with differences, stock lending and borrowing, and penny shares. General content could have been noted. Reference may also have been made to such other requirements as client suitability and suitability letters as well as margin and other requirements.

Question 12.

(a)   The question was concerned with the management of conflicts of interest and maintenance of high ethical standards within regulated institutions.

Two potential sets of conflicts of interest arise between the firm and its clients and between the firm's clients. The main conflict of interest that arises is with the firm acting both as a corporate broker and financial advisor. The need to manage the conflict effectively should have been discussed. Relevant regulatory requirements include PRIN 8 and COB 7.1, as well as 7.16 and 7.17. The means through which conflicts may be managed should have been referred to (including Chinese walls, independence policies, disclosure and declining to act).

Reference should also have been made to the high fee and inducement issues raised (COB 2.2), proper management responsibility and the need to maintain effective systems and controls (SYSC).

Reference may also have been made to the Takeover Panel difficulties that arise with regard to price sensitive information. All relevant PRINs should have been considered and SYSC obligations referred to.

(b)   The main issues that arise are concerned with the breakdown of the Chinese wall and the independence of the analyst's advice. The analyst must be allowed to provide impartial advice to the pension fund. As the analyst is now aware of the potential conflict, it may be appropriate to exclude both companies from any future reports and to decline to respond to the specific enquiry made. A number of difficulties also arise with regard to the conduct of the corporate broker in attempting to place pressure on a colleague to act inappropriately. Reference may also be made to the possibility of insider dealing and market abuse offences arising at this stage.

If the analyst acts on the broker's instruction, he would breach PRIN, SYSC and FIT (approved persons) as well as potentially commit an offence under the Criminal Justice Act (insider dealing), s 118 FSMA (market abuse) or s 397 (misleading statements or practices). It is nevertheless not clear whether inside information has been passed on and the analyst contaminated. Full disclosure should nevertheless be secured of the firm's position and its policy for dealing with conflicts of interest.

(c)   The trading desk should also act independently and not in response to any directions provided by the corporate broker. In light of the imminent merger, the stock should have been placed on a watch list by the compliance department which the trading desk would have been aware of. Any disposal would then have to be confirmed through the compliance department.

The trader cannot increase the firm's position as he may now be guilty of insider trading or market abuse. The only defence may be that he already intended to act although it would be difficult to establish this in court.

Relevant Takeover Panel Code rules could also be considered. Disclosure would be required if further purchases are made. Disposal could nevertheless be effected under the SARs rules if the deal is not public or as bid facilitation if the deal is public.

(d)   The firm is under a fiduciary duty to disclose the interest and would act inappropriately in failing to do so. The broker should disclose his interest and decline to act as appropriate. Breach of relevant PRINs should be considered. The relevance of the Takeover Panel rules in a pre-bid situation could also have been referred to.

The nature of the relationship between Omega and Zeta should also be confirmed. Omega may have entered into an advisory relationship with Zeta and have formed its opinion on the basis of all of the information available. The terms of the advice to be provided would be set out in a client agreement. The provision of this advice would then be protected by the Chinese wall. Any further action by Zeta would be governed by the Takeover Panel's Code.

Question 13.

(a)   Firms have to comply with relevant client classification (COB 4.1) and know your customer (COB 5.2) requirements. Client identity and client profile should be confirmed with relevant documentation and information being requested. As a regulated firm, verification can be carried out through the FSA website.

(b)   Money laundering checks should be carried out as soon as practicable after the initial client meeting, and before regulated activities commence. This may not be required where the money laundering rules do not apply (such as less than €15,000). Information should be updated including on each occasion that new business is conducted.

(c)   Relevant action includes reporting of suspicious transactions to the MLRO, assessment by the MLRO and reporting to NCIS as appropriate with no action being taken for a seven-day holding period, avoiding assisting (14 years), failure to report (five years) and tipping-off (five years). The role and function of the MLRO may have been referred to and the need for staff training and the maintenance of effective procedures. Reference may also have been made to the use of international findings as this is an offshore centre and the keeping of appropriate records.

(d)   All of the main offences under the POCA 2002 should have been referred to (including assisting (Ss 327-329), failure to report (Ss 330-332) and tipping-off (S333)) as well as the requirements under the money laundering regulations and FSA Handbook. Reference may also have been made to the joint guidance notes or other recent initiatives including anti-terrorist laws or FSA money laundering themes.

Question 14.

(a) (i) The trader may be guilty of insider dealing although it is unclear whether specific price sensitive information has been used in this case. The trader has reported to the Head of European Equities but not necessarily to compliance. He was nevertheless acting on an unsolicited client instruction. The trader is required to report any suspicions under the revised Market Abuse Offences (following the coming into effect of the European Market Abuse Directive). The trader could also argue that he had taken all necessary due diligence under S123 FSMA.

(ii) The line manager may be guilty of insider trading, assuming that the information was price sensitive, unpublished and specific. The line manager may also have breached S118 and 397.

(iii) The Head of European Equities may have encouraged an offence and would certainly have breached PRIN 2, APER 6 and SYSC 3.1.1. and 2.1.1.

(iv) The director was clearly indiscreet and may have breached the Takeover Panel Code although it is not certain whether this would apply to him as the company is listed on Euronext Paris and the offence may only have been committed in France. More information would also be required with regard to the nature and content of the information discussed and the person with whom the director was in contact. Insider trading, market abuse and s 397 may all be relevant depending upon the circumstances.

(v) The client may also be guilty of insider dealing, market abuse and breach of S397 depending on whether they had received inside information and was acting on that with a view to making a profit.

(b) Relevant offences, defences and penalties should have been summarised either generally or with regard to the specific parties involved.

Section C

Question 15.

The question was concerned with the effectiveness of the financial promotions regime and its ability to deal with developments in modern telecommunications.

The basic promotions regime set up under the FSMA should have been explained including S21 FSMA and the main provisions contained within the Financial Promotions Order (FPO) and COB 3.

Specific measures dealing with real time and non-real time communications could have been referred to as well as specific measures included with regard to internet promotions. The FSA's Perimeter Guidance Manual (PERG) Chapter 8 'Financial Promotion and Related Activities' could have been discussed.

The Electronic Commerce Directive which imposes a country of origin/home state regulatory approach to financial promotions communicated within the EEA should have been discussed.

Recent FSA disciplinary action should have been mentioned and evaluated e.g. Courtover Investment Management £50k fine in May 2005 for approving a misleading financial promotion. The FSA's financial promotions hotline could have also been mentioned.

Question 16.

The purpose was to assess the scope and extent of the enforcement regime set up under FSMA against the corresponding accountability mechanisms created. The following enforcement powers of the FSA should have been mentioned.

- Information gathering & investigatory powers.
- Unlimited fines.
- Injunctions.
- Restitution & redress.
- Private and public censure.
- Vary/cancel Part IV Permission.
- Vary/cancel approval.
- Intervention against incoming firms.
- Revoke recognition of a CIS.
- Insolvency proceedings.
- S56 Prohibition Orders.
- Pursue criminal proceedings in some cases.

These extensive enforcement powers should have been considered against the accountability regime established. The following ways of accountability should have been mentioned.

- Regulatory objectives & principles of good regulation.
- HM Treasury board appointment and removal.
- FSA Annual Report & annual public meeting.
- Senior management e.g. maintenance of appropriate oversight and disciplinary measures.
- Complaints Investigator.
- Consumer and Practitioner Panels.
- Competition scrutiny.

- The Treasury may also conduct reviews or set up independent investigations.

- Regulatory Decisions Committee (RDC).

- Financial Services and Markets Tribunal and to the courts on a point of law.

- Judicial review.

Question 17.

Please note: the following comments were valid at the time of the exam which was before the implementation of the Takeover Directive.

The nature and role and function of the Takeover Panel should have been explained. Its non statutory basis and essential legal informality should have been noted along with its aim to protect shareholders from abuse.

The following provisions of the Takeover Code should have been discussed.

- Its application to takeovers of plcs and certain private limited companies.

- Definitions of control and concert party.

- The ten general principles.

- The takeover timetable.

- The Substantial Acquisition Rules 1, 2 & 3 (SARS) which aim to prevent dawn raids.

Question 18.

The existing provisions governing senior management responsibility and systems and controls under the FSMA and FSA Handbook should have been explained as well as further changes expected to take place under MIFID and CRD.

The existing regime could have summarised including relevant provisions within PRIN, SYSC and FIT. It is expected that MIFID will introduce detailed new provisions governing management responsibility and conduct of business requirements amongst others although much of the detail remains to be determined by the Committee of European Securities Regulators (CESR).

Operational risk is also included as a new component within the Pillar 1 of the CRD and supervisory review introduced under Pillar 2. The effect of both of these measures will be to strengthen further the responsibilities imposed on management and the need to maintain effective internal systems and controls requirements.

Summer 2005 – Answers

Please note: the answers given have not been updated to reflect technical changes since the date of the exam and therefore this document is only intended to provide guidance on the suggested content of your answers. In particular, we have used bullet points throughout to highlight the areas you could have discussed or considered. In the examination, particularly with Section C questions, it may often be more appropriate to set out certain answers in paragraph form. To see the examiner's report on this exam, please go to www.sii.org.uk.

Section A

1. The general prohibition 'authorisation' is set out in S19 FSMA and provides that a person (usually a business) may not undertake regulated activities in relation to specified investments by way of business in the UK unless they are either authorised or exempt/excluded from authorisation. Authorised persons include

    ▪ Anyone holding a Part IV permission.

    ▪ EEA passport firms.

    ▪ Treaty firms.

    ▪ A person who is otherwise authorised under FSMA.

    Under S20 FSMA authorised persons must also hold the relevant permission to carry on the specific activities conducted in the UK. Applications for permission are made under S40 FSMA and Part IV FSMA.

    Individuals are approved under S59 FSMA. Authorised persons must take reasonable care to ensure that all persons that carry one or more of the controlled functions (listed in SUP10 of the FSA Handbook) are properly approved by the FSA to do so. Approval therefore only applies to individuals within authorised firms. The objective is principally to confirm the individual is fit and proper and is suitable to carry out the particular controlled functions.

2. A breach of S20 FSMA is not a criminal offence and does not mean that transactions are void or unenforceable, but it may give rise to claims from consumers. Breaches will nevertheless constitute a disciplinary matter subject to FSA enforcement including a fine or censure (public or private) or possibly a restriction or variation of permission.

3. You should have listed any four of the following from the Financial Services and Markets Act (Exemption) Order 2001.

    ▪ Appointed representatives.

    ▪ Members of the professions.

    ▪ Lloyd's members.

    ▪ RIEs, ROIEs, RCHs.

    ▪ Other bodies including the Bank of England, other central banks and international financial institutions as well as the UK National Savings Bank and municipal banks, local authorities, charities and certain other government organisations.

4. You should have listed disclosure, declining to act, Chinese walls or maintaining an Independence policy.

5.   You should have listed three of the following customer functions listed in SUP10 and given a brief explanation of the activities covered.

■   CF21 Investment adviser.

■   CF22 Investment adviser (trainee).

■   CF23 Corporate finance adviser.

■   CF24 Pension transfer specialist.

■   CF25 Adviser on syndicate participations at Lloyd's.

■   CF26 Customer trading.

■   CF27 Investment management.

6.   You should have listed any four of the following circumstances where unsolicited real time financial promotions can be made.

■   Communications covered by appropriate exemptions in the Financial Promotion Order (such as certified sophisticated investors.

■   The communication is to a market counterparty or intermediate customer.

■   Existing private customers where the relationship 'envisages' the call.

■   Marketable ungeared packaged products (such as regulated non-derivative collective investment schemes).

■   Services relating to readily realisable securities other than warrants (such as selling share dealing services in a FTSE 100 stock rather than buying the stock directly).

7.   The Regulatory Processes block consists of

■   Authorisation Manual (AUTH).

■   Supervision Manual (SUP).

■   Enforcement Manual (ENF).

■   Decision Making Manual (DEC).

8.   Please note, this question was set before the implementation of the Market Abuse Directive on 1 July 2005. Section 118 FSMA applies with regard to

■   Misuse of information.

■   False or misleading impressions.

■   Market distortion.

The 'regular user' is defined as a reasonable person who regularly deals in qualifying investments on a prescribed market. The objective is to introduce an objective professional standard in determining whether conduct should be considered to constitute market abuse or not.

9.   You should have mentioned three of the following requirements.

■   Firms must ensure that personal account transactions by employees do not conflict with the duties owed to clients.

■   The personal account dealing policy must be contained in a written notice to the employee and included as part of the contract of employment.

■   Permission to deal in designated investments should be expressly required.

■   The policy should apply to all employees and not just approved persons.

10. The Financial Services and Markets Tribunal (FSMT) is part of the Department for Constitutional Affairs and is therefore independent from the FSA/RDC. It will hear appeals against decisions of the Regulatory Decisions Committee (RDC), e.g. Decision Notices and Supervisory Notices. It will completely rehear the case and therefore can take into account new evidence if relevant. This appeal process is distinct from an appeal on a point of law to the courts.

Section B

Question 11.

(a)   The client needs to be classified under COB 4.1. The rules require firms to classify all clients before any designated investment business is undertaken. The client should have been classified as either a private customer, an intermediate customer or a market counterparty. The company would be classified as an intermediate customer if it is either listed in EEA/IOSCO or has had in the last two years net assets or called up share capital of ≥ £5m. Intermediate customers are able to 'opt up' to market counterparty status if both parties agree and the company has either called-up share capital of ≥ £10m or the company satisfies two of the following tests.

- ▓   Balance sheet total of ≥ €12.5m.

- ▓   Net turnover of ≥ €25m.

- ▓   Average number of employees during year ≥ 250.

(b)   Under the Money Laundering Regulations 2003 identification of all applicants for business must occur as soon as is reasonably practicable after initial contact (and before any business is conducted with that client). There are some exceptions where identification need not occur, which include

- ▓   For one-off or linked one-off transactions below €15,000.

- ▓   Where the applicant is a credit or financial institution based in the UK, EU or a country with equivalent money laundering regulations.

- ▓   Where the transaction relates to a small long-term insurance contract (one-off premium not exceeding €2,500 or regular premiums of less than €1,000 p.a.).

- ▓   For a one-off transaction where the applicant is introduced by a credit or financial institution based in the UK, the EU or a country with equivalent money laundering regulations.

In terms of identification of this client, as it is a leading technology company then no further steps are required where it is

- ▓   A company quoted on a recognised, designated or approved exchange.

- ▓   Known to be a subsidiary of such a company.

- ▓   A private company where one or more of the directors/partners are already known to the firm.

The JMLSG Guidance notes provide specific details of appropriate documentation. In addition, the firm should know its customer. This relates to the need to have a benchmark against which to establish suspicious activity. This might include establishing the purpose for the relationship, anticipated nature and level of activity, relationships of signatories to underlying owners and, origin of funds. Records should be kept for all of these matters for at least five years.

(c)   Documentation requirements are set out in COB 4.2 and would generally require a terms of business to be provided to most customers. The following types of customer require a two-way client agreement.

- ▓   Private discretionary customers.

- ▓   Private advisory and private execution only customers dealing in contingent liability investments.

- ▓   Private advisory customers regarding stock lending.

- ▓   Private advisory customers regarding underwriting.

You should have also mentioned the main contents of these documents, e.g. name of regulator, services to be provided, charges & risk warnings etc.

(d)   Where the firm acts as an investment manager for a private customer COB 5.2 and COB 5.3 would apply regarding KYC and suitability. If a private customer deals in derivatives a warrants and derivatives risk warning should have also been given, although it is unlikely the client here is a private customer. If the client is a private/intermediate discretionary customer the firm must, under COB 7.2, ensure it avoids churning. In addition, the firm must also provide periodic statements under COB 8.2. For accounts with uncovered open positions in derivatives a statement should be prepared monthly and dispatched within 10 business days of the end of the period to which the statement relates. This should include the contents and value of the portfolio with the basis of valuation at the end of the relevant period.

(e)   A firm holding client money or assets will have to comply with the Client Assets Sourcebook (CASS) contained in the Business Standards block of the FSA Handbook. This will include obligations with regard to custody, segregation, registration and recording, holding, assessment of custodians, client agreements, client statements, use and reconciliation. Reference may also have been made to the relevant definitions of client money, types of account and account segregation, approved banks, mandates and reconciliation.

Question 12.

(a)   The High Level Standards Block of the FSA Handbook contains over-arching guidelines and principles for both authorised firms and the senior managers of these firms. The Principles for Businesses (PRIN) and the Statement of Principle of Approved Persons (APER) require firms to act with Integrity (PRIN 1 & APER 1), act with Skill, Care and Diligence (PRIN 2 & APER 2) and manage Conflicts of Interest (PRIN 8).

Obligations on senior managers are fleshed out in Senior Management Arrangements, Systems and Controls (SYSC). SYSC requires the head of a division within an investment bank to put in place appropriate systems and controls (SYSC 3.1.1R) given the nature, scale and complexity of the business. Failure to do this could mean a failure by the firm to continue to comply with the Fit and Proper requirements (FIT). Firms are also bound by FSMA 2000 in relation to market abuse (S118 FSMA) and Misleading Statements and Practices (S397 FSMA) and common law duties of obedience, care and skill, good faith and confidentiality.

(b)   Principle 8 – Conflicts of Interest confirms that a firm must manage conflicts of interest fairly, both between itself and its customers and between a customer and another client.

The FSA COB rule Conflicts of Interest (COB 7.1) states that where a firm has a material interest or conflict of interest in a transaction or any other relationship, it must not advise a customer or act in a discretionary capacity for a customer unless it has taken reasonable steps to ensure fair treatment.

Reasonable steps include having a written 'policy of independence' that requires staff to disregard any material interest or conflict of interest and put the interests of customers first. The existence of a policy of independence should also be disclosed to private customers.

Reasonable steps also include disclosing either verbally or in writing that the firm has a conflict.

(c)   Chinese walls (COB 2.4) are administrative, physical and cultural barriers designed to prevent the flow of information. Chinese walls do not have to be used by firms, but if they are COB 2.4 applies. Where Chinese walls are used as a means of managing conflicts they must be effective and monitored. This would require firms to consider using code names, establishing separate IT access, training staff on Chinese walls, having procedures for wall crossing, monitoring trades, and using stop, restricted and watch lists.

A stop list would act to prevent personnel within a firm from dealing in a particular stock either for themselves, the firm or for customers. A restricted list may restrict the persons or amounts of stock that can be traded.

Watch lists tend to have a much more limited circulation. These lists go to the different compliance officers within the firm and are often also sent to the heads of the dealing desks. These lists do not necessarily prevent the firm from entering into trading activity, but serve to highlight those stocks which are more sensitive.

(d)   Possible options including taking no action, declining to act or 'crossing the wall.' The situation may initially be dealt with by asking the PE operation to confirm its valuation and to ensure that proper due diligence has been carried out. It is essential to respect the Chinese wall and to protect the client's interests. In the event that the over valuation is not identified, the PE team may have to be directed to withdraw although this should be confirmed first. Possible insider dealing under the Criminal Justice Act 1993 and S118 FSMA market abuse breaches should be considered in relation to participating in the auction (and then withdrawing) as well as in subsequently dealing (or not dealing) on behalf of other clients. More information may be required to assess the situation fully. Difficult issues must be discussed with compliance and the FSA.

(e)   The discovery of accounting irregularities must initially be brought to the client's attention by the M&A team. This issue would have to be disclosed to the FSA and possibly the relevant accountancy bodies.

The accounting irregularities may mean that the company has breached S397(1) FSMA for the offences of dishonestly/recklessly making a statement, promise or forecast that is misleading, false or deceptive or dishonestly concealing material facts. Alternatively this may breach the market abuse provisions in S118(7) – Dissemination. You could have also mentioned Companies Act implications.

If listed, the additional disclosure obligations will also apply under the UK Listing Rules although from the question it is not clear whether ABC is listed or not.

The firm should carefully handle this issue to avoid anyone possibly breaching insider dealing and market abuse offences.

Question 13.

(a)   The rules for dealing with customer complaints are detailed in the Redress Block of the FSA Handbook in Dispute Resolution: Complaints (DISP). The FSA rules should be applied to complaints which are defined as any oral or written expression of dissatisfaction whether justified or not about a firm's provision or failure to provide a financial service.

Authorised firms must have written procedures to ensure the proper handling of complaints from eligible complainants for example private individuals other than those properly classified as an 'expert' intermediate customer. It must refer to such procedures at the point of sale and supply a copy on request. All employees should be aware of the procedures and be able to use them. A senior uninvolved person with authority to settle the matter should be tasked with investigating the complaint promptly and fully. A copy of all complaint correspondence should be kept for three years.

The FSA sets out strict time limits for dealing with complaints that have not been resolved by close of business on the day after receipt.

▓   Within five business days send a written acknowledgement letter.

▓   Within four weeks either send a final response (informing the complainant of their right to refer to the Financial Ombudsman Service) or a holding letter.

▓   Within eight weeks either send a final response (informing the complainant of their right to refer to the Financial Ombudsman Service) or explain the firm is unable to send a final response and if the complainant is unhappy with the delay, they should complain directly to the Financial Ombudsman Service.

(b)   If the client is unable to resolve the complaint with the firm, they have the option to refer to the Financial Ombudsman Service (FOS), claim a breach of statutory duty under S150 FSMA or S71 FSMA or try to seek a remedy in court due to a breach of common law.

The FOS will review the facts of the case and make an independent decision. A FOS ruling is binding on the authorised firm to a maximum award of up to £100,000 plus costs.

A private person, which includes individuals not doing regulated activities and businesses not doing business of any kind can sue the firm for compensation under S150 FSMA if they have suffered loss due to a relevant rule breach. A private person can sue the firm for compensation under S71 FSMA where they have suffered loss due to dealing with an unapproved individual.

(c)   Factors to be taken into consideration include

⬛   Whether the client had been properly classified and provided with an appropriate terms of business letter or client agreement.

⬛   Whether the firm complied with COB 5.2 Know Your Customer, COB 5.3 Suitability and COB 5.4 Customer Understanding of Risk, including where appropriate the provision of a warrants and derivatives risk warning.

⬛   Whether the firm has acted with Integrity (PRIN 1) and adequate Skill, Care and Diligence (PRIN 2).

⬛   Whether the firm had adequate management oversight required by SYSC and PRIN 3.

⬛   Whether the firm has treated its customer fairly under PRIN 6 and PRIN 9.

(d)   The FSA can assist a client by applying for a restitution order under FSMA (Part XXV). The FSA could also conduct an investigation and take appropriate disciplinary action although this would not assist the client directly. The FSA can otherwise encourage the firm to enter in appropriate settlement arrangements with the client.

(e)   The client should be protected under the Financial Services Compensation Scheme (FSCS). All UK authorised firms are required to contribute to the FSCS. When a firm is declared insolvent or bankrupt only eligible claimants can apply for compensation under the scheme.

The client is likely to be deemed an eligible claimant as individuals (whether classified as private or intermediate customers) are covered unless they are connected to the insolvent firm in some way, e.g. the directors of the insolvent firm and their close relatives are not eligible.

The maximum awards available for investments is £48,000. This is calculated as 100% of the first £30,000 added to 90% of the next £20,000.

Question 14.

(a)   GRAB is a research and advisory broker and an authorised firm. Whilst the issue of financial promotions is not a regulated activity, the following regulations need to be followed.

⬛   S21 FSMA.

⬛   Financial Promotions Order (FPO).

⬛   PRIN 7 and COB 3 Financial Promotions.

S21 FSMA requires financial promotions to be issued or approved by an authorised firm. As GRAB is authorised it appears to be complying with S21.

There are a number of exemptions from S21 FSMA and COB 3 in the FPO, however none of these appear to be relevant, particularly as GRAB is advertising in a major national newspaper.

Regarding PRIN and the FSA rules in COB 3, financial promotions must generally be clear, fair and not misleading. This type of promotion is called a specific non-real time financial promotion and therefore it should have detailed a description of the investment, any commitment and any risks associated. There does not appear to be a risk caveat that the value of the shares and any income received can go down as well as up or that past performance is not necessarily a guide to future performance.

References to past performance must be for a relevant and sufficient period, although full five year performance figures are not required. The promotion should have included the firm's name and address or contact point.

The promotion should have also clarified

■ The differences in risk profile between unlisted and listed company shares and what industry is being referred to.

■ The relevance of the relationship between total assets and sales.

■ Any conditions applicable to commission free dealing.

■ Any other charges imposed.

■ The basis on which the 25% return was calculated and the source of this statistic.

(b) The most likely initial action taken in this case would be to request that the advertisement is initially withdrawn and substantiated. In the event that the company fails to do so, an injunction could be obtained. In the event that the promotion was considered to be misleading, appropriate disciplinary action would be taken including a fine or public and private censure.

■ The FSA's powers relating to supervision and enforcement are found in FSMA, the Supervision Manual (SUP) and the Enforcement Manual (ENF) (both of which are found in the Regulatory Processes block of the FSA Handbook).

■ The FSA staff undertaking the investigation will normally refer disciplinary cases to the Regulatory Decisions Committee (RDC). Firstly, a Warning Notice is sent to the accused setting out the facts of the case. This is then followed by a Decision Notice and a Final Notice. The firm has the right to refer a Decision Notice or Final Notice to the Financial Services and Markets Tribunal. They must normally do this within 28 days.

■ The actions above aim to ensure customers are adequately protected and that market confidence is maintained.

(c) The fact that GRAB was dealing as principal and neither had the necessary Part IV Permission or had disclosed this conflict of interest to customers shows that there insufficient systems and controls in place.

■ The asset figure is also potentially misleading as the company has liabilities of £350 million which have not been taken into account. The interest of the directors should also have been declared.

■ Because of the above, conflicts of interest arise under PRIN (1, 6 and 8), APER (1 and 2) and COB 7.1.

■ There has also been a general failure of PRIN (1, 2, 3 and 7) and APER (5, 6 and 7) as well as SYSC regarding the failure to ensure the advertisement was correctly approved by an individual with appropriate expertise before issue.

(d) GRAB has since clearly breached a number of principles set out in PRIN as well as APER and SYSC. Appropriate fines and public or private censure would be considered. The advertisement would also have to be immediately withdrawn through injunction if this had not already been achieved.

■ Individual action would also be considered against the Chief Executive and other relevant senior managers who have been given significant responsibility for a breach of APER. Fines, censure and S56 Prohibition Orders could also be considered where necessary.

Section C

Question 15.

The purpose of the question is to consider in further detail the increased importance attached to management responsibility and accountability under FSMA. Candidates should have mentioned a good number of the following.

▨ Recent crises may have been referred to including Barings, Sumitomo, Morgan Asset Grenfell as well as Enron and Worldcom.

▨ The nature of the approved person regime set up under FSMA should have been explained. As much detail as possible should have been provided with regard to the obligations imposed under S59 FSMA and availability of redress under S71 FSMA. Relevant information should have been given regarding Governing functions (e.g. CF 1 Director), Required functions (e.g. CF10), Compliance Oversight, Systems and Control functions (e.g. CF 13 Finance), Significant Management functions (e.g. CF 16 Designated investment business) and Customer Functions (e.g. CF 21 Investment Adviser)..

▨ The importance of the Threshold Conditions (COND) as well as the fit and proper tests for approved persons (FIT) should have been referred to.

▨ Reference should also have been made to the general requirements imposed under PRIN, SYSC and APER.

▨ Available remedies under the FSMA and the ENF against weak or even fraudulent management should have been explained.

Question 16.

The nature of the regimes established within the UK and EU concerning market abuse should have been discussed in as much detail as possible within the time available. Candidates should have mentioned a good number of the following.

▨ The relevant UK requirements include insider trading under the Criminal Justice Act / S118 FSMA market abuse and misleading statements and practices under S118 FSMA / 397 FSMA. Relevant offences, defences and penalties should have been explained in each case.

▨ The importance of the new revised requirements imposed under the European Market Abuse Directive (MAD) should have been noted and the main differences between the MAD and the existing UK regime explained. The commencement date of 1st July 2005 should have been referred to.

Question 17.

The general nature of the regime set up in the UK to deal with money laundering and terrorist financing should have been explained. Candidates should have mentioned a good number of the following.

▨ The main statutory and secondary as well as regulatory requirements imposed under the Proceeds of Crime Act, the Money Laundering Regulations, Money Laundering provisions in the SYSC Sourcebook and Terrorism Act 2000.

▨ Reference should also have been made to the Joint Money Laundering Steering Group Guidance Notes (JMLSG).

▨ As the question was not restricted to UK responses, candidates were then able to refer to relevant European and international developments to the extent they considered relevant, e.g. Money Laundering Directives and Financial Action Task Force (FATF) recommendations.

Question 18.

The question required candidates to identify the main types of risk that arise and how these are managed in practice. Candidates should have mentioned a good number of the following.

■ The main financial risks including credit risk, market or position risk, interest rate risk, foreign exchange risk and settlement or delivery risk. The other main risks that should have been referred to include legal risk as well as operational risk.

■ Reference may also have been made to other management or business related risks such as reputational, strategic or management risks.

■ The relevant requirements or standards that apply could either have been explained in terms of the general regulatory regime set up under the FSMA or the more specific compliance systems set up within financial institutions.

Winter 2004 – Answers

Please note: the answers given have not been updated to reflect technical changes since the date of the exam and therefore this document is only intended to provide guidance on the suggested content of your answers. In particular, we have used bullet points throughout to highlight the areas you could have discussed or considered. In the examination, particularly with Section C questions, it may often be more appropriate to set out certain answers in paragraph form. To see the examiner's report on this exam, please go to www.sii.org.uk.

Section A

1. The general prohibition is set out in S19 of FSMA 2000 and provides that a person (usually a business) may not undertake regulated activities in relation to specified investments by way of business in the UK unless they are either authorised or exempt/excluded from authorisation. The penalty for breach is two years' imprisonment and/or an unlimited fine. In addition, contracts may be unenforceable. The purpose of the prohibition is to define the scope of FSMA and ensure that the fitness and propriety of those conducting regulated activities in or into the UK is vetted before services are provided.

2. You should have listed the following categories of authorised person set out in S31 FSMA.

    ▪ A person who has Part IV permission.

    ▪ An EEA firm who qualifies for Passporting.

    ▪ A firm who exercises Treaty rights.

    ▪ A person who is otherwise authorised under FSMA.

3. The general functions of the FSA are set out in S2(4) FSMA. You should have listed any three of the following.

    ▪ Making rules under FSMA.

    ▪ Preparing and issuing codes under FSMA.

    ▪ Giving general advice.

    ▪ Determining general policy and principles.

4. Section 21 FSMA [and specifically S21(1)] requires that financial promotions are issued or approved by an authorised firm. Breach can result in the following consequences (you should list three).

    ▪ The person is guilty of a criminal offence punishable by six months' imprisonment on summary conviction.

    ▪ The person is guilty of a criminal offence punishable by two years' imprisonment on indictment.

    ▪ A fine may be imposed (up to an unlimited amount on indictment).

    ▪ A private warning or public censure may be imposed.

    ▪ An injunction may be issued.

    ▪ The FSA may apply for a restitution order.

5. You should have listed any six of the following.

    ▪ Generic promotions.

    ▪ Promotions to investment professionals.

    ▪ Promotions to overseas recipients.

- Certain deposit and insurance activities.

- One-off communications.

- Promotions to certified high net worth individuals.

- Promotions to associations of certified high net worth individuals.

- Promotions to certified sophisticated investors.

- Promotions to high net worth companies.

6. The purpose of the know your customer (KYC) requirement in COB is to ensure that the firm takes reasonable steps to obtain sufficient personal and financial information about the customer to enable the firm to properly carry out the services that they have agreed to provide. This is separate from KYC requirements under money laundering rules. This might include information about income, outgoings, attitude to risk, etc.

   This is usually conducted via a questionnaire or 'fact find'. Where a customer refuses to provide information the firm should promptly notify them that this may affect the quality of the services it can provide to the customer. Where the firm acts in a discretionary, or on a continuous basis, the information should be kept under regular review.

7. The Fit and Proper test (FIT) is found in the High Level Standards Block of the FSA Handbook.

   - Honesty, integrity and reputation, e.g. civil or criminal convictions.

   - Competence and capability, e.g. compliance with TC Sourcebook.

   - Financial soundness, e.g. bankruptcy proceedings.

8. You should have listed any three of the following.

   - All shareholders of the same class of an offeree company must be treated similarly by an offeror.

   - During the course of an offer, or when an offer is in contemplation, neither an offeror, nor the offeree company, nor any of their respective advisers may furnish information to some shareholders that is not made available to all shareholders. This principle does not apply to the furnishing of information in confidence by the offeree company to a bona fide potential offeror or vice versa.

   - An offeror should only announce an offer after the most careful and responsible consideration. Such an announcement should be made only when the offeror has every reason to believe that it can and will continue to be able to implement the offer. Responsibility in this connection also rests on the financial adviser to the offeror.

   - Shareholders must be given sufficient information and advice to enable them to reach a properly informed decision and must have sufficient time to do so. No relevant information should be withheld from them.

   - Any document or advertisement addressed to shareholders containing information or advice from an offeror or the board of the offeree company or their respective advisers must, as is the case with a prospectus, be prepared with the highest standards of care and accuracy.

   - All parties to an offer must use every endeavour to prevent the creation of a false market in the securities of an offeror or the offeree company. Parties involved in offers must take care that statements are not made which may mislead shareholders or the market.

   - At no time after a bona fide offer has been communicated to the board of the offeree company, or after the board of the offeree company has reason to believe that a bona fide offer might be imminent, may any action be taken by the board of the offeree company in relation to the affairs of the company, without the approval of the shareholders in general meeting, which could effectively result in any bona fide offer being frustrated or in the shareholders being denied an opportunity to decide on its merits.

▩ Rights of control must be exercised in good faith and the oppression of a minority is wholly unacceptable.

▩ Directors of an offeror and the offeree company must always, in advising their shareholders, act only in their capacity as directors and not have regard to their personal or family shareholdings or to their personal relationships with the companies. It is the shareholders' interests taken as a whole, together with those of employees and creditors, which should be considered when the directors are giving advice to shareholders. Directors of the offeree company should give careful consideration before they enter into any commitment with an offeror (or anyone else) which would restrict their freedom to advise their shareholders in the future. Such commitments may give rise to conflicts of interest or result in a breach of the directors' fiduciary duties.

▩ Where control of a company is acquired by a person, or persons acting in concert, a general offer to all other shareholders is normally required – a similar obligation may arise if control is consolidated. Where an acquisition is contemplated as a result of which a person may incur such an obligation, he must, before making the acquisition, ensure that he can and will continue to be able to implement such an offer.

9.　The core requirements are as follows (you should have listed any four).

▩ **Recruitment** – assess and confirm existing knowledge and skills at recruitment.

▩ **Training** – determine and deliver timely, planned, structured and evaluated training.

▩ **Attaining Competence** – employees must either be assessed as competent or supervised. Assessment of competence may require passing an appropriate examination and demonstration of skills and application.

▩ **Examinations** – employees should pass appropriate examinations for each controlled activity within the time-frame set out in TC2.

▩ **Supervising** – until assessed as competent, employees should be supervised. Once competent, employees should continue to be monitored.

▩ **Maintaining Competence** – a firm must assess whether employees remain competent in their technical knowledge and skills in changing markets.

10.　▩ **Warning notice** – this provides the recipient with details of the action the FSA/RDC proposes to take and the recipient's right to make representations.

▩ **Decision notice** – this sets out the reason for the decision, proposed sanction and a notice of the right to refer the matter to the Financial Services and Markets Tribunal.

▩ **Final notice** – this is issued once appeals have been exhausted and sets out the final outcome of the proceeding including the sanction and the date it takes effect.

▩ **Supervisory notice** – This sets out details of action the FSA/RDC will take immediately before formal procedures. This is designed to be preventative and protective.

Section B

Question 11.

This question was concerned with the need for authorisation for commodity-related derivatives activities by an authorised and non-authorised firm.

(a)   S19 FSMA requires that all persons carrying out regulated activities regarding specific investments by way of business are either authorised or exempt. The definitions of Regulated Activity are set out in FSMA and the Regulated Activities Order 2001 (as amended) drafted by HM Treasury. Regulated activities include dealing and arranging deals in investments. Specified investments include futures for investment purposes which includes financial and commodity futures (i.e. fish futures would be included).

The customer will not require authorisation to the extent that their activities are not carried on by way of business. In addition, there are specific exemptions in the Regulated Activities Order excluding dealing as principal where the person is not holding themselves out to the market as doing the activity by way of business. Therefore it would appear likely that the investment bank is conducting the regulated activity of dealing and arranging in investments. The bank is likely to be authorised under S19 already, but would need to ensure its permissions cover these specified activities and investments under S20. The penalty for breaching S19 is two years' imprisonment and/or unlimited fines. The penalty for breaching S20 is FSA discipline including fines and censures but not imprisonment.

(b)   Under COB 4.1, clients must be classified before the firm conducts designated investment business which would include dealing/arranging/advising on futures.

The classifications are

■   Market Counterparty, e.g. government, central bank, state investment body, large company who has opted up.

■   Intermediate Customer, e.g. a company, which is listed in the EEA or IOSCO or has £5m or more share capital or net assets.

■   Private Customer, e.g. unlisted companies with share capital or net assets below £5m and private individuals.

Where a client has opted up or down this classification must be reviewed annually

Documentation requirements are set out in COB 4.2 and would generally require a terms of business to be provided to most customers. Some customers – e.g. private discretionary customers – require a two-way client agreement:

(c)   These additional services would constitute the additional regulated activities of managing investments and possibly providing investment advice. The scope of the investment bank's permissions would need to be extended to cover this under S20. The sanction for failure would be FSA discipline.

Where the firm acts as an investment manager for a private customer

COB 5.2 and COB 5.3 would apply regarding KYC and suitability, although it is unlikely the client here is a private customer. If the client is a discretionary intermediate customer the firm must, under COB 7.2, ensure it avoids churning. In addition, the firm must also provide periodic statements under COB 8.2. For derivatives contracts these should be prepared monthly and dispatched within 10 business days of the end of the period to which the portfolio relates. This should include the contents and value of the portfolio with the basis of valuation at the end of the relevant period.

In addition, where the firm is looking after the client's assets then the firm must also comply with the requirements in the Client Assets Sourcebook (CASS).

(d)   Unless an exemption in the Financial Promotions Order applies, under S21 FSMA financial promotions (i.e. those which invite or induce someone to engage in investment activity) must be issued or approved by an authorised firm. Breach is a criminal offence with a penalty of two years' imprisonment and/or an unlimited fine. Therefore the client should not be promoting these unless they are authorised or the promotion is approved by an authorised firm. It is not possible to approve real-time promotions.

Unless a COB exemption applies, the firm will then have to comply with the provisions of COB 3 regarding the form and content of the promotion.

COB 3 requires that the promotion is clear, fair and not misleading and contains details of the firm and appropriate risk warnings. Where derivatives products are promoted these cannot be sold by direct offer promotion unless directed to those for whom it is suitable. Derivatives may also not generally be the subject of unsolicited real-time financial promotions.

(e)   Financial promotions are not included as core or non-core activities under the ISD, nor are they specifically mentioned in the Banking Consolidation Directive. It is however, possible to passport the services of dealing, arranging and managing under the ISD.

Financial promotions are thus generally subject to host state requirements. Even if the firm is passporting dealing or arranging activities, any promotions will be subject to local Conduct of Business rules. However, where the promotion is made electronically, e.g. via a website, then the E-Commerce Directive provisions will apply and these are subject to home state rules. Thus the marketing rules will differ depending on whether the promotion is made electronically or not.

Finally, where contracts are concluded at a distance the provisions of the Distance Marketing Directive may apply requiring standard information to be provided to the consumer.

[Although not relevant at the time of the exam, you could have mentioned that MIFID will include commodity derivatives business.]

Question 12.

This question is concerned with offering to carry on investment management services outside the EEA through an electronic internet promotion.

(a)   The main services will be investment management as well as dealing and arranging deals and possibly some investment advice. These all constitute Regulated Activities under the Regulated Activities Order 2001 as amended (RAO). The activities will be covered by FSMA to the extent that they are carried on in or into the UK. The term 'into' could include where activities are carried on from a place abroad but on behalf of UK investors. If activities are being carried out into the UK, then S19 and S20 will apply and authorisation and relevant permissions must be obtained. Breach of S19 is a criminal offence carrying a penalty of two years' imprisonment and/or unlimited fines. Breach of S20 will result in FSA discipline.

Separately, the services are being disseminated as a financial promotion under S21 FSMA so the promotion must be issued/approved by an authorised person unless an exemption in the Financial Promotions Order applies. The promotion refers to 'all prospective investors' thus the exemptions for promotions to certified high net worth individuals, sophisticated investors and investment professionals seem unlikely to apply. The penalty for breach of S21 is two years' imprisonment and/or an unlimited fine. In addition, unless exemptions apply (e.g. promotions are to market counterparties and intermediate customers) the promotion must comply with COB 3. A breach of COB 3 will result in FSA discipline plus private persons may sue the firm under S150 FSMA.

(b)   Under COB 3, the promotion would be a non-real time financial promotion. This is because it is communicated to more than one person in identical form, creates a record and does not require an immediate response. Real time promotions by contrast tend to be interactive.

The general non-real time rules in COB 3 require that the promotion

- Is clear, fair and not misleading, e.g. no untrue facts, no material omissions.

- Is checked and approved by a person with appropriate expertise.

- Contains the firm's name.

- Contains the firm's address or a contact point to get an address.

- Contains an adequate description of the nature of the investment, the commitment and the risks.

- For non-packaged products, discloses any conflicts of interest.

- Complies with the requirements on past performance, i.e. for packaged products clear warnings are included and five years of standard data is also included.

In addition, records should be kept for at least three years detailing the person who checked the promotion, evidence for the contents and the date and the medium of the promotion.

(c)   Avoiding a breach of S21 can be achieved most simply by not issuing or approving any promotions which invite or induce persons to engage in investment activity or ensuring it is routed through an authorised firm in the UK who signs off on the promotion.

If a promotion is going to be made but the person wants to avoid making it to or directing it at particular persons (i.e. those in the UK) they can ensure access restrictions via the use of disclaimers and passwords. Disclaimers could state that the site is not intended for those in the UK. It could also reject UK postal addresses. Passwords could be provided only once a telephone interview process has occurred.

The promotion could be addressed to sophisticated or high net worth investors only if the firm has taken steps to ensure the recipients are sophisticated or high net worth, e.g. by obtaining evidence of net worth from an accountant. This appears to be of limited use in this case as the product seems to be directed at the mass market.

(d)   The main powers the FSA has against authorised firms are set out in FSMA and the Enforcement Sourcebook (ENF). These include fines, private warnings, public censures, restitution, withdrawal or variation of authorisation or permissions. These are in addition to their criminal prosecutory powers under S19 and S21 FSMA.

If the entity issuing the promotion is authorised in the UK, then persons carrying out controlled functions, e.g. governing functions, must be approved by the FSA under S59 FSMA. They would have to comply with the Statements of Principle (APER) and could be fined, censured and lose approval if they did not.

If the person is not breaching S19 or S21 and is not authorised/approved by the FSA then the FSA generally will have no remit over the person. Higher level candidates may have referred to the need for the FSA to co-operate with overseas regulators including any memoranda of understanding that may exist.

(e)   If there is a significant or total loss because the firm has become insolvent then under the Financial Services Compensation Scheme there is a maximum claim per investor of £48,000 for investment activity. If the firm is not insolvent but has breached FSA rules then the client may request a remedy from the firm. Where the client is an Eligible Complainant (an individual who is not an expert, or a business with less than £1m turnover, income or net asset value, as applicable) they may use the Financial Ombudsman Service who can award claims of up to £100,000.

Claims against a firm may be based on common laws of tort (e.g. negligence) or contract. In addition, for a Private Person (an individual not doing a regulated activity and a business not acting in the course of business) they can bring their claim under S150 FSMA where there has been an FSA rule breach and loss is suffered.

Question 13.

NOTE THAT S118 FSMA WAS REVISED IN JULY 2005. THIS ANSWER REFLECTS THE POSITION AS AT THE TIME OF THIS EXAM. FOR CURRENT RULES, REFER TO YOUR STUDY BOOK.

This question raises various issues regarding the insider dealing rules under the Criminal Justice Act 1993 (CJA 93) as well as market abuse and market manipulation offences under FSMA.

(a)   The employee of Crimpleton Bains appears to be an insider under the CJA 93. He has inside information as he has unpublished price sensitive information which is specific and precise and relates to a particular issuer of securities, Crimpleton Bains. The knowledge that the company is breaching UN sanctions is likely to have a significant effect on its share price. He is an inside source as he is an employee of Crimpleton Bains. As an insider he then deals. It is unclear whether he deals on a regulated market or through a professional intermediary but this is likely as the shares are listed. Unless he can claim a defence he is liable to prosecution and imprisonment for seven years and the imposition of fines up to an unlimited sum. His possible defences are that he did not expect the dealing to avoid a loss. This defence is debatable as his primary motive may have been a moral stance but can he really claim he didn't think it would avoid a loss? He is unlikely to be able to say that he would have acted as he did anyway as the information triggered his moral stance.

Furthermore, he could be prosecuted by the FSA under the market abuse regime set out in S118 FSMA. His behaviour is in relation to qualifying investments traded on a prescribed market and is based on unavailable information. The one real unknown is what would a regular market user think of this conduct, and would they consider it a failure? In terms of defences under S123 the employee could claim that he believed on reasonable grounds that the behaviour did not amount to market abuse. This would avoid a financial penalty. In addition, he may be able to claim the safe harbour that he was dealing for other reasons, i.e. moral grounds. The penalty under S118 would be fines and censures.

Higher level candidates may also have mentioned the UKLA listing rules as this is price sensitive information which should have been disclosed, and possibly the Model Code, although there is nothing to suggest the employee is a director. Candidates with knowledge of the UN sanctions regime could also have mentioned this although it is not needed for the marks available.

(b)   Pre-release of profit warnings raises issues of insider dealing, market abuse and Listing Rules breaches. The company should not be making disclosures to journalists ahead of the market. The PSI guide makes clear that price sensitive information should be released in a timely fashion to the market via a Regulatory Information Service. The UKLA may discipline the company for breaches of these rules. If the company fails to make the relevant announcements in a timely way there is also a possible breach of S397 FSMA if it can be shown beyond reasonable doubt that there was a dishonest concealment of material facts. The penalty is seven years' imprisonment and/or unlimited fines.

In addition, employees of the company have disclosed inside information to the journalist which is a criminal offence under CJA 93. The disclosure can result in seven years' imprisonment. There is a defence to disclosure where no dealing was expected. On the second occasion the journalist was asked to sign agreements and warnings so that the company could argue that no dealing was expected. A court would decide whether these tests and defences are proved beyond reasonable doubt. Either way, this does not affect the fact that there are UKLA breaches. The journalist does not deal, encourage or disclose any information so he does not appear to have breached CJA 93.

S118 may also be breached by the company/its staff as the behaviour relates to unavailable information. Again the question would be whether a regular market user would consider this a failure on the part of the persons concerned. Some might argue that selective briefings before announcements are commonplace and thus acceptable. The FSA have, however, made clear that such accepted practices are not always, in fact, acceptable. In addition, these practices should not occur, and are increasingly less commonplace, under today's more compliant and ethical regime.

It could also be noted that the journalist's recommendations are excluded from FSA authorisation under the Regulated Activities Order 2001 although the journalist should comply with the Press Complaints Commission's codes of practice.

(c)   The earlier announcements may be a breach of S397 if parties have dishonestly or recklessly made a false or misleading statement, promise or forecast. The case of AIT – regarding profit warnings – looks at similar issues. This would have to be proven beyond reasonable doubt. There are defences if the person reasonably believed that their act or conduct would not create a false or misleading impression. Ultimately, this will come down to a decision as to what was believed at the time by the parties and the due diligence they had adopted.

Under S118, the conduct may also breach the second head of market abuse, i.e. it was behaviour likely to give a regular user a false or misleading impression as to supply, demand, price or value of investments. The term likely here does not necessarily mean over 50%. Again the question is: would a regular market user consider this to be a failure of the person concerned? This would be considered separately for Crimpleton Bains and its corporate finance advisers. The regular market user will have higher expectations on the part of the advisers who are likely to be FSA authorised. Crimpleton Bains is also likely to claim the statutory defences under S123 FSMA, in particular that they took reasonable precautions and exercised due diligence to avoid committing the offence as they were relying on professional advisers.

Additionally, the corporate finance advisers are likely to be FSA authorised and as such may have breached the FSA's Principles for Businesses (PRIN). In particular, PRIN 2 (skill, care and diligence) and PRIN 3 (management and control). Their conduct may also breach the Senior Management Arrangements, Systems and Controls Sourcebook (SYSC) as their employees and agents do not appear to be giving appropriate advice. This may also link into training failures under the Training and Competence Sourcebook (TC). Any approved persons (under S59 FSMA) may also have breached the Statements of Principle (APER). In particular, APER 2 (skill, care and diligence).

(d)   As long as the statements were accurate at the time that they were made there is no breach of S118 or S397 FSMA regarding misleading statements and practices. However, if the statements are no longer accurate then disclosure should be made to the market without delay under the UKLA Listing Rules (via a Regulatory Information Service).

If information which is incorrect is allowed to remain in the public domain then this could breach S397 as allowing incorrect statements to stand can in itself constitute a course of conduct which creates a false or misleading impression about the price of Crimpleton Bains' shares. Failure to remedy this can result in seven years' imprisonment and/or unlimited fines.

In addition, under S118, behaviour can include inaction and thus the inaction could constitute behaviour in relation to qualifying investments traded on a prescribed market. A regular market user may consider such inaction a failure on the part of the company as it is likely to create a false or misleading impression or distort the market. This would only have to be proved by the FSA on the lower (balance of probabilities) burden of proof and can result in fines and censures.

As you are acting as a new adviser to this company you should strongly advise that an appropriate announcement correcting the data and forecasts is made without delay. Any failure by the investment firm to make clear the issues and seriousness involved could result in the firm facing disciplinary action by the FSA for breaches of PRIN – e.g. PRIN 2, which requires the firm to act with skill care and diligence and PRIN 7, which requires communications with clients to be clear, fair and not misleading. As the client is likely to be an intermediate customer or market counterparty the COB rules on suitability of advice, etc., are unlikely to apply. However, the firm should ensure that its common law duties of negligence are not breached.

(e)   Selective briefings of analysts are not generally to be encouraged in particular where price sensitive information may be in danger of being disclosed. Where the company wishes to invite some analysts to a briefing it must ensure that no unpublished price sensitive information is disclosed at that meeting prior to announcement to the market. To disclose unpublished information would be a breach of the insider dealing rules under CJA 93 and the Misuse of Information head of market abuse under S118 FSMA. The penalties have been discussed above.

In order to avoid providing price sensitive information staff must be properly trained and advised on what they may and may not say. Proper records should be kept of what information is provided.

Additionally, there are specific requirements under COB in relation to analysts and their conduct with regards to conflicts of interest. COB 7.16 requires analysts to have proper systems and controls regarding reporting lines and organisation structures. Firms with analysts must have a written policy to manage conflicts of interest. In addition, the analysts must consider whether attending a selective briefing may breach COB 7.1 regarding conflicts generally and COB 2.2 regarding inducements. It could be argued that being invited to a selective briefing is an inducement which may conflict with the duty to provide impartial advice to the firm's customers. However, the firm also has an obligation to provide suitable advice and act with skill, care and diligence in providing the best possible research based on published information.

NOTE THAT PARTS OF POCA WERE REVISED BY THE SERIOUS ORGANISED CRIME AND POLICE ACT (SOCA) IN JULY 2005. THIS ANSWER REFLECTS THE POSITION AS AT THE TIME OF THE EXAM. FOR INFORMATION ON SOCA PLEASE REFER TO YOUR STUDY BOOK. FURTHERMORE, THE REQUIREMENTS OF THE FSA'S MONEY LAUNDERING SOURCEBOOK HAVE NOW BEEN INCORPORATED INTO THE SYSC SOURCEBOOK AND THE JMLSG HAVE ISSUED NEW GUIDANCE NOTES.

Question 14.

(a)   As the head office of the new group will be a UK authorised firm, various UK relevant money laundering requirements will apply including various provisions of the Proceeds of Crime Act 2002 (POCA), Money Laundering regulations 2003 (MLR), the FSA Money Laundering Sourcebook (MLS) and the Joint Money Laundering Steering Group (JMLSG) Guidance Notes. More specifically

- POCA would apply to the extent that there is criminal conduct which would constitute an offence if it occurred in the UK. It does not matter where the offence is conducted (S340 POCA).

- MLR requires various systems and controls to be in place and applies to various organisations carrying on business in the UK via a branch or cross-border services. Business may be carried on in Athens and Delhi but is also being conducted in the UK as the head office is in the UK. MLR requirements are usually applied on a group-wide basis.

- MLS requires systems and controls to be in place and applies to activities carried on from an establishment maintained by the firm or its appointed representative in the UK [now incorporated into SYSC].

Thus, the primary legislation, POCA, applies more broadly whilst the MLR and MLS strictly only apply to activities carried on within the UK. However, in practice it is common for a group to adopt a common policy (usually that of the head office) as well as local offices having to comply with local money laundering requirements. Thus, the Greek operations would need to comply with Greek money laundering regulations if required by the Greek authorities and law and thus local variations must be taken into account.

The Indian call centre is outsourced and should comply with the group money laundering policy as outsourced activities are still deemed to be the activities of the origin business and where it is based. Thus the call centre must comply with UK requirements, and, if dealing with Greek clients, Greek requirements as well.

(b)   The offences include

■   S327-329 POCA – assisting another person to launder the proceeds of criminal conduct, e.g. acquiring, using, retention use or control of funds, concealing, disguising, transferring the proceeds of crime. Defences include where disclosure is made and consent received to continue. The offence carries a penalty of 14 years' imprisonment and/or unlimited fines.

■   S330-332 POCA – failure to report knowledge, suspicion or reasonable grounds for suspicion of laundering. Defences include where there is a reasonable excuse for not reporting. The offence carries a penalty of five years' imprisonment and/or unlimited fines.

■   S333 POCA – tipping off, i.e. alerting a suspected launderer to a potential or actual investigation. Defences include where the person did not believe the disclosure would prejudice an investigation. The offence carries a penalty of five years' imprisonment and/or unlimited fines.

■   MLR – the institution must have internal reporting procedures, identification and know your customer procedures, record-keeping procedures (five years), procedure to recognise suspicious transactions and educational and training programmes. Penalty for breach is two years' imprisonment and/or unlimited fines.

■   Additionally, under the MLS the MLRO must be an approved person, the MLRO must produce an annual report to management and review international findings and staff must be trained at least once every two years.

(c)   Under the MLR, identification of all applicants for business must occur as soon as is reasonably practicable after initial contact (and before any business is conducted with that client). There are some exceptions where identification need not strictly occur, which include

■   For one-off or linked one-off transactions below €15,000.

■   Where the applicant is a credit or financial institution based in the UK, EU or a country with equivalent money laundering regulations.

■   Where the transaction relates to a small long-term insurance contract (one-off premium not exceeding €2,500 or regular premiums of less than €1,000 p.a.).

■   For a one-off transaction where the applicant is introduced by a credit or financial institution based in the UK, EU or a country with equivalent money laundering regulations.

The verification evidence to be obtained depends on the type of client. For example, for a UK resident, individual name and current permanent address should be obtained. This might include providing an original passport and utility bill. For non-UK resident applications, or where there is no face-to-face contact, additional information should be provided, e.g. the initial deposit is drawn on a UK/EU bank in the customer's name. If the client is a company or trust then other documentation evidence would be appropriate such as listed status, memorandum and articles, trust deed, details of settlors and beneficiaries. The JMLSG Guidance notes provide specific details of appropriate documentation.

In addition, the firm should know its customer. This relates to the need to have a benchmark against which to establish suspicious activity. This might include establishing the purpose for the relationship, anticipated nature and level of activity, relationships of signatories to underlying owners and origin of funds.

Records should be kept of all these matters for at least five years.

(d)   Suspicions should be referred to the local MLRO for consideration and assessment. Reference may then be made to the group MLRO and suspicious activity reports should be completed as necessary.

If there are suspicions which require reporting then these should be reported via the MLRO to the National Criminal Intelligence Service (NCIS) [now SOCA] in the UK and consent should be obtained before proceeding with the client activities or transactions. Any failure to report could lead to individuals (including the MLRO) committing an offence under S327-329 POCA for assistance and S330-332 POCA for failure to report.

In order to avoid assistance, NCIS must receive the report and consent to the activity continuing. They have seven days in which to respond. During this time it is important that the firm and individuals do not either further the client's transaction or tip off the client that there is, or may be, an investigation into their activities. If they tip off this is a separate offence under S333 POCA. Juggling these different requirements can prove difficult in practice but must be complied with.

Additionally, separate disclosures may need to be made to the Greek authorities if Greek clients are involved and possibly to the Indian authorities as well (depending on their local requirements).

(e)   Senior management are responsible for ensuring adequate systems and controls in relation to money laundering under the MLR. The penalty for breach includes a maximum penalty of two years' imprisonment and/or an unlimited fine. The FSA may also enforce their rules in the MLS by the use of fines, censures, loss of authorisation or approval for the firm or the management.

In addition, management have obligations under the Senior Management Arrangements, Systems and Controls Sourcebook (SYSC) to ensure that there are systems and controls in place which are appropriate to the nature, scale and complexity of the business. This includes, in particular, appropriate systems and controls to counter financial crime. This links into Principle 3 of the Principles for Businesses (PRIN 3) – management and control. Further, where the management are approved persons they must comply with the Statements of Principle (APER) which include that they ensure proper organisation of the business (APER 5), exercise skill, care and diligence in management (APER 6) and comply with regulatory requirements (APER 7).

Under the MLS, the MLRO must also be a senior person. If the MLRO does not comply with regulatory requirements (APER 7), they will also be liable to fines, censures and loss of approval.

Where a private person suffers a loss as a result of a rule breach by an authorised firm that person can sue the firm under S150 FSMA (in addition to the general common law) and management and the firm should take this into consideration.

Section C

Question 15.

The examiner is seeking primarily a factual account of the High Level Standards Block of the FSA Handbook. Candidates should have referred in as much detail as possible in the time to the following:

The purpose of the High Level Standards is to set out general principles with which authorised (S19) and approved (S59) persons should comply. These set out general ethical conduct expected of these persons, breach of which will attract sanctions including fines, censures, etc.

The main standards are the Principles for Business (PRIN) which apply to authorised persons/firms. The 11 principles should have been listed (integrity, skill, care and diligence, management and control, financial prudence, market conduct, customers' interests, communication with clients, conflicts of interest, customers' relationships of trust, clients' assets and relations with regulators).

PRIN 3 is expanded in Senior Management Arrangements, Systems and Controls Sourcebook (SYSC). This requires apportionment and establishment of appropriate systems and controls, e.g. organisation, compliance, risk assessment, management information, employees and agents, audit, business strategy, remuneration.

The 27 controlled functions that require approval are set out in the Supervision Sourcebook (SUP). However, the Fit and Proper Test for Approved Persons (FIT) is set out in the High Level Standards Block. These criteria include honesty and integrity, competence and capability, and financial soundness. The Statements of Principle (APER) are also set out here and these should have been listed (integrity, skill, care and diligence, market conduct, deal with regulator in an open way) applicable to all approved persons (and proper organisation of business, skill, care and diligence in management and comply with regulatory requirements) applicable to significant influence functions.

Candidates could also have referred to the Threshold Conditions Sourcebook (COND) and the General Provisions Sourcebook (GEN).

Question 16.

NOTE THAT S118 FSMA WAS REVISED IN JULY 2005. THIS ANSWER REFLECTS THE POSITION AS AT THE TIME OF THIS EXAM. FOR CURRENT RULES, REFER TO YOUR STUDY BOOK.

Candidates were expected to compare the relative advantages and disadvantages of the insider dealing offences under CJA 93 to the market abuse regime under S118 FSMA. Relevant points include the following:

Candidates should have explained the offences, defences and penalties under each offence in detail to explain the nature of each set of requirements.

Market abuse is a civil offence, so no prison sentences can be given, just unlimited fines and FSA discipline.

▓ The burden of proof in criminal law is 'beyond reasonable doubt'. In civil law, it is the 'balance of probabilities', the latter being easier to secure convictions.

▓ Territorial issues – insider dealing needs a close UK nexus whereas market abuse is extraterritorial.

▓ Criminal law looks at intention whereas market abuse is effects-based (NB: due diligence defence applies).

▓ Insider dealing only covers dealing on a regulated market or through a professional intermediary. S118 covers behaviour 'in relation' to qualifying investments trading on a prescribed market which is much wider.

▓ Inside information definition of 'specific/precise' is very narrow and hard to prove. Under S118, this would be a relevant factor, but not an absolute test.

■ Insider dealing is asymmetric as it fails to cover not dealing when you would otherwise have dealt. S118 covers actions and inaction although, of course, inaction is hard to prove.

■ Insider dealing can only be committed by individuals not businesses. S118 covers all natural and legal persons.

■ Parts of S118 are arguably unclear, e.g. the use of the word 'likely' in relation to two of the heads of market abuse and the scope of the regular market user.

■ Overall effectiveness of S118 remains unclear due to Human Rights concerns (reference could have been made to the case of the Plumber). The FSA have also reviewed its enforcement policies recently.

Question 17.

This question is looking for a discussion of the scope of regulated activities in relation to financial derivatives products. Candidates should have mentioned a good number of the following.

■ Reference to the general prohibition under S19 FSMA and definition of Regulated Activities and Specified Investments as set out in the Regulated Activities Order 2001 (as amended). The Specified Investments include certain (but not all) options, futures for investment purposes, and contracts for differences. Various activities regarding these investments such as advising, dealing, managing, arranging and agreeing to provide services would be regulated. The need to have specific permission regarding each activity (S20) could also be referred to.

■ The exemptions and exclusions from S19 should have been referred to and examples given, e.g. dealing as principal where not holding out to the market.

■ There are restrictions on the sale of derivative products under S21 (requirement for promotion to be issued/approved by an authorised firm). Additional promotional restrictions under COB 3 include restrictions on the sale via direct offer financial promotions to those to whom the product is not suitable.

■ There are various additional requirements regarding derivatives product set out in COB. These include.

    — COB 4.2 – private customers to receive two-way client agreements

    — COB 5.4 and COB5 Ann1E – requirement to ensure private customer understands risks and receives specific risk warning for derivatives

    — COB 7.10 – requirement to explain and take margin on derivatives trades

    — COB 7.11 – requirement regarding non-exchange traded securities to offer reasonable buy back price

    — COB 8.1 – requirement to provide confirmations

    — COB 8.2 – requirement to provide periodic statements

■ Exchange-traded derivatives must also comply with the rules of the relevant exchanges, e.g. Euronext.liffe, LME, IPE (now ICE Futures) trading rules. The Recognised Investment Exchanges themselves must comply with the provisions of the Recognised Investment Exchanges and Clearing Houses Sourcebook (REC).

■ For over-the-counter (OTC) derivatives contracts where wholesale market counterparties are involved, parties should comply with the provisions of the Inter-Professional Conduct (IPC) set out in the FSA Handbook. Industry terms and conditions (such as ISDA) are also appropriate.

■ Reference could also have been made to the legal issues as exemplified in the cases of Hammersmith and Fulham and Bankers Trust.

Question 18.

Candidates should have discussed the following in detail

* The rights available to European securities firms under the EU Investment Services Directive should have been discussed in detail. This includes setting up a branch or providing cross-border activities. The process for application (establishment and service conditions) and the nature of home and host state regulation should have been discussed. In addition, reference to core/non-core services and Non-ISD business definitions should be referenced.

* Information surrounding the MiFiD could also be referred to.

* The rights available under Treaty rights should also be discussed including application, scope and procedure for using these.

* US and Asian firms do not have the benefit of passporting or Treaty rights. They will therefore be subject to the general prohibition and permission requirements under S19 and S20 FSMA. This will require firms doing these activities by way of business into the UK to be authorised under S31 FSMA, e.g. via an application for Part IV permission. The firm would then have to comply with the FSA Handbook requirements.

Summer 2004 Answers

Please note: the answers given have not been updated to reflect technical changes since the date of the exam and therefore this document is only intended to provide guidance on the suggested content of your answers. In particular, we have used bullet points throughout to highlight the areas you could have discussed or considered. In the examination, particularly with Section C questions, it may often be more appropriate to set out certain answers in paragraph form. To see the examiner's report on this exam, please go to www.sii.org.uk.

Section A

1. This question is talking about S19 of the Financial Services and Markets Act (FSMA) and the permissions regime. All persons (businesses) are required to be authorised or exempt if they carry on a regulated activity in the United Kingdom under S19. This is referred to as the general prohibition. S31 FSMA explains the routes to authorisation, e.g. persons holding a Part IV permission or passporting:

    When a person is authorised this does not mean that they automatically undertake all regulated activities regarding all investments. The scope of their authorisation is limited to the permission they have applied for and been granted. Under S20 it is not a criminal offence for a firm to go beyond its permission but it may lead to FSA discipline and claims from consumers.

    The examiner's report goes into a lot of detail regarding S31 and exempt persons which would not be required for 2 marks.

2. You should have listed any eight of the statutory objectives or principles of good regulation. These consist of

    ▨ S2(2) FSMA Statutory Objectives

        – Maintaining market confidence in the UK financial system (S3)

        – Promoting public understanding of the UK financial system (S4)

        – Securing the appropriate degree of consumer protection (S5)

        – Reducing financial crime (S6).

    ▨ The principles of good regulation are set out in S2(3). These are

        – Efficiency and economy

        – Management responsibility

        – Burden proportionate

        – Facilitate innovation

        – International character

        – Distortion of competition

        – Facilitating competition.

3. You should have listed four of the Threshold conditions set out in Schedule 6 FSMA and COND which consist of

    ▨ Legal status.

    ▨ Location of offices.

    ▨ Close links.

    ▨ Adequate resources.

    ▨ Suitability.

4.   The general prohibition imposed under S19 applies to regulated activities. The purpose of the Financial Services and Markets (Regulated Activities) Order 2001 as amended (RAO) is to specify the scope of the regulated activities covered by FSMA including, in particular, the nature of the specified investments and activities covered and excluded. The purpose of the RAO is to define legally the scope of the investments and investment activities covered by the general prohibition.

5.   The aggregation and allocation rules are set out in COB 7.7. Aggregation is concerned with the grouping together of customers' orders for execution either with those of other clients or with the firm. Firms may not aggregate a customer order with an own account order unless it is likely not to disadvantage each customer and any possible disadvantage has been disclosed to the customer either orally or in writing.

   Allocation must be fair and timely. Fair allocation is concerned with ensuring that no unfair preference is given to any of those for whom the firm has dealt. This will require the firm to allocate orders at the weighted average price and where there is a partial fill customers orders will usually be filled before own account orders. Allocation must occur on a T+1 basis and records of trades and allocations kept.

6.   **NOTE THAT S118 FSMA WAS REVISED IN JULY 2005. THIS ANSWER REFLECTS THE POSITION AS AT THE TIME OF THIS EXAM. FOR CURRENT RULES, REFER TO YOUR STUDY BOOK.**

   The definition of market abuse is set out in S118 of FSMA. The three general offences are

   ▦   Misuse of information.

   ▦   False or misleading impressions.

   ▦   Market distortion.

   You should have listed three defences. You could have listed any of the following.

   The statutory defences against market abuse are set out in S123. These generally consist of

   ▦   The person believed on reasonable grounds that the behaviour did not amount to market abuse, or

   ▦   The person took all reasonable precautions and exercised all due diligence to avoid engaging in market abuse.

   Behaviour will also not amount to market abuse where it complies with a 'safe harbour' set out in the Code of Market Conduct which is in the Market Conduct Sourcebook in the FSA Handbook. These include acting in accordance with the

   ▦   Price stabilisation rules.

   ▦   Chinese walls.

   ▦   Listing Rules.

   ▦   Takeover Code.

7.   The meaning of 'real time' and 'non-real time' are set out in the financial promotions chapter of the FSA Conduct of Business Sourcebook (COB 3).

   A real time financial promotion is one communicated in the course of a personal visit, telephone or other interactive dialogue. Real time generally covers instantaneous or immediate forms of financial promotion involving direct contact between the customer and regulated firm.

   Non-real time refers to promotions not involving any immediate contact between the potential customer and the firm. Relevant factors to be taken into account in determining whether a communication is non-real time include

■ It is communicated to more than one person in identical form.

■ It is communicated in a way that creates a record.

■ It does not require any immediate response.

8. A penny share is a readily realisable security (excluding Government securities, FTSE 100 stocks and other stocks with a market capitalisation in excess of £100m) where the bid/offer spread is greater than or equal to 10% of the offer price.

Under COB 5.4 the firm should make private customers aware of the large difference between the buying and selling price. The warning may be either written or verbal and there is no need for the customer to acknowledge it.

9. The examiner's report refers to the requirement under COB 9.15.2. This is not correct, as they are set out in COB 6.2.

The use of a Key Features Document is provided for under COB 6.2. These are used where a firm sells, personally recommends or arranges life policies, certain investment trusts or regulated collective investment schemes to private customers.

A Key Features Document generally provides information with regard to

■ The product.

■ The terms and conditions.

■ The right to cancel or withdrawal.

All Key Features Documents must have certain headings such as 'Aims' and 'Risk Factors' and have a Questions and Answers section.

10. The Redress block of the FSA Handbook sets out the details of both the Financial Ombudsman Service (FOS) and Financial Services Compensation Scheme (FSCS).

The purpose of the FOS is to provide a mechanism for eligible complainants to make complaints concerning the conduct of regulated firms to an independent party, FOS. The relevant provisions are set out in the Dispute Resolution: Complaints Sourcebook (DISP).

The purpose of the FSCS is to make payment to eligible claimants of regulated firms where a firm is declared insolvent. The relevant provisions are set out in the Compensation Sourcebook (COMP).

Section B

Question 11.

This question was generally concerned with client classification and documentation issues.

(a)   This element is asking you to consider classification issues. Firms must classify all clients before conducting designated investment business (COB 4.1). The three classifications are market counterparties, intermediate customers or private customers.

Where a firm is instructed by another authorised person (or overseas financial institution) which is acting as agent on behalf of underlying clients, the authorised person may be treated as the client unless the firm and the authorised person otherwise agree. If the firm of independent financial advisers is to be treated as the client, it would generally be classified as a market counterparty although it may opt down where it is acting for underlying customers.

The underlying clients may also be treated as the customers of the firm provided that the firm and authorised person agree. The underlying clients may then be classified as private customers although an expert private customer may be classified as an intermediate customer if they have sufficient experience and understanding of the relevant risks (having regard to the client's knowledge, length of time and frequency of dealing, the extent of any advice given, the size and nature of transactions carried out and financial standing). If the firm is classifying an expert private customer as an intermediate customer it must also provide a written warning and receive the customer's consent after sufficient time to consider.

(b)   This element is concerned with documentation issues. Relevant documentation generally includes terms of business letters or client agreements under COB 4.2. Candidates should have given details of which client would need which documentation and mentioned the general content of these letters/agreements.

Reference may also have been made to obtaining KYC information under COB 5.2 and COB 5.3. Money laundering documentation under the Money Laundering Regulations 2003 should also have been referred to.

(c)   This element relates to the FSA's custody rules. Candidates should have referred to the provisions of CASS 2 such as segregation, registration and records, holding rules, assessment of custodian, client and custodian agreements, client statements and reconciliation requirements. Candidates should have briefly explained each in general terms.

(d)   This element relates to client money. Candidates should have referred to CASS 4. Relevant provisions include segregation in approved banks, trust creation, approved bank restrictions, reconciliation and client statements. More general reference could have been made to the purposes of the client money rules. Candidates should have briefly explained each in general terms.

(e)   This element relates to additional requirements. CASS 2 should have been referred to as stock lending requirements include appropriate consent, e.g. prior written consent from private customers to terms and conditions. Under COB 5.4 risk warnings must be sent to private customers regarding the impact on tax and legal rights. Under COB 4.2, private customers entering into stock lending must receive a client agreement. Suitability considerations under COB 5.3 could also have been mentioned. COB 7.10 regarding explaining margin requirements was also relevant.

Question 12.

This question was generally concerned with permissions with regard to the establishment, operation and management of unregulated collective investment schemes, marketing of these schemes and available remedies.

(a) Candidates should have discussed permissions here. All relevant regulated activities would require permission under S20 FSMA. This is in addition to the need to be authorised or exempt under S19 (the general prohibition). Regulated activities are listed in the Regulated Activities Order (RAO), which is secondary legislation written by HM Treasury.

Regulated activities of the London team could include

■ Arranging deals in investments.

■ Possibly investment advice.

■ Dealing in investments may also be involved (using computer-based systems for giving investment instructions).

■ From the information provided, it does not appear that they will be directly involved in establishing the collective investment scheme, managing investments or safeguarding and administering assets directly.

The London team will also be involved in financial promotions although this does not require permission directly as it is not a regulated activity but is governed by S21 FSMA.

Specified investments are also generally detailed in the RAO. They will include units in a collective investment scheme. Collective investment schemes are defined in S235-6 FSMA and cover pooling activities.

(b) If the fund is to be run out of London, additional permissions could include

■ Establishing/operating the scheme.

■ Managing investments.

■ Dealing in investments.

■ Safekeeping or administering.

■ Dealing (electronically) if using computer-based systems for giving investment instructions.

(c) Candidates should have discussed the financial promotions rules. In particular

■ Under S21 FSMA, financial promotions should be issued or approved by an authorised person unless an exemption in the Financial Promotions Order applies. The effect of this is that the authorised person will then have to comply with the relevant marketing requirements set out in the Financial Promotions Order (FPO) and COB 3 in the FSA Handbook as well.

■ Under S238 and the Promotion of Collective Investment Schemes Order 2001, promotion of unregulated schemes is limited. As an unregulated scheme, the fund cannot be promoted to the general public. Authorised unit trusts, OEICs or Recognised schemes may be promoted to the public. Unregulated schemes may only be promoted to

– Persons who are participants (or have been participants within the last 30 months) in a substantially similar scheme

– Established or newly accepted customers where the firm has taken reasonable steps to ensure that the investments are suitable

– Market counterparties and intermediate customers

– Certain persons covered by FPO exemptions, e.g. sophisticated investors

(d)   Candidates should have discussed passporting rights. The firm would have to consider available passporting rights under the European Directives including, in particular, the Investment Services Directive (and Banking Consolidation Directive if relevant). This would apply to establishing a branch or providing cross-border services. The home state would still govern areas such as fitness and propriety and capital adequacy although Conduct of Business rules (including financial promotions) would be subject to host state rules. Reference may also have been made to distinction between core and non-core services under the Investment Services Directive.

Additional rights of establishment and cross-border services may also be available under Treaty rights established under Schedule 4 of FSMA.

Candidates could also have referred to internet activities which would be governed by the E-Commerce Directive, which generally allows promotion on a home state basis. The relevant parts of the FSA Handbook (Electronic Commerce Sourcebook (ECO)) would then apply to any electronic promotions from the UK within the EEA.

(e)   Candidates should discuss Electronic Commerce Activity (ECO). Under ECO, promotions are simplified and can comply with home state rules. However, under certain derogations, essential information such as risk warnings must be provided in the relevant language. The restrictions on selling unregulated collective investment schemes must be recognised including selling to suitable persons and maintaining necessary procedures to prevent unsuitable persons from applying. The promotions are likely to be specific non-real time and these rules must be adhered to, e.g. firm's name and address, commitments and risks.

(f)   Candidates should have referred to the Redress block of the FSA Handbook. Complaints should first be made to the firm under its internal procedures (which must comply with DISP). Further rights of complaint may then be available by using the Financial Ombudsman Service (FOS) set up under FSMA.

(g)   Candidates should have referred to the Redress block of the FSA Handbook. Compensation rights may be available under the Financial Services Compensation Scheme (FSCS) as detailed in the Dispute Resolution: Complaints Sourcebook (COMP). Private persons may bring an action under S150 where a firm breaches a rule, e.g. financial promotions. The FSA may also apply for restitution orders (under S382-386 FSMA).

Question 13.

This question relates to insider dealing, market abuse and the Takeover Code.

(a)   Detailed reference should be made to rules and legislation including

- Insider dealing under the Criminal Justice Act 1993 including the definition and nature of the insider dealing offences as well as relevant defences and penalties.

- Market abuse under S118 FSMA including the definition and nature of the possible offences (e.g. misuse of information) as well as relevant defences and penalties.

- The examiner also suggested reference could also have been made to misleading statements and practices (under S397 FSMA); however, this is not likely to be a core offence based on the facts given.

- Candidates should have mentioned the investigation and enforcement powers of FSA, although this would not be necessary for full marks.

- The main provisions set out in the Takeover Code should have been referred to including the dealing restrictions and general disclosure rules (Rules 4 and 8). While some provisions may only apply during the offer period (from the announcement until the closing date) dealing or recommending another to deal in advance of an offer is expressly prohibited under Rule 4.1. Additional disclosure requirements may also then have arisen under the Companies Act 1985 including any concert party holdings. [Candidates should note that Rules 4 and 8 are no longer on the syllabus].

- Reference may also have been made to the rules governing Substantial Acquisitions of Shares (SARS) and to the Price Sensitive Guide (PSI) issued by the FSA as UKLA. [Candidates should note the PSI Guide and SARS no longer exist.] This would, in particular, require disclosure of any significant movements in share price by the companies concerned.

- The Model Code for Director's Dealings would generally not be applicable to a non-UK company director although equivalent German provisions may be relevant.

- Where the scope of application of any particular provisions was unclear, further enquiry or professional advice would be required.

(b) Relevant market abuse and insider dealing offences should again have been referred to with comment on the location of the manager within the UK providing a UK nexus.

(c) Dealings in the UK companies concerned are involved in this case creating a UK nexus although the purchaser is now overseas. Any available defences may also have been referred to. Relevant German laws would also, of course, apply although no further comment would be expected.

(d) Relevant UK market abuse and insider dealing offences would again apply to the cousin subject to any possible defences available.

(e) Relevant UK provisions would again apply with regard to the staff of the cleaning company. The definition of inside source under CJA 93 would be relevant here (with relevant information having been obtained in the course of their employment). There is uncertainty over whether they 'knew' they had unpublished information and therefore certain defences may be available.

NOTE THAT PARTS OF POCA WERE REVISED BY THE SERIOUS ORGANISED CRIME AND POLICE ACT (SOCA) IN JULY 2005. THIS ANSWER REFLECTS THE POSITION AS AT THE TIME OF THE EXAM. FOR INFORMATION ON SOCA PLEASE REFER TO YOUR STUDY BOOK.

Question 14.

This question was generally concerned with the application of the relevant legal and regulatory requirements that apply with regard to money laundering controls in connection with the operation of a London-based bureau de change.

(a) The definition of money laundering should have been explained here. There are various definitions that could be used, however, FATF defines money laundering as the conversion or transfer of property, the concealment or disguise of its true nature or source or the acquisition, possession or use of property knowing it to be criminally derived. The FATF identifies the three stages of placement, layering and integration. The FATF definition was generally adopted under the 1991 European Directive.

Under the Proceeds of Crime Act (POCA) in the UK, money laundering is an act which constitutes an offence under S327-329 (assistance, e.g. concealing, arrangements, acquisition, use and possession). Money laundering also includes aiding, abetting, counselling or procuring the commission of any such offence. Candidates could also have mentioned that under POCA it covers the proceeds of all crimes.

(b) This element requires you to explain the offences and defences in detail.

The main offences for individuals working in the bureau de change are set out in Part VII of the Proceeds of Crime Act 2002 (POCA). The three main offences are.

- Assistance, i.e. concealing, arrangements, acquisition, use and possession restated as concealing (S327-328).

- Failure to report (S330-332).

- Tipping-off (S333).

Candidates should have discussed the defences, e.g. reasonable excuse and the penalties for each offence.

Reference should also have been made to the obligations imposed on financial institutions under the Money Laundering Regulations 2003 (MLR). The FSA's Money Laundering rules would not apply as bureaux de change are not FSA authorised. The penalties should have been noted.

Higher level candidates may also have mentioned the powers in POCA which create the Assets Recovery Agency (ARA) and its confiscation, cash forfeiture, taxation of criminal proceeds and investigation powers. The bureau de change may face production orders, customer information orders and account monitoring orders.

(c) The identification requirements imposed under the MLR should have been noted. Relevant institutions must, in particular, set up procedures to ensure that satisfactory evidence is obtained that verifies the entity of all applicants for business.

Evidence of identity must be obtained when a business relationship is to be established, the institution undertakes a one-off or series of linked transactions in excess of €15,000, or there is any suspicion of money laundering. Relevant exemptions include one-off or linked transactions under €15,000, dealings with UK or other EU or overseas financial institutions with equivalence, small long-term insurance contracts and certain introduced transactions.

Evidence of identity should be obtained as soon as is reasonably practical. Examples of appropriate evidence should have been noted. The need to obtain Know Your Customer information should also be noted. Candidates should have noted the five-year record-keeping requirement.

(d) Relevant provisions concerning recognition and reporting of suspicious transactions should have been noted. The need to report any suspicious activities to the Money Laundering Reporting Officer (MLRO) or to relevant authorities directly should have been discussed.

All reasonable enquires must be followed up with any necessary questions being asked as part of the general customer identification and KYC obligations. Appropriate records must be kept in all cases even where information is provided voluntarily and any suspicious activity properly reported.

Candidates may have noted that business may still be accepted in exceptional situations although the decision and reasons for this would have to be fully recorded.

(e) Reference could have been made to the financial promotion rules contained in S21 FSMA and Chapter 3 of the Conduct of Business rules (COB 3) in the FSA Handbook although candidates should have noted that currency exchange services would generally not in itself constitute a regulated activity and would thus fall outside of these provisions. Reference could also be made to a possible breach of POCA S327-329 (assistance) and the MLR and to general advertising standards.

Section C

Question 15.

This question wants the candidate to look at the purpose and main rules of the approved persons regime so will be largely a factual discussion. Candidates should have mentioned a good number of the following.

▩ Requirement under S59 of FSMA for those carrying out controlled functions to be approved.

▩ That this requirement is fleshed out in the FSA Handbook, specifically SUP (which lists the controlled functions), and sets out what type of functions are covered. Candidates should list the categories of approved person and some examples of controlled functions.

▩ The rationale for the regime being those who govern or manage firms or carry out customer functions must be fit and proper. This links to the FSA's objectives of market confidence and consumer protection.

▩ Firms must get persons approved by submitting Form A. Firms should ensure people applying for approval meet the criteria in FIT (honest, integrity, etc.). Firms should also notify the FSA of changes to functions of those approved and when they leave the firm.

▩ Firms should ensure that approved persons are aware of the Statements of Principle that apply to them. Candidates should have listed the contents of these principles.

▩ Reference could also have been made to the relationship between firm authorisation (and permission) and individual staff approval.

Question 16.

This question is essentially factual in nature and concerned with the management and control of conflicts of interest especially with regard to research staff within authorised firms. Reference should have been made to the main specific provisions contained in the FSA Handbook and recent FSA consultations in this area. In particular

▩ The conflict between research and the rest of the firm should have been explained, e.g. the need for research to be independent of investment banking or client relationship matters. Recent problems in the US and fines should have been referred to.

▩ Principle 8 of the Principles for Businesses requires firms to manage conflicts of interest fairly.

▩ Under COB 8.1 where a firm has a material interest or conflict of interest, it must not advise the customer or act in a discretionary capacity unless it has taken reasonable steps to ensure fair treatment.

▩ Reasonable steps include disclosure, declining to act, Chinese walls (COB 2.4) or a Policy of Independence. Each of these should have been described briefly.

▩ More specific COB rules may also have been referred to such as with regard to churning and switching (COB 7.2), dealing ahead of publication (COB 7.3). Other related provisions could have been noted such as customer order priority obligations, best execution and timely execution and aggregation and allocation.

▩ Reference ought to have been made to the FSA's consultation (and new rules) concerning research analysts in COB 5.10 and COB 7.16.

▩ Reference may also have been made to other High Level Standards including the Principles for Business (PRIN) and Senior Management Arrangements, Systems and Controls Sourcebook (SYSC).

▩ Higher level candidates may have referred to the common law of agency, more general duties are also imposed with regard to obedience, care and skill, good faith and confidentiality. Remedies may then be available under breach of general common law duties or under S150 of FSMA.

[NB: Since this exam, COB 7.17 has been introduced, which now should be mentioned.]

Question 17.

Note that this question relates to the syllabus prior to the Winter 2004 sitting which covered market regulation in more detail. Current candidates would not be able to answer this question from the Study Book, as this is no longer on the syllabus. We have therefore included the examiner's answer below without comment for information only.

Question 17 was concerned with the regulation of the Eurobond market. The nature and structure of the Eurobond market could have been referred to although detailed information was not required.

Reference should have been made to the relevant provisions that would apply under the FSMA and the FSA Handbook as well as the various trade association rules concerning Eurobond activity. Relevant FSMA requirements would generally include the need for authorisation and permission under the FSMA (S19 and S20) as well as restrictions on financial promotion (S21). Relevant investment and investment activities should also have been noted (S21, 23 and Schedule 2 to FSMA) and reference made to the Regulated Activities Order (RAO).

The general exemptions applicable to wholesale business could have been referred to. This would be subject to available exemptions under the COB and the Financial Promotions Order. The wholesale nature of the activities will generally mean that many of the more specific provisions set out in the FSMA are generally inapplicable although the inter-professional section of MAR will be relevant.

The other functions and rules of the relevant international trade associations including, in particular, the International Primary Markets Association (IPMA) and the International Securities Market Association (ISMA) – now combined to form International Capital Market Association (ICMA)) – should have been referred to. The non-statutory nature of the guidelines and standard form documentation issued could have been noted and the general structure and content of the measures provided referred to.

Reference could also have been made to the Transaction Exchange System (TRAX) or other pricing and dealing systems on the London Stock Exchange. Any related derivative transactions would generally be conducted through the International Swaps Dealing Association (ISDA) master agreements.

Reference may have been made to the main possible clearing systems and the London Clearing House or CREST. The nature and function of the main global custodians including Euroclear and Clearstream could also have been noted.

Question 18.

The examiner is looking for an analysis of the progress towards a single market. Thus, a purely factual answer would be unlikely to score highly. The candidate should be discussing whether the work currently being undertaken is likely to achieve the single market objective. Candidates should have discussed a good number of the following.

▨ Brief history of the single market, Treaty of Rome and Financial Services Action Plan and time-frames.

▨ Progress through Passporting provisions, e.g. ISD, UCITS, BCD but problems, e.g. non-core services and Alternative Trading Systems.

▨ Progress through Lamfalussy proposals should be discussed, e.g. committee structures and framework principles. Has it worked?

▨ E-Commerce Directive. Does it create confusion, will it be properly implemented?

▨ Review of ISD in MiFID – good idea too slow, too late?

▨ Market Abuse Directive – lots of uncertainty about implementation and problems with lists of insiders.

▨ Prospectus Directive – anti-competitive? Member states want home state issuance.

▨ Takeovers – opt outs for important provisions like frustration reduce harmonisation.

- Can laws create a single market? Shouldn't this be market driven? Candidates could discuss consolidation of clearing and settlement and exchanges.

- Lots of barriers still exist, e.g. political (protectionist behaviour), cultural, cost, language, law, no clear vision.

- Will expansion of the EU hamper the creation of a single market?

Winter 2003 – Answers

Please note: the answers given have not been updated to reflect technical changes since the date of the exam and therefore this document is only intended to provide guidance on the suggested content of your answers. In particular, we have used bullet points throughout to highlight the areas you could have discussed or considered. In the examination, particularly with Section C questions, it may often be more appropriate to set out certain answers in paragraph form. To see the examiner's report on this exam, please go to www.sii.org.uk.

Section A

1. The question is talking about a breach of S19 of FSMA, known as the General Prohibition. You should have identified the following sanctions set out primarily in Sections 23-24 of FSMA

   ▨ Criminal sanctions – breach of S19 is an offence punishable by two years in prison and/or an unlimited fine.

   ▨ Agreements are voidable – any agreement made by an unauthorised person will be unenforceable against the other party. However, the innocent party may be allowed to enforce the agreement against the other party even though this is still strictly a criminal offence.

   ▨ Compensation – the innocent party is entitled to compensation if the agreement is made unenforceable.

   ▨ An injunction to stop the person continuing to breach S19.

   ▨ Restitution order to put the injured party back in the pre-breach situation.

   The examiner's report also mentions the possibility of referring to the defence under S23(3), although this should not have been required to achieve four marks where sufficient details of sanctions were given.

2. You should have listed the following categories of authorised person set out in S31 of FSMA

   ▨ A person who has Part IV permission.

   ▨ An EEA firm who qualifies for passporting.

   ▨ A firm who exercises treaty rights.

   ▨ A person who is otherwise authorised under FSMA.

   The examiners' report refers to this being under S30(1). This should actually be S31 as stated above.

3. You should have listed and explained briefly four of the following conditions set out in Part IV and Schedule 6 of FSMA.

   ▨ Legal status.

   ▨ Location of offices.

   ▨ Close links.

   ▨ Adequate resource.

   ▨ Suitability.

4. COB 7.5 (Best Execution) requires firms to take reasonable care to ascertain the best price for the transaction in terms of its type, time and size and execute at a no less advantageous price. The best execution obligation applies to all customers.

    The best execution obligation does not apply in the following circumstances. You should have identified two of these situations

    ▨   On purchase of a life policy.

    ▨   On purchase or units in a CIS.

    ▨   For market counterparties.

    ▨   Where an intermediate customer has opted out (unless they are trustees of OPS/CIS or firms acting as 'permitted third parties' who cannot opt out).

    The examiner's report also refers to the Best Execution Discussion Paper 2001 which may in the future lead to further exemptions being provided, although reference to this was not essential for three marks.

5. COB 5.3 provides rules on suitability which stem from Principle 9 of the Principles for Businesses. The COB rule requires firms to ensure that the advice or transaction is suitable, having regard to the facts disclosed by him and any other facts of which the firm should reasonably be aware. This would cover both advice and where a firm undertakes discretionary transactions. The suitability rule applies where a firm is advising a private customer or acting as an investment manager for a private customer or managing an occupational or stakeholder pension scheme.

    A firm is required to provide the customer with a suitability letter explaining the main consequences and possible disadvantages of the transaction where a private customer then subsequently invests in

    ▨   A life policy.

    ▨   A stakeholder pension.

    ▨   A pension transfer.

    ▨   Investment trust shares where they are acquired via an ITSS or are held in an ISA/PEP.

    ▨   A regulated CIS (except where the firm is acting as an investment manager for the customer).

6. Appointed representatives are businesses or self-employed individuals who act on behalf an authorised firm through an agency contract for services. The exemption removes them from the scope of authorisation under S19 so long as they act solely on behalf of the authorised firm and the firm takes complete responsibility for their actions. Individuals selling products within the appointed representative may, however, need to be approved persons.

7. You could have mentioned any three of the following requirements under COB 9 (now CASS).

    ▨   Segregation – a firm must ensure that client assets are clearly segregated from its own assets.

    ▨   Registration and recording – a firm must effect appropriate registration or recording of legal title to a safe custody investment in the name of the client, a nominee company, a custodian or in certain circumstances in the name of the firm or in the name of another person on the client's specific instruction.

    ▨   Holding – the firm must ensure that an appropriate level of protection is afforded to safe custody investments that the firm physically holds.

    ▨   Assessment of custodian – a firm that holds safe custody investments with a custodian or arranges for registration through a custodian must have undertaken a risk assessment.

- Client agreements – before a firm provides safe custody services to a client, it must notify the client as to the applicable terms and conditions that apply to the service. Private customers must sign the agreement.

- Custodian agreement – before a firm holds safe custody investments for or on behalf of a client with a custodian, it must agree in writing, appropriate terms and conditions with the custodian.

- Reconciliation – a firm must carry out a reconciliation of all safe custody investments held physically at least every six months. It must also reconcile other safe custody investments for which it is accountable but which it does not physically hold at least every 25 business days. It can use the total count method or the rolling reconciliation method.

8. The Financial Services Compensation Scheme is able to award a maximum of £48,000 for investment business (100% of the first £30,000 and 90% of the next £20,000) and £31,700 for deposit-taking business (100% of £2,000 and 90% of the next £33,000).

    The examiners' report also refers to the limits for insurance. As this is not part of the question, we assume this is for information purposes only.

9. You could have listed any four of the following.

    - HM Treasury.

    - General public meeting on annual report.

    - Internal mechanisms such as RDC/non-executive directors.

    - Complaints Commissioner.

    - Competition scrutiny.

    - Judicial review.

    - Consumer and practitioner groups.

    - Financial Services & Markets Tribunal.

10. The FSA has immunity from prosecution unless it has acted in bad faith or has breached the Human Rights Act 1998.

Section B

Question 11.

This question was generally concerned with client classification, account opening procedures and documentation.

(a)   This element is asking you to consider client classification issues. You should have considered the following.

■   The obligation in COB to classify before carrying out designated investment business.

■   The prospective client appears to be a private customer from the information given. The reference to a sophisticated investor is not relevant to the client classification as this relates to the Financial Promotions Order exemptions. However, if he met the criteria for opting up to expert status he could be classified as an intermediate customer.

■   As a private customer, the individual could be either a private discretionary, private advisory or private execution-only customer.

■   To make any proper determination you would need to establish what type of relationship and services the individual is looking for and his degree of expertise.

The examiner's report also refers to the need to keep records of the classification and review opt-ups annually. These were not strictly required by the question.

(b)   You should have set out the possible ability to opt up and down under the client classification rules

■   You should have discussed the criteria for opting an individual up to expert status. Does the individual have the knowledge and experience of the products and the risks involved? This would include considering activity in the market, length of time dealing, size of trades, etc. Have the risk warnings been provided? What should the risk warnings say? Do both parties agree to opting up?

■   You should have stated that as an individual he cannot opt up to a market counterparty.

■   Where a customer has previously opted up, this must be reviewed annually and where the criteria are not met on the review they should be reclassified.

(c)   You could have considered the following documents.

■   Client agreement if he/she is a private discretionary or a private customer entering into contingent liability transactions, underwriting or stock lending, unless as an overseas customer the firm reasonably believes that he/she does not want to receive it. If so, only a terms of business needs to be sent.

■   Terms of business for other activities. Client agreement/terms of business should set out investment objectives, charges, details of the firm, etc.

■   The terms of business/client agreement should also set out relevant risk warnings for penny shares, non-readily realisable investments, stock lending, etc.

■   You should have noted when these must be sent out, i.e. for private customers generally in advance of business being conducted or for intermediate customers within a reasonable period of time.

(d)   Further COB requirements include

■   Two-way client agreement for contingent liability transactions if none provided before.

■   Two-way risk warning for derivatives must be provided unless an overseas customer and the firm reasonably believes that the client does not wish to receive it. The content of the warning is set out in Annex 1 to COB 5.

■ Special rules for securitised derivatives, e.g. provision of listing particulars.

■ Consideration of general understanding of risk and suitability under COB rules.

■ Explanation of margin rules and requirements under COB rules.

(e) You should have considered the following.

■ Firms are required to review the classification of experts and opted up intermediates at least annually (unless the account has remained dormant over the last 12 months).

■ Firms must continue to comply with suitability and risk requirements in Chapter 5 of COB.

■ If the client wishes to invest in packaged products, they require a key features document and should be provided with cancellation rights (COB 6).

■ Confirmation notes after each trade for all customers (COB 8).

■ Periodic statements where the firm acts as investment manager and where accounts contain uncovered derivatives (COB 8).

■ Compliance with client asset rules.

■ Record-keeping rules.

Question 12.

This question was generally concerned with the rules and restrictions relating to carrying out regulated activities, passporting and financial promotions rules.

(a) Candidates should have discussed the following.

■ Section 19 of FSMA – the General Prohibition that requires the US firm to be authorised or exempt in order to provide regulated activities in the UK by way of business. The firm should have applied for Part IV permission. It cannot passport as it is not an EEA firm..

The penalties for breaching S19 should have been discussed, i.e. criminal sanctions (S23-24) and civil consequences (S28)

■ The requirements for authorisation set out in Schedule 6 of FSMA and the High Level Standards Block of the FSA Handbook, i.e. the Threshold Conditions, which are: Location of Offices, Legal Status, Close Links, Adequate Resources and Suitability. As this is a US company, the FSA will want to consider their group structure and location of offices and may liaise with the US regulators to gain more information.

(b) Candidates should have referred to the Regulated Activities Order 2001 which sets out those regulated activities that require authorisation. The activities in the order include 'establishing or operating a collective investment scheme'. Candidates should have discussed the meaning of a collective investment scheme, i.e. that it relates to pooling of investors' funds. Examples of such schemes include unit trusts and OEICs.

Here, the scheme is a property scheme and candidates should have discussed that while property is not itself a specified investment under the Regulated Activities Order, the regulated activity of establishing or operating a collective investment scheme is interested in the activity of pooling rather than the underlying assets in the pooled fund. The activity clearly appears to be pooling, so falls within the definition of a collective investment scheme.

(c)   Candidates should have discussed any other regulated activities in the Regulated Activities Order 2001 which may also be being undertaken by the US firm. It is unclear from the facts what other activities, if any, are being done but possibilities include:

■   Dealing as principal or as agent in investments. The activities of investment management are clearly likely to include dealing on an agency basis and they may also be undertaking proprietary trades.

■   Arranging deals in investments as their activities bring together buyers and sellers to a transaction(s).

■   Managing investments is also very likely to be undertaken as the funds are to be managed by the US firm.

■   Advising on investments may also take place where they advise investors on the merits of the investments.

■   Safeguarding and administering investments may also be relevant where the firm proposes to undertake custody activities in relation to the property assets within the firm. It is also unclear whether they propose to hold client money.

(d)   This part of the question is asking you to focus on the marketing rules relating to collective investment schemes. Candidates should have discussed

■   The requirement that financial promotions must be issued or approved by an authorised firm under S21 FSMA and the penalties for breach. It is unlikely that any exemptions apply in this case based on the facts given.

■   That the further rules on selling will depend on whether the scheme is a regulated or unregulated collective investment scheme. A regulated scheme is a scheme that complies with the collective investment scheme sourcebook (or New Collective Investment schemes sourcebook) and has been granted authorised status by the FSA. An unregulated scheme is a scheme that does not meet these criteria. It is unclear whether the proposed scheme in the question is regulated or not.

■   If the scheme is a regulated collective investment scheme, it can be freely marketed, including being cold-called to private customers and sold via direct offer financial promotions. However, the firm must comply with the general real-time rules in COB, e.g. calling at an allowable time and not making any untrue claims.

■   If the scheme is unregulated then under S238 FSMA it may only be promoted to existing or recent participants in similar schemes, customers for whom the firm has assessed suitability, market counterparties and intermediate customers and some persons in limited FPO exemptions, e.g. sophisticated investors.

(e)   This part of the question is asking you to consider passporting and treaty rights issues. Candidates should have discussed

■   If the firm was already established within the EEA, then it may be able to passport the investment management services into the UK using the passporting provisions in the Investment Services Directive. It would apply to its home state regulator for the passport and the home regulator would liaise with the FSA. Since managing is a core service, this can be passported.

■   Where a firm is seeking to passport a fund itself rather than services relating to it, the firm may use the UCITS Directives to passport the fund. Higher level candidates may have mentioned that it has not always been as straightforward to passport property funds as for standard securities funds.

■   Where no passporting or UCITS rights exist it may be possible to use treaty rights under EU case law to provide the cross-border services.

■   Using any of these methods will ensure the firm meets the definition of authorised under S31 FSMA.

Question 13.

This question is focused on money laundering rules and requirements.

(a)   You could have discussed the following.

- Concerns over money laundering due to the source of funds, identity of client, selection of high risk investments (with no concern of loss), no introduction and no obvious reason for using the firm.

- Need to comply with money laundering regulations and FSA ML rules (now in SYSC). Detailed discussion should be made of when identity must be verified, exceptions and possible form of evidence. Reference to KYC checks should also be made, e.g. source of funds, expected trading patterns.

- You could also have mentioned the need to carry out classification checks and comply with COB documentation requirements.

(b)   You should have discussed in rigorous detail the offences, defences and penalties under the following legislation.

- Proceeds of Crime Act 2002 (POCA) – individual offences of assistance, failure to report and tipping off. Defences such as disclosure and sign off by NCIS or failure to be trained.

- Money laundering regulations – institutional requirements to have procedures for identification, reporting, MLRO, record keeping, recognition of suspicions, training and penalties for failure to comply.

- FSA Money Laundering rules (now in SYSC) – institutional requirements to have procedures similar to ML regulations plus additional training and MLRO requirements should have been noted.

(c)   Candidates would have been expected to mention areas such as

- FATF requirements and typologies.

- EU money laundering legislation in progress.

- Higher level candidates may have also referred to US requirements under the PATRIOT Act relating to terrorism.

- Need to cooperate with overseas authorities.

(d)   Candidates should have discussed the need to avoid tipping off under POCA. Relevant defences could be mentioned.

(e)   Candidates should have discussed that POCA covers the proceeds of all crimes, including terrorism. Candidates should have noted that there is additional separate anti-terrorism legislation in the UK such as the Terrorism Act 2000 and the Anti Terrorism, Crime and Security Act 2001.

Question 14.

This question is asking you to consider the issues relating to internet-related financial services.

(a)   Considerations should have included

- Need to comply with S21 FSMA, offences and penalties.

- If website is a financial promotion, the need to comply with FSMA/COB3.

- Difference between real and non-real time financial promotions.

- General reference to E-Commerce Directive rules could have been made.

(b)   Discussion should have been made of

- Section 19 General prohibition restrictions and possible exemptions for certain overseas persons acting through an authorised firm.

- SYSC and PRIN 3 regarding the outsourcing issues – can the firm control the business properly?

- Live chat facility may result in making real-time financial promotions which must be issued by authorised firms and must comply with COB 3, e.g. clear, fair and not misleading. There may also be suitability issues under COB 5.

(c)   Discussion should have been made of the restrictions on the sale of unregulated collective investment schemes (S238 FSMA). In order to sell to existing participants and those for whom it is suitable, password operated protections would be required.

(d)   This is a tricky part of the question. Candidates should have mentioned that the 'hoster' may still be communicating a financial promotion and S21 and COB may apply. There is an exception for mere conduits in the Financial Promotions Order, although it is unclear whether that would apply here. Candidates could also have mentioned that the activities may constitute arranging deals under the Regulated Activities Order.

(e)   A hypertext link is unlikely to be a financial promotion but the advertorial listing may be a financial promotion. If it is a financial promotion S21 applies. Again, the company may also be arranging deals under the Regulated Activities Order.

Section C

Question 15.

This question is asking you to consider the rules and guidance in the FSA Handbook relating to conflicts of interest. In particular, it is asking for you to focus on the High Level Standards Block and then consider any other relevant areas of the FSA Handbook.

You could have started by discussing the types of conflicts that can arise in the financial services industry and by then referring to these throughout the essay when discussing the rules. Conflicts can occur, for example, between the firm and client; between different clients, between areas of a firm, e.g. sales and research/corporate finance; and between the firm and employees.

Detailed discussion should have been made of Block 1 (High Level Standards) including

▓   The Principles for Businesses (PRIN). The main principle relating to conflicts is PRIN 8 and this should have been discussed in detail. In addition, a number of other Principles have relevance to conflict management such as PRIN 3 (Management and Control), PRIN 6 (Customer's interests), PRIN 1 (Integrity), PRIN 9 (Suitability) and a number of these could be mentioned.

▓   The Statements of Principle for Approved Persons (APER). Clearly, employees may suffer conflicts of interest in their dealings with customers and a number of the APER have relevance here, e.g. APER 1 (Integrity), APER 5 (Organisation of the business) and these could have been discussed.

▓   The Senior Management Arrangements, Systems and Controls Sourcebook (SYSC) has a number of important provisions which relate to conflict management. You could have mentioned the provisions in SYSC relating to organisation, compliance, management information and remuneration policies as examples of areas where management must consider procedures to deal with and manage conflicts.

The question also asks how conflicts are otherwise dealt with under the Handbook. You should have discussed the Conduct of Business Rules (COB) relating to conflicts, in particular

▓   COB 7.1 rules requiring firms to ensure they do not act where they have a material interest or a conflict of interest unless they have taken reasonable steps to ensure fair treatment. Discussion should have been made of the types of reasonable steps, e.g. Chinese walls, Policies of Independence, Disclosure and Declining to Act.

▓   Higher level candidates could also have discussed some other areas in COB which seek to manage conflicts such as the rules regarding personal account dealing, dealing ahead of publication, research churning, best execution, timely execution, customer order priority, aggregation of orders, realisation and lending.

▓   Higher level candidates may also have mentioned the common law which governs fiduciary relationships.

The question asks candidates to comment on the extent to which these rules control conflicts. Candidates should have discussed this. Some relevant points could include

▓   Existing rules provide a good standard of protection for conflict management within firms.

▓   Rules recognise the different nature and extent of conflicts that can arise and are largely not unduly prescriptive, which is laudable.

▓   Rules did not prevent a number of high profile conflicts scandals..

You could have mentioned the issues relating to analysts' research and FSA consultations and responses. Higher level candidates may have mentioned that COB rules are to be amended in 2004 to deal with a number of these issues and that there have been reports on similar issues in the US/IOSCO [now implemented in COB 7.16-17].

■ Conflicts still arise over remuneration tensions where sales generate commission/bonuses. You could have referred to misselling scandals such as split capital trusts, precipice bonds and endowments as examples of these problems.

■ Can conflicts ever fully be managed in large multiproduct, multidisciplinary firms?

Question 16.

This question is mainly factual in nature asking you to outline the FSA's enforcement powers in FSMA and the Handbook.

You should have discussed the main provisions in FSMA, including

■ Information gathering and investigation (S165).

■ Investigations (S167/8).

■ Support of overseas regulators (S169).

■ Obstructing an investigation (S177).

■ Reports by skilled persons (S169).

■ Varying/canceling permission (S45).

■ Vary/canceling approval.

■ Prohibition Orders (S56).

■ Redress.

■ Injunctions (S380).

■ Fines and censures.

■ Prosecutory powers for criminal/market abuse offences.

You should have discussed the fact that the details of the FSA enforcement powers are fleshed out in greater detail in the Enforcement Manual (ENF), which covers largely the same powers but explains the scope and criteria for use in further detail. You could have discussed the enforcement criteria and process of discipline. [You could mention the FSA's Enforcement Process Review of October 2005.]

Question 17.

NOTE THAT S118 FSMA WAS REVISED IN JULY 2005. THIS ANSWER REFLECTS THE POSITION AS AT THE TIME OF THIS EXAM. FOR CURRENT RULES, REFER TO YOUR STUDY BOOK.

This question is asking for a discussion of the market abuse regime and thus whilst the factual detail of the regime should have been fully discussed, candidates should also have discussed the extent to which the regime controls market abuse in reality.

Detailed explanation of the following should have been included

■ S118.

■ S119 and Code of Market Conduct (MAR).

■ Civil offence/penalties.

■ Scope of offence.

■ Regular market user test.

■ The three heads of abuse.

■ Defences and safe harbours.

Candidates should also have discussed some of the following.

◼ Rationale for introduction of regime.

◼ Role of exchanges in market abuse.

◼ Uncertainty of regime/will it work?

◼ Recent cases.

◼ Market Abuse Directive.

Question 18.

NOTE THAT THE SARS WERE ABOLISHED IN MAY 2006. THIS ANSWER REFLECTS THE POSITION AS AT THE TIME OF THIS EXAM. FOR CURRENT RULES, REFER TO YOUR STUDY BOOK.

This question is factual in nature and requires you to focus on both the purpose and the content of the Companies Act share disclosure rules and Substantial Acquisition Rules (SARS).

Candidates should have discussed the purpose of the disclosure rules. These include

◼ To ensure that public limited companies know who owns shares in the plc and that changes in ownership are promptly notified to the company to enable them to monitor ownership of the plc.

◼ In the case of the SARS, to prevent dawn raids of certain plcs and to ensure that a plc is aware of anyone building a substantial stake in the plc, which is often a precursor to a takeover bid. Disclosures have to be made earlier than under standard Companies Act requirements.

◼ The rationale for disclosures generally is that shareholder interests are paramount in companies and they must be treated fairly, not oppressed and have access to proper information.

◼ The rules also ensure proper markets, prevent distortion and encourage share ownership in the UK.

Candidates should have discussed the content of the rules, including

◼ Sections 198-211 Companies Act 1985 relating to disclosure of material and notifiable interests in plcs at 3% and 10% thresholds, ongoing disclosures up and down across a percentage point, concert parties, timing of disclosures (T + 2) and penalties for non-compliance.

◼ Section 212 Companies Act 1985 power to request information from shareholders of plcs regarding beneficial ownership, right of 10% shareholders to request this and penalties for non-compliance.

◼ The SARS written by The Panel on Takeovers and Mergers. Application to plcs listed on London Stock Exchange, AIM or OFEX.

◼ SARS Rule 1 and 2 restrict purchase of 10% or more shares, in the same seven-day period, from more than one shareholder, taking total holding to 15% or more.

◼ SARS Rule 3 disclosure to panel and market (via a Regulatory Information Service) by noon T + 1 of acquisitions reaching 15% or above and rising across each percentage point.

You could also have briefly mentioned the role of the Takeover Code and the general principles, as well as rule 8/38 of the Takeover Code regarding disclosures of interests in shares during a takeover.

Summer 2003 – Answers

Please note: the answers given have not been updated to reflect technical changes since the date of the exam and therefore this document is only intended to provide guidance on the suggested content of your answers. In particular, we have used bullet points throughout to highlight the areas you could have discussed or considered. In the examination, particularly with Section C questions, it may often be more appropriate to set out certain answers in paragraph form. To see the examiner's report on this exam, please go to www.sii.org.uk.

Section A

1.   The general functions of the FSA are set out in S2(4) of FSMA.

   ▪   Making rules under the FSMA.

   ▪   Preparing and issuing codes under FSMA.

   ▪   Giving general advice.

   ▪   Determining general policy and principles.

2.   You could have listed any four of the following:

   ▪   PRIN 1 – Integrity.

   ▪   PRIN 2 – Skill, Care and Diligence.

   ▪   PRIN 3 – Management and Control.

   ▪   PRIN 4 – Financial Prudence.

   ▪   PRIN 5 – Market Conduct.

   ▪   PRIN 6 – Customers Interests.

   ▪   PRIN 7 – Communication with Clients.

   ▪   PRIN 8 – Conflicts of Interest.

   ▪   PRIN 9 – Customers relationships of trust.

   ▪   PRIN 10 – Client Assets.

   ▪   PRIN 11 – Relations with Regulators.

3.   The financial promotion rules restrict to whom these promotions may be made. You could have listed three of the following.

   ▪   The communication is to a person covered by a relevant Financial Promotions Order exemption, e.g. a certified sophisticated investor.

   ▪   The communication is to market counterparty or intermediate customer.

   ▪   The communication is to an existing customer where the relationship envisages the call.

   ▪   The promotion relates to marketable non-geared packaged products.

   ▪   The promotion relates to services relating to readily realisable investments.

4.   You could have listed any three of the following.

   ▪   Money need not be segregated where an intermediate customer or market counterparty has opted out of client money and the appropriate notifications made.

   ▪   Where money is not to be treated as client money because it is due and payable to the firm, i.e. settlement money or fees payable to the firm.

■ Where the firm is itself an approved bank it need not segregate client funds from its own funds.

■ Money received from a client that is an affiliated company unless an arm's length customer.

■ Money held in connection with a delivery versus payment transaction.

5. You could have listed any four of each of the relevant functions as set out in SUP 10, e.g. Significant Influence Functions

These include functions 1-20 (please refer to your manual for the full list), for example

■ Director.

■ Money Laundering Reporting Officer.

■ Compliance Oversight.

■ Designated Investment Business.

NB: Please note that whilst the question asks you to refer to 'significant influence functions' which covers functions 1-20 the examiner's report only lists functions 16-20 which are the 'significant management functions'.

Customer Functions

These are functions 21-27 (please refer to your manual for the full list), for example:

■ Customer trading.

■ Investment adviser.

■ Investment management.

■ Corporate finance adviser.

6. NB: This question is rather ambiguous and it is unclear whether it is referring to controlled functions, provisions in SYSC or other requirements. The examiner's report refers to Principles 5, 6, and 7 of the Statements of Principle (APER).

7. You could have listed any three of the following.

■ Accountability to HM Treasury via annual report.

■ HM Treasury appointment of the FSA board and chairman.

■ Accountability to public via annual meeting.

■ Internal processes, e.g. corporate governance structures/Regulatory Decisions Committee.

■ Financial Services and Markets Tribunal final right to determine authorisation/ enforcement cases.

■ Competition scrutiny under S150 FSMA.

■ Requirement to consult on proposed new rules S155 FSMA.

■ Independent complaints commissioner as set out in COAF.

■ Principles of good regulation in S2 FSMA.

■ Judicial review.

■ Practitioner and consumer panels.

8. This question is asking you to consider the defences to market abuse.

    Under S123 FSMA, the FSA will not impose a financial penalty in two cases

    ■   Where a person believed on reasonable grounds that they were not committing market abuse or.

    ■   The person took all precautions and exercised all due diligence to avoid committing market abuse.

    In addition, behaviour will not amount to market abuse where the behaviour conforms with the Code of Market Conduct, e.g. where there is a safe harbour.

9. Cancellation rights include pre-sale withdrawal (seven days) and post-sale cancellation (14-30 days). These can be used for packaged products and you could have listed two packaged products, for example

    ■   Units in a unit trust.

    ■   Life policies.

10. You could have listed any of the examples set out in the manual, e.g.

    Recognised Investment Exchanges

    ■   London Stock Exchange.

    ■   London Metal Exchange.

    ■   International Petroleum Exchange (now ICE Futures).

    NB: The examiner's report refers to Tradepoint as an RIE; however, please be aware that Tradepoint was renamed as virt-x several years ago.

    Recognised Clearing Houses

    ■   London Clearing House (now known as LCH.Clearnet).

Section B

Question 11.

This question was concerned with client classification and documentation.

The classification rules are set out in Chapter 4 of COB and the glossary of terms. The documentation rules are also found in Chapter 4 of COB. According to Rule 4.1 of COB, before conducting designated investment business with a client the firm must classify them.

(a) As the fund is Cayman and non-regulated it does not appear to be an authorised firm although it may be an overseas financial services institution if regulated outside the UK. Unless it is an overseas financial services institution, it cannot be classified initially as a market counterparty.

If it is not an overseas financial services institution it is likely to be an unregulated collective investment scheme and would be classified as an intermediate customer. It would be possible for an unregulated collective investment scheme to opt up to market counterparty status if it is either a company or trust which meets the size criteria laid down in COB 4, e.g. £10m share capitalisation if a company and if a trust has assets of £10m or more and has received appropriate documentation.

If it is an intermediate customer, they will need to receive a terms of business unless they are execution only, in which case no agreement is required although you might suggest the firm provides documentation in any case to ensure the terms of the relationship are established.

(b) This client is an unregulated collective investment scheme. Under the classification rules, an unregulated collective investment scheme would automatically be treated as an intermediate customer.

They may opt up if they meet the criteria as discussed in (a). The securities firm may decide to treat some or all of its customers as private customers for ease of application of the rules. If they wish to do so they will have to send a written warning to the client advising them of this fact and that the client, whilst treated as a private customer, will be unable to use the Financial Ombudsman Service.

As above, they will need to receive a terms of business unless they are execution only, in which case no agreement is required.

(c) Megabank appears to be FSA authorised. This should be verified by checking on the FSA's register. If so they will be treated as a market counterparty. If the bank is acting for underlying customers, it may wish to opt down to intermediate customer status if Megabank and the securities firm agree.

If treated as a market counterparty, no client agreement or terms of business is required under COB rules. However, guidance in the FSA sourcebook entitled Inter-Professional Conduct (IPC) recommends that agreements are entered into as a matter of best practice.

(d) The treasury department of a company is responsible for the fund-raising and cash flow management of the company. Nothing in the question indicates the FTSE listed company is also an FSA authorised firm so you should not assume this.

The company will be an intermediate customer, as they are listed within the EEA. They may however wish to opt up to market counterparty status, which they can do if they have a share capitalisation of £10m or more, or meet any two of the following three tests: balance sheet total ≥ €12.5m; turnover ≥ €25m; or average employees in the year ≥ 250. In addition, both parties must agree and the company must receive a one-way warning of the protections that they will lose (such as the right to best execution).

If classified as an intermediate customer, they will require a terms of business.

(e)   The overseas individual must still be classified in the same way as a UK individual. Prima facie, he would appear to be a private customer. We know he has one year's experience of equities trading. Whether he can be treated as an intermediate customer (expert) will depend on whether we can establish that he has sufficient experience and understanding to be treated as an expert and understand the risks involved. We do not have enough information here. We should ascertain the frequency of previous trading, whether it was done on a discretionary/advisory basis, his financial standing and his knowledge of the markets he wishes to trade in with us. Following that assessment, if we reasonably believe he has enough knowledge and experience and wants to opt up, we can treat him as an expert provided he has received a written warning of the protections he will lose and has consented to treatment as an expert either orally or in writing after sufficient time to consider.

If he is a private customer, he will require a two-way client agreement if he is to be a discretionary customer, or be involved in stock lending, underwriting or derivatives trades. The only exception is that as an overseas customer if he does not want to receive a two-way agreement, we can send him a one-way terms of business. If he is an expert he will receive a terms of business.

Question 12.

This question was generally concerned with the authorisation, passporting, stock lending and financial promotions rules.

(a)   You should have considered the following.

- ▓   The provision of regulated activities by way of business in or into the UK requires authorisation under S19 of the FSMA. The penalties for breaching should have been mentioned.

- ▓   Where an authorised firm wishes to expand the scope of the regulated activities or specified investments that it wishes to undertake it must apply for an extension to its permissions.

Where a person goes beyond their permitted permissions, this is an offence under S20 FSMA, which is punishable primarily by FSA fines and censures although it is not an imprisonable offence as it is a breach of S19.

- ▓   The additional regulated activities under the Regulated Activities Order appear to be safeguarding and administering investments, although the specified investments are unclear but would presumably cover investments such as shares and tradable debt.

(b)   You should have considered the following.

- ▓   The Spanish bank has a branch in London. This branch may be operating under existing passporting rights established under the Banking Consolidation Directives (BCD) and/or the Investment Services Directive (ISD). To passport, the Spanish bank would have approached its home state regulator that it wished to open a branch in the UK. The Spanish regulators would have liaised with the FSA to determine any additional requirements that the FSA had for the Spanish firm. The provision of the passport would mean that the Spanish branch was authorised for the purposes of S19 FSMA.

- ▓   However, any passport only relates to the activities notified when the passport was provided so the Spanish Bank would have to re-approach the Spanish regulators/FSA and explain their further plans. If the activity is covered by the BCD as an Annex activity there should be no major issue as long as the firm is deemed fit and proper to provide these activities. If the passport falls under the ISD custody it is a non-core activity so can only be passported if the bank is also passporting core activities such as dealing.

(c)   You should have considered the following.

▪   The passporting directives establish home and host state responsibilities, so it is clear which regulator, i.e. Spanish or UK, has responsibility for the passporting firm. Generally, the Spanish regulator would retain jurisdiction over the bank for prudential supervision (capital adequacy), authorisation and the determination of fitness and propriety. The prudential requirements should not be dissimilar between the two regulators due to the EU Capital Adequacy Directive. The host state regulator, i.e. FSA, would govern compliance with UK Conduct of Business (COB) rules generally.

▪   In terms of the relationship with customers generally when providing services to UK customers, UK COB will apply so the bank must apply the classification, dealing and managing rules, etc. of the COB. In terms of the provision of custody services, these are found within the client assets chapter of COB (Chapter 9). [Note this has since been moved to CASS.] The rules on client assets are actually reserved to the home state regulator, so when providing custody services in the UK, the bank must apply the Spanish custody rules. This is largely to ensure assets are held in accordance with the rules that would govern the bank's insolvency if this were to occur.

(d)   You should have considered the following.

▪   The requirement for a two-way client agreement before any stock lending were to occur.

▪   The requirement to send a risk warning of the risks attached to stock lending, i.e. the fact that and lending may create a disposal for tax purposes (CGT) and that legal rights attaching to the shares such as voting rights will pass to the borrower. This warning can be written or verbal and does not need to be acknowledged by the customer.

(e)   You should have considered the following.

▪   Any sales and promotion of the custody services would be likely to constitute a financial promotion as defined in FSMA. As a result under S21 FSMA, it would have to be issued or approved by an authorised firm. If the passport is extended, then the bank will be authorised.

▪   Under Chapter 3 of COB, the bank must follow the detailed rules relating to the form and contents of such financial promotions and some examples should be given, e.g. all promotions must be clear, fair and not misleading (fleshing out PRIN 7), real and non-real time rules.

▪   You could have mentioned the impact of the E-Commerce Directive which may affect the rules which apply to the financial promotion if the promotion originates from Spain, i.e. electronically at a distance.

Question 13.

This question requires you to identify and discuss the issues and problems that arise rather than search for an absolute right answer in terms of the advice you give. The question covers the Principles for Businesses, Market Abuse, Insider Dealing and Misleading Statements.

(a)   The concern with this proposal relates to conflicts of interest and concerns relating to the acquisition of inside information. You should have discussed the following.

▪   The requirement to control conflicts of interest under the FSA's Principles for Businesses (PRIN 8) and the specific Conduct of Business Rules in this area including Chinese walls. The conflict here occurs because the corporate finance department want to win the work they are pitching for. The equity analysts should be issuing research based on the merits of a stock or transaction. By having an analyst at the pitch, this may undermine the integrity of the analyst's research going forward. The firm must remember that it owes duties to all of its clients when it issues that research to them. Mr Neck should be aware that whilst the practice of taking analysts to pitches has been common in the past, as a result of recent major conflicts of interest in the US, the FSA has recently proposed new rules to restrict this practice in Consultation Paper 171. [Note these have since been implemented in COB.]

■ The problems where an analyst becomes an Insider under the Criminal Justice Act 1993 and S118 and 397 of FSMA.

(b) The concern with this proposal is that Neck appears to be considering the order flow and profit generation of the firm and his department over the interests of the client. You should have discussed the following.

■ The private client department's obligations to their customers under PRIN 6 – Customers interests, PRIN 9 – Customers relationships of trust.

■ COB rules on best execution, which requires the firm to obtain the best price for a transaction's time, kind and size. If the firm is obtaining the best price, this is not objectionable but clear controls and checks would need to be implemented to ensure that this is the case. He should be reminded that execution via SETS currently evidentially proves best execution.

■ COB suitability rules.

■ You could have mentioned that it is unclear where the large lines of stock that he wants to give the private client department are coming from. If these are as a result of IPOs, CP 171 also addressed issues of spinning in new issues and recommends that allocation of IPOs is centralised and controlled with proper oversight. If the firm has proprietary positions in these stocks, this must be disclosed to clients [now implemented in COB].

■ There could also be concern that these allocations are to create commission for the equities division which needs 'reinvigorating' and this could be construed as churning.

(c) This is unlikely to be allowable. You should have discussed the offences, defences and penalties in relation to

■ Insider Dealing (CJA 93).

■ Market Abuse (S118 FSMA).

■ S397 FSMA.

■ You could have mentioned breaches of the UKLA listing rules.

The corporate finance department may conduct a briefing once the announcement is made to the market, but this should only cover information that has been made public.

(d) I would question why the equities division staff want this information. The point of S212 is to allow the company to find out who the underlying beneficial owners are, often to ascertain whether a takeover bid is imminent. The nominee and safe custody department owe duties of confidentiality to the shareholders they act for and should not breach this. You should have discussed:

■ Conflicts of interest.

■ Insider dealing.

■ Market abuse.

■ Section 397.

NOTE THAT PARTS OF POCA WERE REVISED BY THE SERIOUS ORGANISED CRIME AND POLICE ACT (SOCA) IN JULY 2005 AND THE MONEY LAUNDERING SOURCEBOOK HAS BEEN INTEGRATED INTO SYSC. THIS ANSWER REFLECTS THE POSITION AS AT THE TIME OF THE EXAM. FOR INFORMATION ON SOCA PLEASE REFER TO YOUR STUDY BOOK.

14. This question relates to money laundering issues and requires you to identify and discuss the issues and problems that arise. You should have discussed primarily the Proceeds of Crime Act 2002 and the FSA Money Laundering Sourcebook (MLS).

NB: Although the question does not ask us specifically to consider the Money Laundering Regulations 1993 and 2001 (MLR) the examiner's report does cover these in detail. There is much overlap between the MLS and the MLR.

Proceeds of Crime Act 2002 (POCA) – this should have been covered in detail including:

■ POCA applies to the proceeds of criminal activity whether the crime was committed in the UK or abroad as long as it would be an offence if it had been committed in the UK. The issue is that Esteban made his money from bullfighting, which may be legal in his native country, but appears to be illegal in the UK. De facto, therefore, it appears the funds he is going to invest may be the proceeds of crime under POCA definitions.

■ The assistance offence: including definition of assistance and penalties (14 years' imprisonment and/or an unlimited fine). The requirement for knowledge or suspicion. The defences should have been discussed including reporting to NCIS and getting their agreement to proceed.

■ The reporting offence: Coverage of the regulated sector. The need to report any knowledge, suspicion or reasonable grounds for suspicion to NCIS and penalties (five years' imprisonment and/or an unlimited fine).

■ The tipping off offence: The definition and penalties (five years' imprisonment and/or an unlimited fine). This offence is important regarding the call from Esteban about the delay. You must ensure he is not aroused to the concerns.

The MLS and MLR requirements

■ Identification and Know Your Customer requirements. What clients need to be identified and any exceptions, suitable forms of identity. We must establish the reason for establishing the relationship. Why does Esteban want to start using Poundwise? The expected pattern of activity and source of funds.

■ The requirement to ensure all staff are aware of what might be suspicious, how and where to report suspicions and ensure these are followed up. This involves proper training.

■ Additional requirements in the MLS for the MLRO, i.e. approved person status, review international findings such as that of FATF and prepare an annual report to senior management.

■ Effect of breach of these requirements can result in FSA discipline such as censures, fine and loss of authorisation. Breach of MLR a criminal offence (two years and unlimited fines).

Section C

Remember that Section C answers are often subjective and as such, there is no real 'model' answer. In the exam, you should have written these as essays rather than using bullet point format. However, the answers set out below simply list some of the areas or arguments that you could have raised and these are listed in bullet point for ease of review.

Question 15.

This question is asking for a discussion of the provisions of S19/20 and 21 FSMA, although the main focus should have been the financial promotions rules. Candidates could have considered the following.

- Describe the authorisation and permission system under S19 and S20, i.e.

    - The general prohibition requirement to be authorised if doing regulated activities regarding specified investment and not exempt or excluded

    - Criminal/civil penalties for breaching the general prohibition

    - Requirement not to go beyond permissions granted (S20) and consequences of going beyond permissions, i.e. not criminal but fines, censures, etc.

- Describe the financial promotions regime under S21, i.e.

    - Financial promotions made or directed at persons in the UK must be issued/approved by an authorised firm

    - What is a financial promotion? An invitation or inducement to engage in investment activity communicated in the course of business

    - Mention exemptions exist as set out in the Financial Promotions Order

    - Penalties for breach of S21, i.e. criminal offence – two years' imprisonment, fines, injunctions, etc.

- Discuss the separate but parallel nature of the two regimes – issuing a financial promotion is not in itself a regulated activity, so don't need authorisation to issue it under S19, but under S21, an authorised firm would have to approve it. You could have discussed why the rules are structured this way, e.g. the FSA must consider principles of good regulation – arguably as long as an authorised firm signs off, the issuer need not be authorised, i.e. regulation must be proportionate.

- The COB financial promotions rules (exemptions, real and non-real time rules).

- Your conclusion could have commented on the success of the financial promotions rules, e.g. split capital investment trusts.

Question 16.

This question is asking you to consider the extent to which, under FSMA, the FSA are now expecting firms to take more internal controls proactively rather than relying on FSA external supervision.

Candidates could have opened with a discussion of some the following points.

- Focus on senior management responsibility post-Barings.

- Lots of examples of misselling, e.g. pensions. Why were failures not picked up at senior levels?

- Equitable Life management – have they been held accountable enough for their actions?

- The FSA has limited resources and approximately 14,000 [as at Summer 2003] firms to supervise, thus possibly inevitably they need firms to use more internal controls. Traditional supervision based on prudential returns and report and occasional meetings no longer enough.

- Focus on placing responsibility with the right people.

Detailed discussion should have been made of the relevant provisions within the FSA Handbook and what they require senior management to consider and implement within the firm, e.g.

■ Principles for Businesses – PRIN 3 (management and control).

■ Statements of Principle – APER 5,6,7 (for significant influence functions).

■ Senior Management Arrangements, Systems and Controls (SYSC) – rules and guidance, e.g. apportionment and recording, compliance functions, audit, employees, risk management, remuneration.

■ Threshold Conditions and the Fit and Proper test for approved persons.

■ Requirements on senior management to implement training and competence requirements under the TC sourcebook.

Contrast with external supervisory powers of FSA, e.g.

■ FSA investigation.

■ FSA discipline and enforcement.

The conclusion could have covered a number of areas, e.g.

■ That some rules are new, e.g. SYSC.

■ Some rules have been fleshed out in more detail, e.g. TC, APER.

■ Perhaps, the major shift will be in FSA enforcement policy on a more top-down basis. However, you could have mentioned that recent fines for the questionable spread bet placed by the plumber and others fined individuals rather than their firms or senior managers!.

■ Finally, why is this focus on controls and responsibilities important? Reference to the FSA regulatory objectives would be a good reason, e.g. market confidence.

Question 17.

This question is essentially factual in nature asking you to explain takeover and acquisition rules and principles that apply in the UK. It is not seeking detailed discussion of the merits of such principles, simply an explanation of those requirements. You should have covered

■ The fact that takeovers are regulated primarily by the Panel on Takeovers and Mergers and explain briefly its structure.

■ The ten principles laid down in the Takeover Code [now 6].

■ The bid timetable.

■ Possibly more detail on a couple of the main rules of the takeover code, e.g.

    — Rule 8/38 Disclosures

    — Rule 4 Insider dealing

    — Rule 5 Acquisition of control

    — Rule 9 Mandatory bids.

    [Note that some of the rules are no longer on the syllabus.]

■ The Substantial Acquisition Rules [now abolished].

■ Companies Act notification requirements.

■ Higher level candidates could have mentioned the FSA jurisdiction in respect of market abuse and the memorandum of understanding between the FSA and the panel and the takeover directive.

■ A detailed conclusion would not be necessary as this essay is factual in nature.

Question 18.

This question is essentially factual in nature and should cover the main markets and trading systems.

[Note that the level of detail for this question is no longer on the syllabus. Also SEAQ International has now been replaced by the International Order Book, the International Bulletin Board and the International Retail Service.]

Main LSE markets

▓ The domestic equity market – where the exchange ensures an adequate and liquid secondary market in UK shares.

▓ The international equity market. Analogous to the domestic equity market where the exchange ensures a liquid market place in selected international shares using the SEAQ International system.

▓ The gilt-edged market. One of the requirements for market makers is that they are also members of the Stock Exchange and therefore abide by the Stock Exchange's dealing rules. These rules will also cover domestic fixed interest securities.

▓ The traditional options market. The traditional options market is a very limited market place, offering highly tailored options into any equity available on the exchange.

Main trading systems with dealing and reporting requirements

A good number of the following should have been outlined.

▓ LSE Rule 3000 limits the trades which can be done on the exchange.

▓ LSE Rule 3040 the exchange can prohibit or suspend dealings in certain circumstances.

▓ Outline the main trading systems (SETS, SEAQ, SEATS Plus and SEAQ International).

▓ SETS orders (Limit orders, At Best orders, Execute and Eliminate orders, Fill or Kill orders or Market orders). Different characteristics, trading limits as to the minimum tick and order size, T – 3 settlement.

▓ SEAQ system – must attract a minimum of two market makers. Only market makers can display quotes on the SEAQ screen, becoming a market maker, requirement to quote firm two-way prices during the Mandatory Quote Period up to the Minimum Quote Size.

▓ SEATS Plus system – combination of a quote and order-driven system.

▓ SEAQI – MarketMatch system for screen-based order book trades but also market maker support.

▓ Trade reporting for market transparency. SETS trades automatic, hierarchy of reporting, contents and time of report.

▓ Transaction reporting for regulatory purposes. Both parties to report via a designated systems, time limits and contents.

▓ A detailed conclusion would not be necessary as this essay is factual in nature.

NB: The examiner's report suggests reference to alternative market rules such as virt-x, OFEX or ATS's should have been mentioned although the question does not specifically request this.

Winter 2002 – Answers

Please note: the answers given have not been updated to reflect technical changes since the date of the exam and therefore this document is only intended to provide guidance on the suggested content of your answers. In particular, we have used bullet points throughout to highlight the areas you could have discussed or considered. In the examination, particularly with Section C questions, it may often be more appropriate to set out certain answers in paragraph form. To see the examiner's report on this exam, please go to www.sii.org.uk.

Section A

1. The four statutory objectives of the FSA are as follows.

    ▪ Maintaining confidence in the UK financial system.

    ▪ Promoting public awareness of the UK financial system.

    ▪ Securing the appropriate degree of protection for consumers.

    ▪ Reducing the extent to which it is possible for financial businesses to be sued for financial crime.

    You could have listed any four of the following principles of good regulation.

    ▪ The need to use its resources in the most efficient and economic way (economic efficiency).

    ▪ The responsibilities of those who manage the affairs of authorised persons (management function and responsibility).

    ▪ The principle that a burden or restriction that is imposed on a person (or the carrying on of an activity) should be proportionate to benefits considered in general terms expected to result from the burden or restriction (proportionality or subsidiarity).

    ▪ The desirability of facilitating innovation in connection with regulated activities (innovation).

    ▪ The international character of financial services and markets and the desirability of maintaining the competitive position of the United Kingdom (international competition).

    ▪ The need to minimise the adverse effects on competition that may arise from anything done in the discharge of the FSA's functions (competitive damage).

    ▪ The desirability of facilitating competition between those who are subject to any form of regulation by the FSA (general competition).

2. An authorised person is a natural or legal person who has been given permission under Part IV of the Financial Services and Markets Act 2000 (FSMA) to undertake regulated activities by way of business in the UK. A person who is carrying out such regulated activities regarding specified investments must seek authorisation in order to comply with S19 of FSMA unless they have an exemption. Failure to do so may result in criminal and civil penalties. Authorisation can be obtained by obtaining Part IV permission, via passporting or treaty rights.

    An exempt person is a natural or legal person who would appear to require authorisation under S19 FSMA, but falls within an exemption. The exemptions are set out in secondary legislation drafted by HM Treasury (2001 Exemptions Order). Examples of an exempt person would include certain institutions such as the Bank of England, members of professions (e.g. lawyers) carrying out incidental regulated activities and the activities of recognised investment exchanges and clearing houses.

3. You could have listed any four of the following Threshold Conditions.

    ▓   Legal Status – this requires that where certain activities are being undertaken, such as deposit taking, that the institution is structured in a particular legal fashion.

    ▓   Adequate Resources – a firm must have adequate financial and human resources.

    ▓   Location of offices – generally, if a firm is incorporated in the UK, it must have its head and registered offices located in the UK.

    ▓   Suitability – the firm must be suitable to undertake the activities it seeks permission to undertake.

    ▓   Close Links – will any close links with other companies or entities hinder effective supervision by the FSA?

4. You should have picked any four regulated activities covered by FSMA, e.g.

    ▓   Dealing in investments as principal or agent.

    ▓   Arranging deals in investments.

    ▓   Safeguarding and administering investments.

    ▓   Establishing or operating a collective investment scheme.

    You should have picked any four investments covered by FSMA, e.g.

    ▓   Deposits.

    ▓   Futures for investment purposes.

    ▓   Shares in any company.

    ▓   Government or corporate debt.

    Other examples of activities and investments you could have listed can be found on pages 9-10 of Chapter 1 of your Study Book.

5. In certain circumstances a firm can treat an intermediate customer as a private customer. A firm can treat any intermediate customer as private customer (other than an authorised firm or overseas financial services institution) under Chapter 4 of the Conduct of Business rules where it notifies the intermediate customer of this fact. This is often done for administrative ease and ease of applicability of rules.

    The firm should however warn the intermediate customer it is treating as a private customer that they may not be treated as a private customer for the purposes of other rules such as the right to use the Financial Ombudsman Service or Financial Services Compensation Scheme.

6. You could have referred to any two key obligations relating to management functions as set out in

    ▓   Senior Management Arrangements, Systems and Controls (SYSC).

    ▓   The Statements of Principle for Approved Persons (APER), in particular numbers 5-7, which only apply to those carrying out a significant influence function.

    ▓   The Supervision manual (SUP).

    ▓   The Principles for Businesses (PRIN).

    ▓   The Interim Prudential sourcebooks (IPRU).

7.   The first main requirement relating to financial promotions is found in S21 of FSMA. This provides that a financial promotion must be issued or approved by an authorised person. The purpose of this is to ensure that an authorised firm takes responsibility for promotions that invite or induce others to enter into investment agreements. In addition, there are further requirements in the Conduct of Business rules (Chapter 3), which apply primarily where a firm is promoting to a private customer. COB 3 covers rules relating to the content and format of promotions and who they can be made to. The main exceptions to these rules are set out in both the Financial Promotions Order (which is drafted by HM Treasury) and in COB itself.

8.   **NOTE THAT S118 FSMA WAS REVISED IN JULY 2005. THIS ANSWER REFLECTS THE POSITION AS AT THE TIME OF THIS EXAM. FOR CURRENT RULES, REFER TO YOUR STUDY BOOK.**

The Regular Market User test relates to the offence of market abuse set out in S118 of FSMA. In particular, it determines whether the three types of abuse (misuse of information, false/misleading impressions or market distortion) have occurred. The meaning of this test is fleshed out in the FSA's Code of Market Conduct. The regular market user is a hypothetical reasonable person who trades regularly on the market in question. Behaviour must fall below the standards expected of the regular market user in order to constitute market abuse.

9.   You could have listed any four of the following types of administrative sanction:

   ▓   Private warning.

   ▓   Public censure.

   ▓   Fines.

   ▓   Withdrawal/variation of permission.

   ▓   Injunctions.

   ▓   Restitution.

10.   Three forms of redress are set out in Block 4 of the FSA Handbook.

   ▓   Dispute resolution, including utilising the Financial Ombudsman System (DISP).

   ▓   Utilising the Financial Services Compensation Scheme (COMP).

   ▓   Making a complaint against the FSA to the Complaints Commissioner (COAF).

Section B

Question 11.

This question was generally concerned with the financial promotions regime with specific reference to offering financial services over the internet. Additional issues arose with the EU nature of the activities involved (being offered from Italy)

(a)　This element is asking whether FSMA may apply to the activities of an Italian firm. You could have considered the following issues.

    ▪   Offering financial services which constitute financial promotions may be subject to the restriction set out in S21 of FSMA, which requires that a person must not, in the course of business, communicate an invitation or inducement to engage in investment activity unless the person is either authorised or the content of the communication has been approved by an authorised person. This constitutes a separate statutory restriction in addition to the general prohibition imposed under S19.

        The restriction in S21 applies to communications originating outside the United Kingdom where the communication is capable of having an effect in the United Kingdom because it is made to or directed at UK individuals. Applicable exemptions are set out in the Financial Promotions Order issued by the Treasury although we do not have enough information to determine whether any will apply.

        The unenforceability of agreements resulting from unlawful communications is dealt with under S30 FSMA.

    ▪   In addition to the above higher level, candidates may have discussed the territorial scope in more detail. Traditionally, FSMA will apply whenever a financial promotion is 'made to' or 'directed at' persons in the UK. However, as a result of the EU E-Commerce Directive, which was implemented in 2002, 'E-Commerce Activities' (i.e. those that are provided electronically at a distance in the EEA) are subject to 'Home State' rules. Therefore, if the Italian company's promotion falls within the definition of E-Commerce Activities, whilst the company would need permission to offer these services in the UK, the Italian rule book and regulations will apply to the internet promotions rather than FSMA and associated UK rules.

(b)　The Regulated Activities Order sets out a number of regulated activities in respect of specified investments. If a person is conducting such activities in the UK by way of business then the provisions of FSMA will apply. It is clear that the Italian firm is considering providing financial services and issuing promotions in respect of them, and the regulated activities of dealing, arranging, advising or managing may well apply although we do not have enough detail to be clear which activities apply.

Candidates should have discussed the fact that if the activities were deemed to constitute the carrying out of regulated activities in the UK the company would be required under S19 of FSMA to be authorised unless it was exempt or excluded from authorisation under the secondary legislation. You should have mentioned the civil and criminal penalties for breach of S19 and that there is a defence if the person exercised reasonable precautions and due diligence to avoid committing the offence.

In addition, stronger candidates may have mentioned that the company would have to consider the best means of obtaining authorisation (Part IV permission, passporting, treaty rights) and would also have to consider other effects such as whether their capital adequacy requirements are altered by their cross-border activities. This is likely to be the case due to the Capital Adequacy Directive, which would be likely to apply.

(c)   Candidates should have discussed in some detail the three main methods of becoming an authorised person.

■   Applying to the FSA for Part IV permission.

■   Passporting rights.

■   Treaty rights.

(d)   Candidates could have mentioned the following.

■   COB specific guidance on the internet and use of electronic media. In particular, the rules/guidance relating to key features documents, application forms and where a firm markets unregulated collective investment schemes.

■   General Conduct of Business rules (COB) regarding ensuring that an individual with appropriate expertise checks that the promotion is clear, fair and not misleading, monitoring the promotion to ensure that it continues to meet this requirement, and ensuring the promotion must contain details of the firm's name and address or a contact point from which the address may be obtained.

■   Stronger candidates may have mentioned that the firm should consider other general laws such as the Data Protection Act (although candidates are not required to know the detail of the Act).

(e)   Candidates should explain that where the company is conducting Designated Investment Business with clients, it must classify them under COB rules and explain the different classifications available and the ability to opt up or down. They should then have explained who gets what agreements, e.g. Private Discretionary Customers, Private Customers undertaking contingent liability, underwriting or stock lending transactions need two-way client agreements, etc., and when they should be provided.

Question 12.

The question is generally concerned with the marketing and sale of unregulated collective investment schemes.

(a)   Candidates should have explained that the activities of establishing and operating a collective investment scheme are regulated activities under the Regulated Activities Order as long as they are carried out by way of business in the UK and that units in a collective investment scheme are specified investments. They therefore require authorisation under S19 of FSMA.

(b)   In this element, candidates should have discussed S238 of FSMA and the Promotion of Collective Investment Schemes Order 2001 which provide that Unregulated CISs can only be sold to existing or recent participants or those the firm deems it is suitable for. You should explain that the definition of Unregulated CIS excludes authorised unit trusts or authorised OEICs. You should also mention that these cannot be sold by way of direct offer financial promotion unless directed to suitable candidates. Where sold via the internet, it is important that there is a very clear indication to whom they are being marketed.

(c)   The firm should ensure that these persons do meet the criteria to be Certified High Net Worth Individuals (i.e. explain in detail the asset/income tests) and that they have signed an agreement agreeing to be certified as such. Candidates should have explained that the exemption is set out in the Financial Promotions Order and applies only to unlisted securities so procedures should be put in place to ensure this is the case. In addition, the firm should ensure that Principle 7 of PRIN is complied with in that the promotion must be clear, fair and not misleading.

(d)   You could have listed any four of the following.

- Existing participants of a substantially similar scheme.

- Persons who have participated in substantially similar schemes in the last 30 months.

- Market counterparties.

- Investment professionals.

- High net worth companies.

- Sophisticated investors.

- Those for whom the firm has taken steps to ensure the investment is suitable.

(e)   As discussed, S238 limits who a promotion of an unregulated CIS can be made to. In addition, the form of promotion suggested is a direct offer financial promotion as it can be bought directly off the page/website. The firm must ensure that the promotion is made to those for whom it is suitable so it must not be on a general web page which can be accessed by all internet users. The firm could consider a password system for existing customers, clear disclaimers as to whom the promotion is directed at and ensure that applications made by customers who are not suitable or not already investing in similar schemes are not processed. All of the above procedures should be properly documented and staff trained on the procedures.

Question 13.

The question is generally concerned with the conditions for determining whether market abuse or an insider dealing offence have been committed. Chinese walls and high level standards are also relevant as well as other dealing and listing requirements.

(a)   At this stage, you should consider in detail the offences of

- Insider dealing. Are Basil/Norbert 'inside sources'? Is it 'inside information'? Have they dealt, encouraged, disclosed? Defences and penalties. In particular, is the information specific/precise and price sensitive and has it been obtained by virtue of office, employment or duties?

- Market abuse offence relating to the above. You should have set out the tests and defences and in particular discussed whether the information was generally available. It is unlikely that either false or misleading impressions or market distortion have occurred.

- S397 – have any of the parties made false or misleading statements?

- Stronger candidates may also have mentioned whether there have been breaches of the listing rules by Popcat or SYSC/PRIN by Dumbarton Bank or APER by any approved persons.

(b)   This question wants you to focus on Max's behaviour not Basil's.

- Has Max committed insider dealing? You should have worked through the tests for insider dealing and the offences (disclosure, encourage) and the tests for market applying these to facts.

- Apply the disclosure to the market abuse offence detailed earlier.

- Stronger candidates may have mentioned that there seems to have been a breach of fiduciary duties by Max that he owes to the shareholders of Popcat. His actions may also have breached the Listing Rules and that the procedures in place appear to be weak as to the dissemination of price-sensitive information.

(c)   Basil cannot change sell recommendation to buy as that would be using inside information.

■   Basil cannot leave as a sell as this would be a breach of S397/market abuse.

■   The best course of action is to speak to compliance. The analyst would usually be removed from acting until the information was made public.

■   The company should be encouraged to make a disclosure as soon as possible to the market.

(d)   Concerns now include the following.

■   Breach of Chinese walls between research and sales in the firm and PRIN 8.

■   Raises issues regarding systems and controls and training due to the breakdown of systems.

■   Reapply the insider dealing/market abuse/S397 offences to the further actions by each party.

■   The last part of the question regarding whether the position would change if Dallas had solicited the order from Stan without telling Stan why, is driving at the offence of 'encouraging'. Candidates should have noted that no information needs to have passed for someone to be guilty of encouraging under the insider dealing legislation.

Question 14.

It is important, particularly in a lengthy question such as this, to appropriately structure the response and answer precisely. The question wants you to identify suspicions, concerns and action rather than waffle generally! Some of the areas you could have mentioned are as follows.

Case 1

Suspicions and Concerns

■   Cash payment of balance could be placement of funds.

■   Obtaining loan and reselling cars and receiving cheques looks like layering. Is it unusual client activity?

■   Activities which may lead to losses, i.e. the early redemption of loans leading to a penalty raise suspicions.

■   Frequent buying and selling of cars raises suspicions where there is no real rationale for the actions other than boredom.

■   Appears to be money laundering.

Actions

■   A report should be made to the company's nominated officer/police authorities and on to NCIS.

■   Management should be advised of the issue.

■   Ensure no one tips off Ray that a report has been made as under the Criminal Justice Act (now POCA) this is a criminal offence.

■   There is concern that previous transactions have not raised suspicions, consider internal procedures and training requirements and look for similar patterns of behaviour with other clients.

Case 2

Suspicions and Concerns

■   Money exchange offices/bureaux de change commonly used to launder funds.

■   Potentially no discernible need to use the firm as he has accounts elsewhere and not clear why this one is needed.

■   Unusual activity concerning multiple currency exchanges for a personal account.

- Evidence of potential fraud/theft by manager of money from exchange office.

- Staff should be aware of level of transactions even if they did not effect them (e.g. via electronic records being updated and accessible), are procedures adequate in the bank? (SYSC) and training.

- Third-party payments rouse suspicions.

- Payment to jurisdiction with historic banking secrecy laws arouses some suspicions (although it is not a FATF non-cooperative jurisdiction).

- The remitter is the manager not the firm, which looks like layering to muddy the audit trail.

Actions

- The bank must follow the Money Laundering Regulations 1993. [Note that these have since been updated to 2003 version] and the FSA Money Laundering sourcebook if it is an authorised firm which is highly likely [Note this has since moved into SYSC].

- A report should be made to the MLRO/NCIS without delay.

- The firm should ensure they do not tip him off, and you should delay the transfer whilst waiting for NCIS to respond by saying there is not enough credit in the account (it is unclear whether this is the case).

- Ensure that full records of identification and all transactions are available should there be an investigation by the authorities.

- Review the business account for any other suspicious activity.

- Consider whether this business relationship should be allowed to continue.

- Customer activity should be closely monitored.

Case 3

Suspicions and Concerns

- Are these suspicious jurisdictions? Not according to FATF guidelines but offshore centres should be treated more carefully. Why does he need an account here?

- If the company is setting up property funds this is a regulated activity, so are they authorised?

- Identification has occurred but do we have enough KYC information?

- Wire transfers and cash withdrawals appear to be layering.

- Payment to a law firm is not in accordance with KYC information – what has this to do with housing schemes in deprived areas?

- Excessive inward wire transfers do not appear to have been contemplated when the account was set up.

Actions

- Depending on the type of entity, the Money Laundering Regulations and/or FSA rules may apply.

- Make a suspicious transaction report to NCIS.

- You must carefully weigh up offences of assistance and tipping off under the CJA 93 (now POCA) to ensure neither committed and seek advice from NCIS as to whether to make the payment immediately as there is enough money in the account.

- Consider with the authorities whether the relationship can continue or whether the account should be closed.

Case 4

Suspicions and Concerns

- Holding and transferring commodities in bearer form in large quantities may raise suspicions of layering, particularly given the security risk of collecting bullion personally, so why would he take this risk?

- Fraud issues as paid for by company but controlled by him?

- How could Midas buy bullion from the bank and sell it for such a profit when considering the additional costs of security and transportation involved?

- The absence of a clear commercial rationale for the business and the nature of the trade, precious metals, should arouse concerns about money laundering.

- Could Midas be evading Customs Duty by smuggling gold overseas for sale in the open market?

- Third-party payments into the account may be suspicious but could just reflect regular commercial activity – consider whether the payments came from a UK or EU authorised bank.

Actions

- Whilst there is no proof that the funds into the account are the proceeds of any crime, it would be appropriate to submit a suspicious report to NCIS.

- If sufficiently concerned, the account relationship should be terminated, subject to approval by any investigation authority.

- Consider alerting Customs.

- Have proper ID and KYC procedures for both Midas and the company been undertaken? These should be reviewed to assess the pattern of activity.

- Ensure risk of fraud is minimised by checking signatories relating to the company account.

Section C

Remember that Section C answers are often subjective and as such, there is no real 'model' answer. In the exam, you should have written these as essays rather than using bullet point format. However, the answers set out below simply list some of the areas or arguments that you could have raised and these are listed in bullet point format for ease of review.

Question 15.

This question is asking more for factual detail than for a journalistic view of whether the FSA is accountable or not. Candidates could have considered the following.

■ Accountability to HM Treasury (annual report, attending select committees).

■ Public meetings.

■ The processes set out in DEC, i.e. the use of the RDC and the Financial Services and Markets Tribunal.

■ Internal corporate governance.

■ The Consumer and Practitioner panels that the FSA must have regard to.

■ The requirement under FSMA to consult on rules.

■ The role of the Complaints Commissioner for complaints against the FSA.

■ The ability to use judicial review.

■ The regulatory objectives and principles of good regulation that they must consider.

■ The jurisdiction of the competition authorities to deal with anti-competitive behaviour by the FSA.

Question 16.

This question wants the candidate to look at the purpose and main rules so will be largely a factual discussion. Candidates should have mentioned a good number of the following.

■ Requirement under S59 of FSMA for those carrying out controlled functions to be approved.

■ That this requirement is fleshed out in the Handbook, specifically SUP (which lists the controlled functions), and set out what types of function are covered.

■ The rationale for the regime being those who govern or manage firms or do customer functions must be fit and proper. This links to FSA's objectives of market confidence and consumer protection.

■ Firms must get persons approved by submitting Form A. Firms should ensure persons applying for approval should meet the criteria in FIT (honesty, integrity, etc.). Firms should also notify the FSA of changes to functions of those approved and when they leave the firm.

■ Firms should ensure approved persons are aware of the Statements of Principle that apply to them.

■ Senior management must comply with the statements of principle (and note Principles 4-7 apply to those carrying out a significant influence function).

■ Approved persons will often fall within Chapter 2 of the T&C rules and the firm must ensure these criteria are met, e.g. exams, supervision, appraisals, etc.

■ Stronger candidates may have mentioned that SYSC talks about ensuring employees are 'suitable' as part of the control functions that should be exercised by senior management.

Question 17.

Here, the examiner is looking for a factual explanation and also for you to comment on their main powers, so you should express your view of these powers although the main focus should be the factual analysis. Candidates could have included the following.

- The FSA approach to supervision reflects regulatory objectives set out in FSMA.

- Approach recognises that senior management have responsibilities.

- Reflects the principles of good regulation, e.g. proportionality.

- Main method is 'risk-based supervision' – explain what this means.

- FSA powers fleshed out in SUP and include.

    - Desk-based reviews

    - Meetings

    - Inspections

    - Baseline monitoring.

- Stronger candidates will have mentioned that the FSA also supervise through sectoral reviews and themed approaches such as the Money Laundering theme.

- Stronger candidates would have mentioned that senior management are largely the front line of regulation for the firm under their responsibilities under PRIN 11/APER 7 and SYSC.

- The question here is asking more about supervision than enforcement, but it would be worth mentioning briefly that the supervisory relationship can lead to enforcement actions and the FSA's main powers there.

- You could finish by commenting on these powers – are they too great? Are they really any greater than the old SROs? Are they necessary?

Question 18.

The examiner is looking for an analysis of the progress towards a single market and what is currently in the pipeline to achieve this. Thus, a purely factual answer would be unlikely to score highly. The candidate should be discussing whether the work currently being undertaken is likely to achieve the single market objective. Candidates could have discussed the following.

- History of single market, Treaty of Rome and Financial Services Action Plan and time-frames.

- Progress so far

    - Passporting provisions

    - Lamfalussy proposals should be discussed, e.g. committee structures and framework principles. Has it worked?

    - Some directives already enacted, e.g. E-Commerce Directive. Does it create confusion, will it be properly implemented?

- Work being undertaken [Note that since 2002, some of these directives have now been implemented – refer to the Study book for further details.]

    - Review ISD (MiFID) – good idea, too slow, too late?

    - Market Abuse Directive – lots of uncertainty about implementation. Journalists critiqued it heavily

    - Prospectus directive – anti-competitive? Member states want home state issuance

    - Takeovers – fourteen years in negotiation and weak directive with opt outs at the end – shows political allegiances stronger than European allegiance?

- Can laws create a single market? Shouldn't this be market driven? Candidates could discuss consolidation of clearing and settlement and exchanges.

- Could argue that reasons for failure to integrate markets not regulatory ones, but

  - Political (protectionist behaviour)

  - Cultural (some regulators are more consensus based, other more ivory tower)

  - Cost (small businesses cannot compete in Europe if they have to comply with multitudes of additional 'general good' laws and linguistic barriers).

- Will expansion of the EU hamper the creation of a single market?